EMBATTLED MAIDEN

"Shall the biography of Anna Dickinson ever be truly written, its readers will wonder what spirit possessed her contemporaries to make parts of it possible."

—MAY WRIGHT SEWALL, 1885

Anna Dickinson

EMBATTLED MAIDEN

THE LIFE OF ANNA DICKINSON

BY

Giraud Chester

G. P. PUTNAM'S SONS

NEW YORK

COPYRIGHT, 1951, BY GIRAUD CHESTER

Published on the same day in the Dominion of Canada by
Thomas Allen, Ltd., Toronto.

Manufactured in the United States of America

Van Rees Press • New York

TO THE MEMORY OF MY PARENTS

ACKNOWLEDGMENTS

In Orange County, New York, almost twenty years ago, a probate judge was confronted with the task of disposing of several trunks of old letters and documents, the property of a woman who had died intestate at the age of ninety. Fortunately the surrogate sensed the possible value of the papers and offered them to the Library of Congress. An acknowledgment of gratitude is therefore due this county judge, for without the vast collection of letters, clippings, and scrapbooks that jammed the old trunks, it would not have been possible to reconstruct the life of one of the most remarkable women this nation has produced.

I also want to record my appreciation to the following individuals who offered me varying kinds and degrees of assistance: Drs. Powell and McPherson, and Mr. Devereaux, of the Manuscript Division of the Library of Congress; Messrs. Whitelaw Reid and Luke Carroll, of the *New York Herald Tribune,* and the Reid family which found and made available to me the Anna Dickinson letters included in the private papers of the senior Whitelaw Reid; Dr. James Harvey Young, of Emory University, and Dr. J. Calvin Callaghan, of Syracuse University, both of whom are engaged in extensive research on Miss Dickinson's life and who spoke freely to me about her career in several conversations; Miss Leonore Rice, of the Scranton Public Library; Miss Bertha Ackley, of Goshen, New York; Miss Ruth D. Keener, Mrs. Virginia B. Carrick, and Mr. Archibald G. Ogden, who encouraged me to pursue the research leading to this book. I also stand greatly in debt to Mr. Vito D. Matti who saw the manuscript in its various stages of development and offered me the benefit of his editorial judgments. Needless to say, none of these good people, who gave so generously of their time and energy, bears any responsibility for errors of fact or inference that may have inadvertently crept into the manuscript. That is a responsibility I rightfully assume alone.

New York   G. C.
1951

CONTENTS

ILLUSTRATIONS

EMBATTLED MAIDEN

CHAPTER 1

PROLOGUE: JANUARY 16, 1864

FOR even the most seasoned veteran of Washington society, it was hard to recall, in the three winters of war, so memorable a week end. It began early, on Thursday evening, with the dinner at the Secretary of State's and continued the next night with the first public reception of the season at Speaker Colfax's. President and Mrs. Lincoln held open house Saturday afternoon, and later that evening, there was the special convocation on Capitol Hill to hear the Quaker maiden, recently turned twenty-one, tell the Congress of the United States, the President, the Cabinet, and the Supreme Court how to win the war and make a lasting peace.

It was January, 1864, and armies of Americans faced each other in battle. The war had moved slowly and bloodily from the eager raising of militia following the fall of Fort Sumter through the disaster at Bull Run, then through two long years of defeats finally brought to a halt some six months before at Gettysburg and Vicksburg. The city had seen insane panic over exaggerated reverses and insane exultation over exaggerated victories. It had seen Rebel flags flying unharmed within sight of the White House, and it now hardly suspected that in another six months it would once again see enemy guns standing within sight of its fortifications.

Winter had terminated the field campaigns, which must await the coming of spring, but the newspapers were full of the latest reports from the front. Moseby was still harassing the Rebel rear. Union forces had been badly whipped near Harper's Ferry, the Virginia arsenal made famous by John Brown. Word leaked out that General Ben

3

Butler had laid plans before the Confederate authorities for an exchange of prisoners, but had not yet received an answer.

There was comfort in current reports from the South. A refugee from Richmond described the "terribly demoralized" state of the Rebel capital for the *Memphis Bulletin,* and his story was avidly reprinted by the Washington papers. Everyone was delighted by the news that the Confederate Congress, desperate for man power, had entertained a motion to draft Negroes as soldiers; only the opposition of Virginia, Georgia, and South Carolina prevented adoption of the revolutionary move.

But whatever satisfaction the North might take in the plight of the Confederacy was tempered, in mid-January, 1864, by its own unsolved and pressing problems: how to carry the war to the enemy and how to maintain popular support until victory was won. In the public mind, the Emancipation Proclamation had transformed the conflict from a war to restore the Union to a crusade against slavery, and grumblings were heard in many quarters. The year before, division within the North had almost lost the Congress and several governorships to the Peace Democrats. Those had been the darkest months, when it seemed the war would be lost not on the battlefield, but on the electoral front.

A war that goes on year after year with the end nowhere clearly in sight wearies even the most fervent fighters, and for those less impassioned it becomes unbearable. There had been draft riots in New York and Pennsylvania. Eight men of the Army of the Potomac in one day were sentenced to be executed for desertion. The situation was serious, and it would grow worse before better days would come. The fate of the nation was in the balance; the time called for inspired leadership. The people of the North wanted and needed a hero or heroine to give them courage and confidence, to transport them from despair to victory. They found such a leader, and upon her they bestowed all the homage they felt due a messenger dispatched by Providence. The name of their heroine was Anna Dickinson, and the year of her triumph was 1864.

Anna Dickinson was the maiden girl who, in an age when women were not yet deemed fit for political responsibility, left home to speak the cause of war—war to the bitter end for freedom and against slavery —to a people at first unwilling to listen, but later unable to desist. She left home unheralded and penniless, but not without an acute awareness of purpose, a constancy of concern for self and nation backed up by a storehouse of knowledge and oratorical talent amazingly well trained for a person of not yet twenty years. In the 1863 elections, when the loss of a state to the Peace Democrats meant the loss of an army in the field, she swung into action on the political stump and marched through the North in a succession of well-publicized triumphs that made her name legendary before the year was out. In two weeks of speaking to enthralled audiences it was commonly believed that she had singlehandedly saved Connecticut from certain defeat. People read how she had campaigned in New Hampshire and New York and Pennsylvania where rioting miners greeted her with derision, and a bullet fired from the audience had whipped off a lock of her hair, but she carried on, and soon the men were cheering. Her name was on every lip.

Now, less than a year out of anonymity, this incredible girl, borne to the height of fame by the spirit of war and her ability to make use of it, was in Washington, on invitation of the Congress itself. A resolution of the House of Representatives granted use of the newly decorated Hall to hear her, and a formal invitation signed by the Vice-President and the Speaker and a long list of senators and congressmen was sent to Philadelphia to bid her to come to the capitol and address the lawmakers as she saw fit on the topic she chose, the proceeds to be used as she alone pleased. The President gave his blessing to the invitation by dispatching his personal secretary, John Nicolay, along with Congressman William D. Kelley, to deliver the invitation.

The offer was accepted. Anna Dickinson designated Saturday, January 16, 1864, as the day she would speak to Congress; the topic: "Words for the Hour"; the proceeds to be turned over to the Freedmen's Bureau.

On the eve of the speech, she made her first appearance in Washington at the gala reception held by Speaker Colfax, and a reporter for the *National Republican,* eager to draw a vivid portrait for his readers, observed her every movement. "The target for all eyes," he noted, was barely five feet tall, modestly dressed, and certainly not more than twenty or twenty-one, though the ease and assurance of her manner belied her years. She was not beautiful, but her face was "highly intellectual"; at times it assumed "the highest order of beauty." Her "large-speaking" blue eyes expressed more than her lips revealed, and when she smiled she revealed "a most perfect and beautiful set of teeth." Her hair was jet black, cut short, parted Madonna-wise, and curled slightly.

Her dress was rich and neat with few ornaments. Those who were not satisfied with his description could go to the Hall of the House of Representatives and see for themselves the next night. Her "extraordinary powers and romantic history have made her famous throughout the country," remarked the *National Republican*. Readers who had not yet bought tickets were urged "to procure them at the earliest possible moment."

Long before 7:30 P.M. the next day, the capacious Hall and the galleries were filled to overflowing. Tickets were sold out by noon, and seats for five hundred were arranged on the floor. A temporary platform was erected in the space fronting the Speaker's desk. Senators and representatives vied for seats with the cabinet and foreign emissaries. President and Mrs. Lincoln announced they would attend, but when the hour came for the speech to begin, they had not yet arrived.

At precisely half past seven, a hush fell upon the expectant audience as Anna Dickinson, clothed in simple Quaker raiment, entered the Hall arm in arm with Vice-President Hamlin, followed closely by Speaker Colfax. Hamlin rose to make a speech of introduction. He did not tarry long. He recalled her triumphs of the preceding year and noted how she seemed to have been sent by Providence to save the nation. He compared her to Joan of Arc.

Anna Dickinson rose, silenced the audience with a dignified acknowledgment, and began to speak.

She was an orator to remember. Her rich, vibrant voice carried to every corner of the chamber without obvious effort, yet when she dropped it to underscore an impelling point, its grim intensity made it audible to every listener. Her poise was manifest and her earnestness overwhelming. Each word bore the stamp of conviction, as if she was prepared to stake her life upon its truth. This was the day of deliverance; this was the sacred cause; this was the great crusade for liberty and justice which many felt she had been born to lead. The crusade must sweep everything before it, exacting in its triumph the last particle of penance from the brutal and dishonored enemy.

"This is a people's war," she said, in words that would ring familiar a century later. "Today we are fighting an oligarchy built upon the degradation of four million black men and eight millions of white men."

With biting sarcasm she drew up a savage indictment of the enemy: "It has sustained freedom of speech by rifling the mails, and maiming and murdering innocent men for the simple expression of opinion. It has shut out schools and churches. It has come into our pulpits and made the truth a lie."

There was no common ground for reconciliation with such an enemy. To those who called for compromise, she issued a ringing reply: "Let no man prate of compromise! Defeated by ballots, the South has appealed to bullets. Now let it stand by that appeal! There is not an arm of compromise in all the North long enough to stretch over the sea of blood and the mound of fallen Northern soldiers to shake hands with their murderers on the other side!"

She had not spoken long when Mr. and Mrs. Lincoln came into the chamber. It was a dramatic moment for both speaker and audience: at the very moment the President entered, Anna Dickinson was openly criticizing him for his December Amnesty Proclamation and was turning her fire on the Supreme Court for denying the rights of black men in the infamous Dred Scott case. The audience, as if feeling it to be its duty to applaud a sentiment it shared even at the expense of courtesy, sustained the criticism with a round of cheers. "Mr. Lincoln sat meekly through it, not in the least displeased," observed the reporter for the *New York Post*. Perhaps the President knew there were sweeter things to come, and they did. When Anna Dickinson again alluded to Lincoln she made a dramatic call for his renomination and re-election that surprised and delighted the assemblage.

After almost an hour and a half of speaking, she drew toward her conclusion. "It is hard to die," she said in a final appeal to the nation's young men to rush to the aid of their brethren, "but a cause not worth dying for is not worth living for." The future was bright. The people were scaling and overcoming the prejudices of the past, were rising above the mists and thick darknesses of slavery and wrong, and would soon stand triumphant in the glad light of universal freedom.

She returned to her seat midst a volley of cheers and applause. As if protecting a young bird, the Vice-President and Speaker harbored her into an anteroom where she might fittingly meet the assembled dignitaries. Mr. and Mrs. Lincoln were announced, and the President, only recently recovered from a mild case of smallpox, paid his respects under the watchful eyes of his wife. Then came the Cabinet, the ambassadors, the judges, the congressmen.

As he gazed upon the brilliant audience gathered in the Hall, the correspondent of the *St. Louis Missouri Democrat* could think only of Macaulay's description of the attendance at the trial of Warren Hastings. Not so the skeptical correspondent of the anti-Union *London Telegraph* who derided this "crazy Jane in a red jacket" and used the episode to emphasize the uncouthness of the Americans as compared with the French. "At least the Jacobins did not suffer the tricoteuses to mount the tribune," he wrote. "They kept them in the galleries." However, Whitelaw Reid, the able young war correspondent of the *Cincinnati Gazette,* judged the situation in an entirely different light:

> Washington has witnessed strange scenes, betokening stranger changes, in the last two years [he wrote in his weekly dispatch], but I can recall none so strange as that witnessed in the Hall of the House of Representatives last Saturday night. Before the largest and most distinguished audience ever assembled there, there came a young Quaker girl, eight months before a humble employee in the mint, tonight the bravest advocate for the integrity of the Republic and the demand for universal liberty throughout it. Her success has been the most remarkable ever won at the capitol; and all who love the cause of the people, of the soldiers, and of liberty, will follow her with their prayers and benedictions.

The *Washington Chronicle* the next Monday threw restraint to the winds: "Joan of Arc never was grander, and could not have been better, in her mail of battle, than was this Philadelphia maid. . . . Sister of the Heroic—younger sister of the Free and the True—thou Fille du Regiment of this great war of freedom in America, let us humbly, very humbly, give you the hand of political brotherhood."

> There was never such a furore about an orator in this country [wrote three historians twenty years later, in describing a period they had lived through themselves]. The period of her advent; the excited condition of the people; her youth, beauty, and wonderful voice, all heightened the effect of her genius. . . . Ministers preached about her, prayed for her as a second Jeanne d'Arc raised up by

God to save the State to the loyal party. The excitement of the crowds knew no bounds; they shouted and hurrahed for Anna Dickinson; serenaded her with full bands of music; sent her gifts of flowers, books, and ornaments; manifesting in every way their love and loyalty to this gifted girl who had won this period of success in her country's cause.

When he wrote *Washington in Lincoln's Time,* thirty years later, Noah Brooks, a prominent journalist and an intimate friend of Lincoln, could still recall the evening of January 16, 1864. "Anna Dickinson," he wrote with fond nostalgia "made a figure long to be remembered."

But Noah Brooks had a sharper memory and a longer life than most. The memory of Anna Dickinson had died in the minds of most of her countrymen before his book appeared in print. Changing times and interests had swept her into oblivion, though the war of which she was a part continued to live on in pensions, parades, and politics. But the story of Anna Dickinson, for achievement and turbulence hardly paralleled in the history of the nation, was written in the public record of the United States. There it would remain undisturbed until several score years later when the record would be rediscovered and the story of Anna Dickinson, a maiden and a woman who knew both triumph and tragedy, who saw an unmatched fame raise and an impenetrable obscurity lower the standard of her name, would exalt anew the hearts and minds of all who can read and feel.

CHAPTER 2

THE MAID OF PHILADELPHIA

ANNA ELIZABETH DICKINSON was born on October 28, 1842, and grew to maturity in an age when the Declaration of Independence was adjudged a thoroughly masculine document, inapplicable in philosophy and practice to widows, wives, and unmarried maidens who, by decree of God and man, had no rights beyond those that men, in occasional moments of weakness, granted them.

Women might work with men in factories at less than equal pay for equal work, but they might not work at any rate of pay in the professions, for which by nature and intellect they were obviously unfit. If they were married, they could not own property in their own name and their lives were wholly circumscribed by husband, home, and children. If they were not married, their sole legitimate objective was to achieve that notoriously blissful state. It was an age of the double moral standard, when men, at the risk of mild social disapproval, might partake of the pleasures of the flesh before and outside of the pale of matrimony, while women might do so only at the risk of utter social ruin or corporal punishment inflicted by outraged husbands who at worst faced trial by understanding all-male juries.

Women were not consulted, at least not officially, in the making of laws nor in their enforcement. Together with idiots and criminals, they were denied the ballot for reasons most male editorial writers found eminently satisfactory. Not having the right to make political decisions, women were hardly expected to participate in political discussions, and few did. Spread-eagle oratory was a male monopoly, though here and there a few adventurous women, in crinoline and petticoats, braved the public platform. Most respectable women would not risk being seen in the audience.

It was an age of male supremacy, when millions of disenfranchised and subjugated women lived busy and reasonably happy lives.

It was also an age of ferment. The division between North and South grew more marked and irreconcilable each year, and the struggle for political and economic control moved inexorably toward a climax. The birth of a new political party, the Republican, in 1856, signaled the impending downfall of the long-entrenched Jacksonian Democracy and augured profound changes on the national scene.

In a nation committed to the principle of human freedom and dignity, the presence of four million black men held in bondage created its own ferment of tension and agitation. Unable to compromise liberty and slavery, most white-skinned people preferred to let the problem simmer to its own solution, though occasionally they were moved to emotion by fictionalized accounts of facts they preferred not to face directly. More sensitive and principled people, though less knowing in the ways of men and politics, refused to sanction human bondage or subordinate it to any greater principle, whether it be the preservation of the Union or economic advancement. Some became abolitionists—agitators for immediate emancipation—who bore the scorn of social disapproval from their fellow whites North and South, and who formed antislavery societies under the leadership of men like William Lloyd Garrison, Theodore Parker, and Wendell Phillips. What they suffered from smallness of numbers they made up in passion of sentiment, courage, and native ability.

The world in which Anna Dickinson grew up was a confused and disintegrating world. She took her learning at a time when great wrongs were being perpetrated with the acquiescence of the many over the objections of the few. She was reared in the era of the crusader, the social reformer out to awaken the consciousness of his fellow men to the evils that lay about them. Most of the reformers and social gad-flies were men, but there were a few women, like Lucretia Mott and Lucy Stone and Frances Wright, who dared to ride in advance of their time, speaking in behalf of freedom for their sex and for the Negro. Their principle was liberty, liberty not merely for the white man, but for the black man, and for women, too, both black and white.

Of the religious sects in the nation, none was more clear or more unbending in opposition to slavery of man or woman than the Quakers who, though committed to the principle of peaceful reform, found themselves in their zeal skirting dangerously close to militancy. Dressed in their broad-brimmed hats and Quaker coats, they held meetings and discussed issues and pondered solutions. The more fervent among them joined the ranks of abolitionist orators and spent whatever time they could spare from their daily labors to speak to those who would listen.

It was into such a Quaker and abolitionist family in Philadelphia that Anna Dickinson was born in 1842, the youngest of five children of a poor but respectable merchant, who threw himself into the cause of liberty with such passion that he collapsed and died from heart failure shortly after delivering an impassioned antislavery address. John Dickinson was a thorough-going Quaker, tracing his ancestry to the earliest Maryland Friends who came up into Pennsylvania early in the seventeenth century. He was fortified in the knowledge that both his grandmothers had been great and eloquent Quaker preachers. The Dickinson home was poor in material possessions, but there was a plenitude of morality, education, and Bible reading. At times the house, which was used as an active station of the underground railway, took on an air of conspiracy. Among the many wild and eerie tales of those years, the one that seemed to please the Dickinson children most was of a hapless slave, so closely pursued as to prevent any safe hiding, whom John Dickinson whirled into the nursery where his two little boys lay sleeping. Flinging back the covers he thrust the cowering fugitive between his sons. When the law officers passed through the room, they saw nothing but a tumbled mass of linen that small and restless sleepers normally make, and continued their search elsewhere, the Negro finally being passed down and out through the labyrinth of cellars to a carriage and safe driver, and on to Canada.

Old Guard abolitionists like James and Lucretia Mott said of John Dickinson, "He gave to the cause of the slave not alone wise and generous aid, but a logical and impassioned oratory." He apparently was an able and forceful speaker, but he died before he could engrave any lasting trace of himself on the mind of his youngest child. John Dickinson died in his forties, bequeathing to his wife Mary, three boys and two girls, the eldest about thirteen, the youngest, Anna, two, and no money to speak of.

By all reports Mary Edmondson Dickinson was a woman of uncommon beauty and grace. She was descended from a long line of Quakers, too, and was a devout member of the Orthodox Society of Friends. She married John Dickinson when she was more than thirty, after a thirteen year courtship. Heavy losses before her husband's sudden death left Mary and the children in straitened circumstances, and they were perpetually pressed for money to provide food, clothing, and fuel. Mary Dickinson never remarried, but struggled along as father and mother combined. To make a go of things she took in boarders and did some private teaching. A finely educated woman, she made a school of her home, and reared her children in the strict Quaker way of life, instilling in them a high regard for moral courage, learning, and temperance, and a pride in their poor but noble heritage.

Mary Dickinson raised the family on a classical literary diet. She introduced her children to the beauties of Shakespeare and the Bible and ordered their reading in history, poetry, ethics, and biography. Samuel and Edwin took their training dutifully, showing no marked aptitudes for the life of learning, but John forsook his Quaker background to train for the Methodist ministry and, in later years, became a college teacher of religion and mathematics. Samuel and Edwin were both devout but sickly young men, the former going into retail trade, which quickly tired his limited physical stamina; Edwin, the more adventurous, left home to sail to California, where he had a brief and unsuccessful teaching career. Susan, nine years older than her sister, shared with Anna the love of the arts and of politics, a combination of interests both would carry to their graves. Susan was a wisp of a girl, never growing to a full five feet and weighing scarcely one hundred pounds. Her plainness seemed to destine her for spinsterhood, but she liked the good things in life, she enjoyed conversation on literature and painting, and she dabbled with the piano and writing, selling her first poem to the *Saturday Evening Post* when she was sixteen. As the older sister she assumed many of the household duties, relieving Mary Dickinson who was already approaching sixty by the time her youngest child reached her teens.

Anna was the precocious one in the family. She was a crying baby, petulant and irritable, and undoubtedly spoiled as the youngest of the tribe. She exhibited unusual mental capacities at an early age and read voraciously. Not satisfied with the classical learning she daily absorbed from Mary Dickinson, she risked maternal disfavor by secretly reading the verses of that scandalous young romantic, Lord Byron. Later she busied herself with the newspapers of the day, which carried extracts of the great debates over the nature of the Union and were brimful with news of the impending crisis. She was both a buoyant and pensive child, sometimes bubbling with energy and play, at other times given to long solitary walks about the city, wrapped in a tangle of private thoughts. She was not a pretty girl, but there was a clean-cut cast of feature and freshness of spirit that endeared her to her family and friends who felt that she was singularly gifted in the art of language, for in conversation with them she could pursue a point with such fluency and so hammer away at an argument that no reply was possible. One day when she was thirteen she read in a local paper of how a Kentucky schoolmaster was tarred and feathered because he had written an antislavery letter to an Ohio paper. "Can any man in this country . . . stand up firmly and say 'I am free,' when such evils and wrongs are constantly being enacted among us, without one word or act of denunciation?" the inflamed youngster confided to her notebook. "This was done in a state professedly the most free and liberal of the slave States. If this is the best, what must be the worst? If this is done in a State nearest to emancipation, what must be the condition of the farthest from it?" She concluded with a question she doubtless heard repeated many times in abolitionist circles: "How long will Northern men watch the struggle between Freedom and Slavery? How long will they see their rights trampled on, their liberty sacrificed, their highest and most lofty sentiments crushed beneath the iron heel of oppression? How long will they bear all this without an effort of resistance?"

The ardent youngster decided that her notes deserved public distribution and submitted her fiery outcry to the *Liberator,* the antislavery journal published in Boston by William Lloyd Garrison. Garrison ran the piece in the February 22, 1856, issue, and Anna experienced the pleasure of her first publication.

Anna was now beyond the tutorial limitations of her mother. Mrs. Dickinson had enrolled her in the Friends' Select School of Philadelphia before she was ten, under the patronage of the Forrest Estate, a local philanthropic trust. She attended the Quaker school for two terms and then was transferred to the Westtown Boarding School, also in Philadelphia, where she remained until the Forrest Estate sponsored her return to the Friends' School where she continued for another three years, or until she was about fifteen. This seems to have been the last formal training Anna ever received. Determined to stand on her own feet she left school and became a copyist for a publishing house and for various law firms in Philadelphia. After that there was a brief period at a district school, at New Brighton in Beaver County, where she served as an assistant teacher and pursued her own reading. When she heard that there was an opening at a neighboring school, she applied for it. The town committeeman told her that the position had formerly been held by a man at a salary of $28 a month. For a female the pay would be $16. Anna's rebellious spirit produced a show of adolescent heroics that undoubtedly took the supervisor by surprise. "Sir," she is reported to have replied with great vehemence, "are you a fool or do you take me for one? Though I am too poor today to buy a pair of cotton gloves, I would rather go in rags than degrade my womanhood by accepting anything at your hands." She rose from her seat and stalked out of the room defiantly.

At home the Dickinsons fumbled along, with few material comforts or pleasures, living a life of devotion to religion and literature. They were a talkative family; they talked and argued over books and politics. For Susan and Anna there seemed to be but two issues in the whole world worth discussing—the enslavement of black men and the rights of women. In her own mildly rebellious circle of friends Anna acquired a reputation for brightness of mind and a tongue that seemed prematurely gifted with the weapons of sarcasm, wit, and invective. Mindful of her paternal great-grandmothers and their preaching prowess, Anna understandably came to regard the platform and the forum as being legitimately within the sphere of her sex; she liked to attend the political meetings of her elders at which she picked up an understanding of laws and constitutions, of the rights of man, and of the fundamental principles of government. Then one Sunday, in late January, 1860, when she was seventeen, Anna had her first opportunity to express herself before a public gathering. The effect was notable.

That morning her eye caught a notice in the Philadelphia Public Ledger of the day before announcing a meeting of the "Friends of Progress" at Clarkson Hall, Cherry Street above Sixth, for Sunday at 2:30. The subject was "The Rights and Wrongs of Women," and the limit on debate was to be ten minutes. Though similar advertisements had been published for years, Anna had never before noted it. Indeed, until that day she had never attended any meeting on the Sabbath except where Quakers gathered "slow and calm." But this day, as Anna later recalled, she somehow felt a stirring within her; she was now fairly convinced against all older advice that she rivaled Solomon and she longed for the opportunity to demonstrate her ability. This meeting looked inviting; she would attend it and would not stop to learn whether her mother approved or not. She put on her hat, cast a cloak over her shoulders, and was on her way.

She soon found herself in old Clarkson Hall, the very walls of which breathed sedition and revolutionary fire. The meeting was held in a room that seated about eight hundred people and had been used for many years to advocate various reforms. It was then in possession of a group of people who named themselves "Friends of Progress." Among them were to be found learned and simple men, practical helpers and self-seeking hinderers, devotees and atheists, some men and women sound in purse and position, and others with little of either, and a fair attendance of those special creatures who have so much to say that they will burst if they are not given a rostrum from which to expound their views.

Anna walked into the midst of this gathering and seated herself on the center aisle. She listened quietly to a succession of talks and debates, some worth while, some foolish, until one of the special creatures—a bristling, dictatorial man with an unsufferable manner rose to speak and, prowling to and fro in the center aisle, suddenly stopped before a most intent listener, shook his forefinger under Anna's nose, and gave vent to an outcry in a lost cause: "I have daughters. My daughters are as good and as bright and can do as much as any man's daughters. But they cannot be doctors, nor lawyers, nor priests, nor orators. They are not fit to be bank presidents, nor college professors, nor brokers, nor business heads. They cannot be anything but just what they are—homekeepers, nothing that their brothers could be." Wagging his finger vigorously under Anna's nose, he concluded: "And if my daughters cannot be, no man's daughters can!"

A good many years later Anna could still feel the blood run like flame as she started to her feet. She knew little of parliamentary forms or of the order of debate. She leaped up without looking to the presiding officer and cried out to the man who had so enraged her:

"You, sir! You say that what your daughters cannot be, no man's daughters can be; that your daughters are incapable of being doctors, lawyers, priests, businessmen, bank presidents, authors, editors. In one word, sir, as you yourself have summed it up, your daughters are fools!"

Then, shaking her own finger in his face as the startled audience listened in wonderment, "And, in heaven's name, what else is to be expected of the daughters of such a father?"

The irate man slipped out of the auditorium as the delighted assemblage applauded. Anna went back next week and this time, when a man in the audience sneered disparagingly about women's rights, Anna unleashed such a direct and audacious reply that the audience again applauded her. It was evident that here was a worthy addition to the "Friends of Progress" who could be counted on to spark a Sunday meeting. Mr. Ellwood Longshore, who happened to be present, took a personal interest in Anna, and he and his wife, Dr. Hannah Longshore, a pioneer physician, invited Anna to their home. A warm friendship was struck up, and the Longshores became Anna's closest advisers outside her own family. In their home Anna received encouragement and instruction and such cordial welcome that she became a constant visitor and grew to depend upon her benefactors more and more.

Requests soon came from neighboring towns to hear the young Quaker girl who could hold her own in heated argument, and in response to these invitations, Anna occasionally ventured out of her sheltered environs to make short talks before strange audiences. Through the spring and summer of 1860 she attended weekly meetings and forged her speaking skill each time she voiced her sentiments publicly. Mary Dickinson, meanwhile, kept a close eye on her younger daughter. She required her to continue her reading of history, forbade her to enter the theater, which to the orthodox Quaker mind was a den of iniquity, and generally gave much thought to the proper religious training of her most talented child. Anna's favorite historical figure, surprising for a girl with democratic leanings, was Napoleon. In literature her model was Shakespeare.

When fall arrived, Anna went back to teaching though she had discovered by this time that she had no love for the work. Indeed she disliked it intensely, being no more pleased by the niggardly pay than thousands of other teachers before and since her time. But she also found the work dull. She felt cut out for more exciting and rewarding pursuits than the instruction of dolts who wanted nothing more than freedom from the compulsion to learn. She had no other way to earn her keep, however, so after passing an examination for a teacher's certificate in Bucks County, she accepted a position teaching classes at Middleton, at Wild Man's Corner. The pay was small, but we may suppose it was equally small for the men on the faculty, and Anna left home and her circle of friends to settle down at the school.

"How are thy blistered ancles by this time?" Susan inquired solicitously of Anna, opening a correspondence between the two sisters that would run for more than a score of years. "We have not heard whether thee got fairly started on first day evening or not, but supposed so." Susan passed on neighborhood gossip. "Who does thee suppose we are to have across the way in Allison's old home? A bride—I shall not give thee any further clue, now guess." The family was already looking forward to Anna's small earnings. "Mother wants thee, if thee can," Susan wrote, "to come home next seventh day prepared to pay the ice bill." Susan, herself a teacher, was having trouble collecting her salary, but she had "considerable hopes" since learning that the school treasurer had succeeded in obtaining a loan. And if Anna had a collar of the new fashion, "long points down in front, by all means let us have it as soon as possible. Mrs. Lippincott is in a bad way for want of the pattern."

The first weeks of the school term passed uneventfully until Anna received an invitation to attend the twenty-third anniversary meeting of the Pennsylvania Anti-Slavery Society at Kennett Square, a small village about thirty miles from Philadelphia. She seized the opportunity to mingle once again with people whose sentiments she shared and where, moreover, she might possibly be given an opportunity to talk. Her decision to attend was fortunate, as it later turned out, for it was at the Kennett Square meeting that Anna won her first important publicity in abolitionist circles. This was made possible by the *Philadelphia Press,* which, looking for a story, had sent out a feature writer.

The meeting attracted some of the leading abolitionists of the

Whitelaw Reid

The World belongs to
those who take it.
Truly Yours
Anna Dickinson

A popular contemporary picture of Miss Dickinson. The motto and the handwriting are both characteristic.

East: James and Lucretia Mott, Thomas Garrett, Robert Purvis, Thomas Whitson, and Oliver Johnson, editor of the New York *Anti-Slavery Standard*. The hero of the abolitionists, William Lloyd Garrison, was unable to deliver the main address because a severe attack of bronchitis bedded him down in Boston. With the national Presidential election only a few weeks off, the members of the Society found themselves facing an unhappy choice. Four candidates were in the field, three of whom were wholly objectionable to them, and the fourth, Abraham Lincoln, had disavowed their support by defending the Fugitive Slave Law and opposing the abolition of slavery in the District of Columbia. Nevertheless, being realists to a limited extent at least, the society endorsed the Republican candidate on the grounds that "as between him and his opponents, and on the issues involved in the present contest, the election of Abraham Lincoln will be a great and encouraging triumph." From Lincoln's administration of the Presidency, they expected little.

Of course, the slavery question was the topic of the meeting, and it was discussed heatedly in a series of speeches that differed from each other mainly in the fervidness of the speakers. In many speeches, however, there could be detected an honest searching for the underlying principles justifying emancipation of the Negro in the face of the Supreme Court's Dred Scott decision that used the Bill of Rights to defend the slave holder's property, rather than to defend the slave himself. In the face of this opinion, abolitionists had three lawful alternatives: they could call for an amendment to the Constitution, an impossible solution to people impatient in the presence of palpable injustice; they could hope for a new court ruling when the present court retired, similarly a hopelessly prolonged process; or else they could withdraw their call for the Federal government to emancipate slaves, which would undo their basic program.

The speakers tangled with the problem from every point of view, until finally Anna was given the floor.

"Miss Anna E. Dickinson, of Philadelphia, aged 17 years, handsome, of an expressive countenance, plainly dressed, and eloquent beyond her years, made the speech of the occasion," wrote the *Philadelphia Press* reporter, introducing Anna to the public of newspaper readers. "Frequently interrupted, she maintained her presence of mind."

Now it was time for Anna to repeat what she had been studying and

discussing for the past year. She spoke about a law higher than constitutions, and turned to natural law to defend a program of abolition of
slavery that a man-made compact prohibited. "We are told to maintain
constitutions because they are constitutions," she said, "and compromises because they are compromises. But," she asked, "what are compromises, and what is laid down in those constitutions?

"Eminent lawyers have said that certain fundamental ideas of right
are common to the world, and that all laws of man's making which
trample on these ideas, are null and void—wrong to obey, right to dis-
obey. The Constitution of the United States recognizes human slavery,
and makes the souls of men articles of purchase and sale."

A Dr. Stebbins rose in the audience and begged leave to differ. "The
Constitution does not speak of slaves as property," he said. A Rev. Hi-
ram Crozier stood up, too, and shouted impatiently: "If Miss Dickinson persists in intruding her ideas of the constitutional question, I am
bound to answer her if it keeps me here till midnight." Dr. Stebbins
joined in: "So am I!"

The audience commenced clapping hands and stamping feet, and
Anna was observed to tremble somewhat. The *Press* reporter noted
gallantly that she rallied with pluck and a resolution extraordinary for
a girl of her years. She advanced a step or two toward the audience, and
holding forth her hands, continued in a louder and clearer tone, which
rang musically and forcibly in the now perfect silence of the hall.

"I say," she said, "that the Constitution *does* recognize property in
human souls. Does it not do so in a dozen implied ways?" She cited
a half-dozen examples of the use of the law to protect the slaveowner
and to deprive the slaves of human rights. "You are to send back fugi-
tives from labor, to remand the bleeding victims of the overseer and
the slave driver, who are classed, for no crimes of theirs with the crim-
inal who has broken, of his own will, a compact that he made with the
law. The slave can make no compact; he who has been trampled with
the beasts, who has been all his lifetime a chattel, whose volition is dis-
owned, whose tears are disregarded, whose wrongs are not wrongs,
since he has no rights, is incapable of making a compact." Her point
was simple: "If the word slave is not in the Constitution, the *idea* is.
Say what you will, the Constitution of this Government *does* recognize property in human souls."

"No, it don't!" broke in Dr. Stebbins, at which there was some slight applause, but Anna went on.

"What did the Republican party of Lincoln maintain?" she asked. "Only that it was opposed to the *extension* into the territories of the evils of slavery. It had virtually said to the slave driver: Go into your caves and brutal fastnesses, crush there the bones of your victims, bend them, break them, and we will not interfere. The Constitution gives you such rights; we simply claim that we shall not hear you, nor see you."

Dr. Stebbins again protested, stating that Anna labored under a misapprehension.

Anna replied with a sweeping statement whose irrelevance seemed to escape the audience. No law could prevent the reclaiming of stolen goods, she said; the forefathers of the Negroes had been taken from their native land and no length of possession on the part of the slave holder could make his slaves other than stolen property. She gave full vent to her emotions: "The cry comes up from the mothers and children of the South, 'Am I not a man and a brother?'"

Dr. Stebbins here arose with a copious interruption. He could not go beyond the law that gave the slave holder certain rights, and he would be a traitor to set aside the guarantees of the Constitution.

"But any human enactment or constitution," Anna replied, "coming in contact with fundamental truths is not law but injustice."

"No, it is not," the doctor snapped. "You have no right to go behind the Constitution."

Anna turned upon him. "But, sir," she asked with a misleading air of naïveté, "as you go tonight to your happy home and see in his sleep that brave boy of yours, and a single hand stronger than yours were stretched forth to take him from you and make him a slave forever, what would you do?"

"I would kill him!" said the doctor, to the approval of the audience.

"You would not plead for the law then," Anna replied, "and speak of constitutions, nor should you do so now, since the children of your brethren are thus snatched from their homes every day that you live."

She had scored her point, but Dr. Stebbins was reluctant to give her the last word. He persisted until a gentleman on the platform, obviously misinformed on the skill and tenacity of the adversaries, rose to state that Miss Dickinson was but seventeen years of age and necessarily timid, while the doctor was used to public speaking. He asked him as a gentleman to discontinue his interruptions until the lady was done. Dr. Stebbins apologized, and Anna resumed her speech.

The reporter of the *Philadelphia Press,* disposed to burlesque the whole meeting, nevertheless wrote of Anna: "However erratic, enthusiastic, or impracticable her sentiments, they were remarked with the closest attention. The beauty and talent of the young woman exercised a talismanic effect upon even the rudest." At home the Dickinsons read the long account in the *Press* with glowing pride.

The speech established Anna as an up-and-coming speaker in abolitionist circles and won her many new and important friends. Oliver Johnson, a warmhearted man, took Anna under his wing, and invited her to New York. Kindly Lucretia Mott looked with affection and admiration on the girl young enough to be her granddaughter, and encouraged her to keep up her studies and her speaking. She accepted a kind of responsibility to promote Anna in reform circles, to introduce her to the women's rights leaders who might be able to secure some speaking engagements for her. But progress in career making was slow. "It was not unexpected that no way opened, for the present, to promote our young friend Anna Dickinson's lecturing tour," she wrote to her cousin Lydia Mott several months later. "We know well the difficulties attendant on one's going forth without means. Anna has been lecturing around Kennett and in the neighborhood of this city, which may be as well, until she shall be more matured."

When the fall semester ended, Anna terminated her brief teaching career and went to New York City, apparently to visit with some of her new friends. The winter of 1860-61 was uncertain for the nation, as it was for Anna and the Dickinson family. Lincoln was due to take over the Presidency in March, but rumblings of secession boded ill for the republic. The Dickinsons were finding it very difficult to hold their home together. Mary Dickinson was ailing badly, her sons were fully occupied trying unsuccessfully to make their own way in life, Anna was desperately hoping that good fortune in some ill-defined fashion would soon shine upon her, and Susan was on the brink of despair as she surveyed a dismal future for herself.

Unhappy at home and discouraged in her work, Susan wrote to her younger sister in New York to ask a favor. Would Anna be willing to ask a Mrs. Savin to make inquiry among her wealthy friends to see whether Susan could obtain a situation as a governess at $100 a year plus room and board. "I want to give up this life of public school teaching at once," Susan wrote. The Philadelphia home was too great a burden for the children, and Susan felt she would be happier on her own. Moreover, she wanted to continue her study of the piano.

"If I can secure such a situation as I speak of for a year," Susan wrote, "I shall then have a home, and enough to take music lessons for the year, which I have been trying to compass, and to get what I shall need in the way of clothing for that time, which won't be much, as I am already pretty well supplied, including bonnets and coats and dresses, and muslin for underclothes. In the meantime I shall have an easier life and a chance to write, and with a year's start I believe I can get along, while it is necessary for me to make the effort.... See if thee can do anything for me."

Instead of going to New York as she hoped, however, Susan stayed home. Anna returned to Philadelphia with exciting tidings. She had made new and influential friends who were much impressed with her and had suggested presenting her formally to the public in a full-dress lecture. True, it would be unusual for an eighteen-year-old girl to be announced for a public lecture when the public was accustomed to paying money only for well-established platform figures, but the very novelty might attract many people out of curiosity. The publicity from the speech would prepare the way for lecture engagements elsewhere, and, it was hoped, the young girl, rightly now a young lady, might be able to make her way as a paid speaker serving both herself and the cause of womanhood. The guiding influence of Lucretia Mott and Hannah Longshore could be detected behind the plan. At any rate, an auditorium was hired and tickets sold, and on February 27, 1861, Anna delivered her first full-length speech in Concert Hall before eight hundred people. The title of her lecture was "The Rights and Wrongs of Women." Mrs. Mott, presenting a strange contrast to her protégée with her hawklike, albeit friendly face, wrinkled and thin, was assigned the task of introducing a tense and fearful Anna to the expectant audience. It was undoubtedly a thrilling moment for Anna; she had sole responsibility for the evening's program with a sizable audience on her hands.

The *Philadelphia Evening Bulletin,* identifying Anna as "a young Quakeress," who "bids fair to become widely known," noted that

Anna seemed hesitant at first. There was a lack of coherence, "but as she warmed to her subject, she really made a speech that many a popular speaker might have been proud of." Using anecdotes and examples, she took up in turn the main arguments advanced against the admission of women into the various professions. To those whose sense of propriety was outraged by the prospect of a female physician, Anna replied that if it was glorious for Florence Nightingale to care for sick soldiers, it certainly was decent for women to attend their sick sisters as physicians. As to women voting, she asked ironically why, if a woman could go among a crowd of men to pay her taxes, she was to be considered indecent if she went to the polls, with the same men standing before and behind her. Of women lawyers, she said: "Lawyers say they could not be so rude as to use the same strength of argument against a female lawyer that they would against one of their own sex, and yet," she pointed out, "they will cross-question and browbeat the most refined lady witnesses past all endurance."

Finally she came to the subject of prostitution, for an unmarried girl of eighteen then as now a fairly uncomfortable topic, and argued that prostitution was a social evil brought on not by the moral depravity of the practitioners, but by poverty. "One could not but believe her innocent and pure," noted the *Evening Bulletin* with evident satisfaction. "She stood there in the strength of purity and handled well and clearly a subject which it is so difficult for a young woman to handle in public." Any disposition toward rowdyism in the audience, the paper noted, "was fairly cowed by her clear, earnest utterance of her awful statistics."

Already Anna's style was making itself manifest: an overpowering array of facts, examples, and testimony interlarded with a graphic sense of the dramatic, a vividness of expression, a sense of climax, and a richness of voice that could respond with infinite variations to the emotional demands of her subject. Those present knew this was no ordinary speaker—no ordinary girl. What she said was hardly new—indeed nothing she said by itself was new. What was new and different and impelling was the effect she created, as if at one moment of time, righteousness, equity, and truth converged in one mind and flowed out of a single mouth with such modulated fluency and earnestness of statement that listeners somehow felt they were in the presence of some transcendent inspiration. No less surprised by this effect was

Anna herself, who was anything but vague in her objectives and methods, but she was keen enough to discern this mystical reaction of people to her speaking, to sense the sources of her strength, and to cultivate and prepare herself for more imposing assignments.

The speech ran two hours and was pronounced a success by both the press and the notables present. Anna had spoken from only the briefest notes, relying on her knowledge of the subject to move her to direct speech. She was somewhat embarrassed by the undue length of the talk and was perhaps more aware of its lack of point and order than her auditors who could find nothing but good in it. One enthusiastic woman, obviously nearsighted, left the hall with Anna in her thoughts. Her only regret was that the large crowd prevented her from getting near enough to Anna to see her well. "I do not think that I could tell you if I should meet you," she wrote, "but I could distinguish your voice anywhere."

Midst the plaudits came one unpleasant chiding from an individual who apparently was able to resist the charms of the speaker. "Take my advice," wrote this anonymous man in what was perhaps one of the least effectual bits of advice given anyone in 1861. "Leave the rostrum. It is preposterous to vend such schoolgirl nonsense as you have given tonight. If your friends demand an explanation contrive to have a bronchial difficulty—affect debility or be suddenly liable to vertigo. Anything under heavens for an excuse."

But Anna was hardly to be dissuaded from what she now felt was her chosen career. She was eighteen, she had successfully surmounted her debut, she had vindicated the faith of her backers. Soon she would have followers and that would make her a leader. Family and friends agreed: with good fortune and proper guidance this gifted girl might really make a name for herself.

CHAPTER 3

"IF SHE WAS BORN A QUAKER, SHE HAS GOT BRAVELY OVER IT!"

LESS than a week later Abraham Lincoln was inaugurated President of the United States and the country stood on the brink of open war. Southern extremists, determined not to submit to a Republican in the White House, seized Fort Sumter and forced a show of Federal authority. They chose division and war instead of union and limitations on the extension of slavery. To the new President, division meant dissolution and rather than this he accepted war. For the abolitionists the war was not merely to be accepted but welcomed as a resolution of a mighty issue that words no longer could resolve: Will the nation stand slave or free?

Like her abolitionist friends, Anna was caught up in the war spirit. With all its evils, utterly destructive as it is of moral and material values, war nevertheless seems to give a sense of purpose to many people. It arouses in them a militancy of zeal, inspires a unity of effort, and directs energies toward immediate objectives. For those who find righteous cause in the resort to violence, war comes as a satisfying outlet for previously untapped energies and emotions. But Northerners did not at first share a commonness of ultimate purpose; millions, including the President, sought only to restore the Federal union with little or no thought to the liberation of the black man. Anna was not one of these; she shared the sympathies of her abolitionist friends who felt the war was waged for one great objective—emancipation. To her and to them the war was righteously ordained; its outcome would see the final smashing of the slave system and the establishment of the principle of equality of all men, and, Anna hoped, of all women. She

26

prayed for a speedy and triumphant conclusion, but she was not content merely with seeking Divine aid. What she could do herself she would do. What she could not do, she would prepare herself to do. She was keenly conscious of her intellectual abilities, she was an omnivorous reader, an enthusiastic and fluent talker. What more natural than that she should become an amateur military strategist like so many of her countrymen? She read the news dispatches appearing in the daily press, plotted the lines of battle, noted the character of the generals, assessed comparative military positions, and displayed an uncanny ability to command the facts of war.

All this was very interesting, no doubt, to Anna and her friends to whom she so often expressed her determined views, but meanwhile the Dickinsons must live and eat. It was pleasant to have a daughter and sister who was so bright, but the rent still had to be paid and the grocer's bills met. Samuel was ill and could barely care for himself. The meager income from Susan's teaching and the occasional contributions from John and Edwin, both of whom were then in California, could not meet the expenses of running a home with prices rising at every turn. Obviously so self-assertive a young woman as Anna must accept her share of family responsibility and go to work. Since her experience with teaching was so disagreeable and financially so unremunerative, she looked for prospects elsewhere. Young men were going into the Army in droves and it was now somewhat easier for a girl to obtain a regular position than theretofore. Anna applied for a position at the United States Mint in Philadelphia and was made an adjuster. In the mint she worked six days a week from seven in the morning until six at night for $28 a month. It was a good job, as jobs for girls went, but Anna had no love for the work, finding it a great bore. This did not in any way affect her efficiency, however, for soon after coming to the mint she was acknowledged its fastest adjuster, and she worked there through the first year of war. It was a wholesome experience in independence for Anna—she worked hard, but she made her own living and more beside, and she gradually grew out of the tremulous, uncertain, almost childish Quaker girl into a self-assertive young lady, confident, and reliable, who was learning the meaning of responsibility and preparing to enter adulthood. She began to emerge somewhat from the circle of her family. It was not that she grew to love them less—she persisted, as she did throughout her life, in complete devotion to them—but she was no longer wholly wrapped up in the world of a family. Evenings and Sundays she was with her abolitionist friends, and with them she talked over the war and its progress.

The North looked forward to an easy victory, but the first months of the war brought total disappointment. The initial engagement with the Confederates at Bull Run in July, 1861, brought disaster to the Federal forces. After that George B. McClellan, a new general, was put in command and was charged with organizing the unruly Northern troops and working out a plan of victory. McClellan was an able military man, but inordinately sensitive to criticism, and slow to move. Politically he was a Democrat, opposed to the party of Lincoln, in no way interested in the issue of slavery. Many abolitionists wondered whether his slowness to attack stemmed from a desire to avoid an outright Union victory. But most Northerners, seeking their first military hero, idolized George McClellan, and he sat firmly in the military saddle.

Not until the end of September did McClellan move, and when he finally rolled his forces forward at Manassas, he discovered not a massed Confederate army, as he expected, but a camouflage of mock guns that for weeks had held him and his great Army at bay. Not until sometime later was there an actual engagement with the enemy, and this occurred at Ball's Bluff, on the upper Potomac. The result of the encounter was a complete fiasco for the Union. The Union forces were trapped between a cliff and the river, with insufficient boats to take them back to their own shore. Many were captured, while some were shot in the water, and others drowned. Military bungling was manifest, but abolitionists felt that something worse was afoot. The general who had ordered the action was a Northern Democrat who had shown tolerance to Maryland slave holders. McClellan, his superior, was a Democrat. The colonel who was killed leading the detachment had been a Republican senator from Oregon before joining the Army. To a suspicious mind the facts bespoke treachery.

A few days after the defeat at Ball's Bluff, the Pennsylvania Anti-Slavery Society held its annual conclave at Kennett Square and Anna again received an invitation to attend. This time William Lloyd Garrison was there, along with other well-known abolitionists who gathered to evaluate the conduct of the war and to formulate abolitionist policy. It was a meeting of devotees, and Anna was happy and proud to be among them. It was good, too, to be away from the mint, if only for a few days, and it was exhilarating to mingle with dedicated folk of like mind. Older abolitionists who recalled her outspoken if immature address of the year before greeted her warmly and inquired about her plans and progress in speechmaking. Anna replied pleasantly that they would be able to judge for themselves; she was scheduled to speak at one of the meetings. When her turn came Anna took the platform. Calling upon the store of military information she had acquired during the year, she traced the course of the war to date. It was an informed, though highly partisan, account. Finally she came to Ball's Bluff and retold the sordid facts of that engagement. Then, in a display of youthful daring she said publicly what many of her listeners feared to say even privately. "Future history will show," she asserted impetuously, "that this battle was lost not through ignorance and incompetence, but through the treason of the commanding general, George B. McClellan, and time will vindicate the truth of my assertion!"

It was an irresponsible statement. Anna could not prove it and though the word treason once passed from the lips of Abraham Lincoln in a strained conversation with McClellan, no evidence has ever been advanced to support her assertion. It was an emotional outburst, and it showed that Anna had not yet matured to the responsibilities of public discourse. But she delivered her statement with such an overpowering sense of conviction and certainty that the audience, disposed against McClellan to begin with, could not but suspect that perhaps she was right. Anna was introduced to Garrison who congratulated her on her speech and promised to do what he could for Anna if she ever ventured into New England.

All aglow over her talk and her contact with the famous antislavery spokesman, Anna returned home to resume work at the mint. But already word of the charge against McClellan had reached the ears of James Pollock, the director of the mint and a former governor of Pennsylvania. Anna was fired without further ado. In time of war the government could not tolerate an employee who questioned the loyalty of the commanding general.

In some ways Pollock's action was the best service the government could have rendered Anna, since it had the effect of inducing her once again to pursue a public career. The immediate result of her discharge was grave: she had to earn her living in one way or another, and for a brief time she worked in a millinery shop. But of greater significance was her decision to labor no longer with her hands than absolutely necessary, and to find some new path for herself that would utilize her gift of speech.

Those first months were very difficult. Leaving home and the millinery shop behind her, she visited with some of the friends she had made the year before and spent several weeks in Valley Falls, Rhode Island, with her good friend, Lillie Chace. Lillie's mother, Elizabeth Buffum Chace, arranged for Anna to speak before several community groups in and around Providence. All in all, Anna's stay with the Chaces tended to continue the process by which she left behind the naïvetés of adolescence and steadily acquired an independence of manner and thought that characterized her throughout her later life. Years later, in writing a biography of her distinguished mother, Lillie Chace recalled Anna's visit. Anna was a handsome brunette, girlish looking, as Lillie remembered her, possessed of a glowing complexion and magnificent eyes. Her black hair rippled in loose waves about her head. She wore it short, according to a fashion not then unusual for young women. She said "thee" with all Quaker propriety, and her dress was of a style halfway between that of Quakerism and the world. She wore a scoop-shaped, black velvet bonnet. But when she looked at New England girls, who, were they Quaker-affiliated or not, then mostly wore hats, "her spirit rose within her," Lillie Chace related. "She borrowed my best hat to wear. She bought one like it, cut up her bonnet, and used the velvet for trimming."

Mrs. Chace, Lillie's mother, was a little amused and somewhat disturbed by Anna's action.

"Why," she exclaimed, "thee can never make up that bonnet again."

"No," said Anna, "I have put that temptation behind me."

One day in February Anna delivered a talk on "The National Crisis" before an antislavery group in Newport. Word of her power as a speaker must already have spread somewhat for the Democratic correspondent of the *Providence Press,* probably acting out of curiosity, made it a point to attend.

"Who she is, any further than is expressed by her nomenclature, whence she came, and whither she is tending, is beyond my ken," wrote the correspondent, "but this we will venture to say—that if she was born a Quaker, *she has got bravely over it.* To witness the boldness of her manner, speech, and gesticulation, one is almost led to the conclusion that she only needs the sword, the charger, and the opportunity to become a second Joan of Arc, and placing herself in the stead of McClellan, whom she affects to underrate, lead the 'grand army' on to victory and glory."

"Aside from her peculiar sentiments," wrote another paper, "we have seldom heard a more eloquent speaker, with a power of argument and command of language that a man of years might be proud to possess; with a musical voice and clear utterance that could not fail to attract the most careless listener, together with her youthful appearance and winning address, make it a pleasure to listen, even though she advanced the most unwelcome statements, and made war on our favorite political theories."

It is curious that people should have been so willing to sit and listen to a girl not yet twenty speak on the war for an hour or two at a stretch. Two explanations suggest themselves. For one thing, in the nineteenth century people were much more accustomed to listening to platform speeches than twentieth-century folk nurtured on films and radio. Lecturing then was a very popular form of education and even entertainment, though the field was generally regarded as reserved for distinguished men of letters. Secondly, Anna's speaking ability was so remarkable that listeners came to hear her talks on recommendation of friends, much as one might attend the performance of a brilliant pianist or actor. Oratory was accepted as an art, and the audiences looked upon Anna as a child prodigy in this field. Her savage attacks on McClellan, stated in powerful denunciations based on classical models she had studied in her reading, held her listeners spellbound. Her absolute confidence, her complete command of the facts, her rich voice, her unfailing fluency were the marks of a master. She had at her disposal a virtuoso's technique: a great gift of language, a mind that could retain a tremendous array of facts in orderly fashion, and a logic that could unerringly turn up sham and inconsistency. When she was done, as one reporter wrote, "the people would not rise and go away, until she consented to deliver another lecture."

Nor did the listeners leave Anna's speeches behind them in the hall; discussions continued after the hall was closed for the evening and into the next day. One Rhode Island town after another was feeling the impact of Anna's strange magnificence. "The lecture of Miss Dickerson [*sic*] last evening formed a subject of considerable comment about the streets this morning," went one newspaper report. "At several corners small groups were seen discussing its merits. While some spoke of her arguments in terms of the highest praise, others denounced them in the most bitter language and regretted that such sentiments should find a refuge from a storm of indignation protected as they were by calico and crinoline."

In March, Anna was ready to return home to Philadelphia. In response to an invitation extended by a group of prominent friends to deliver "the lecture on the present war which you have given with so much effect in other cities," she made her talk on the national crisis at Concert Hall. Again the speech was a success and now within her limited abolitionist circle Anna had clearly established her ability in discussing politics. The real question, however, was to find some means by which she could reach new audiences, build up a public reputation, and make some money out of it, for since she left the millinery shop she had lived off her friends. Anna decided to appeal for aid to Garrison, hoping that he would remember his promise of the previous fall. Garrison was the most prominent name in the abolitionist movement; with his aid, Anna thought, a solution could perhaps be found to the problem of career making. She sat down and wrote a long letter to Garrison in Boston and asked him if he could work up some speaking engagements for her that would pay in money as well as in prestige. It was a respectful letter and bespoke a young woman considerably more mature and responsible than the girl of a year before.

Philadelphia, Pa.
Tuesday Morning
March 16, 1862

My Friend—You will let me call you so? I have thought often of the conversation which we had together last Autumn and of your kindly promise to do what you could for me if I should come to New England.

I wish to trespass on that kindness.

Some two months since I was discharged from the U.S. Mint in consequence of my abolition sentiments and the yet grave offense, being a woman, of expressing them in public. So Gov. Pollock stated to others.

Since then I have been lecturing, discussing the Woman's Rights Question once or twice, but giving almost exclusively a lecture on the times: "The National Crisis"—this was delivered to a crowded house at Concert Hall last Tuesday evening.

I should like to give this in Boston—and the other if desired. I write you this—to ask if I would be welcome, if I would have a good audience, if it would pay, if, in short, you think it well for me to come.

If you do—I should like to speak about Friday the 28th, but you will know best.

I spoke of its paying. Depending wholly on my own exertions, I must work to live. I have nothing to do. I need labor and profit.

I do not wish to tax your kindness nor trespass on the generous promise made months ago. I should like to come, but I leave it wholly with you to decide. May I hope for a speedy answer either yea or nay.

Very Respectfully and Truly Yours,
Anna E. Dickinson

Garrison replied within the week, and his letter must have quickened Anna's heart. He advised, first, against hiring a hall to lecture in Boston because Anna was not publicly known there, and so many speeches on the war had already been delivered in the city. He had another and better suggestion to make. He had spoken to the committee of the late Theodore Parker's congregation, and the committee, on the strength of his assurances, had consented to have Anna lecture from their pulpit at one of their Sunday morning meetings in April. "This will insure you the immense Music Hall," Garrison wrote, "without any cost, a good audience, and I presume the usual fee of twenty dollars."

From this platform, on the other Sundays of April, Ralph Waldo Emerson, Wendell Phillips, and Moncure D. Conway were scheduled to lecture. The invitation to a girl without position or reputation to speak of was unprecedented for the congregation, and an unexpected tribute to Anna.

Garrison had also conferred with the local antislavery committee, and reported that it wanted Anna to deliver her lecture in various towns in Massachusetts, averaging three evenings a week for four weeks. If Anna was willing, the committee would make all the arrangements, send her to reliable families where she would be made welcome, and see that she received "satisfactory remuneration."

"This will furnish you a good opportunity to make yourself known to the public as a lecturer," Garrison advised, "and I trust will be but the beginning of extended labors in the field of freedom, humanity, and progress."

Garrison himself would be at the depot the Friday evening prior to the meeting to greet Anna and take her to his home where she might stay. It might be, he added in a postscript, that there would also be an opportunity for Anna to speak on women's rights.

Anna leaped at the wonderful opportunity Garrison had gained for her, and quickly wrote to him to accept the invitation and express her gratitude. Acknowledging her acceptance, Garrison offered some fatherly advice on how to handle herself in giving her speech.

"You will need all the voice you can well command to be distinctly heard in Music Hall, on account of its immense size," he wrote. "It is some 80 feet from the floor to the wall, and much better adapted to singing than speaking. Most of the female lecturers fail for lack of voice and this has led those who are opposed to female speaking sneeringly to say, that if God had intended it, he would have given the necessary vocal powers. I am pretty confident that you will be able to make yourself heard generally, and the more you practice, the easier it will be for you. Do not feel hurried, but speak with deliberation, and do not allow yourself to be confined to the reading of your manuscript more than you can help, as that restrains action, and more or less affects the quantity of the voice."

On the last score, Garrison's advice was hardly necessary, for Anna habitually used no manuscript at all, speaking extemporaneously from none or the briefest of notes. She took Garrison's advice to heart only to the extent that she used the back of his letter and the small envelope it came in to jot down some notes for the April talk.

Anna was to speak on Sunday, April 27, following Emerson and Phillips, who spoke on the thirteenth and twentieth. Meantime, Garrison arranged for her to lecture on the ninth at Fall River, and wrote her again to urge her that she keep that engagement before coming to Boston. Apparently having great trust in her oratorical powers, but little confidence in her knowledge of business methods, he asked Anna to reply promptly whether she was prepared to go to Fall River, advising her to telegraph if necessary, and even supplied a suggested text: "Cannot go to Fall River. Particulars by letter."

Anna replied that she would make the trip by boat "if it be not exceedingly stormy and the water rough in which case I will take the cars for Boston." She arranged to deliver two lectures in Providence and one in Newport in the days preceding the Boston speech. To a committee in Rhode Island, she wrote, "I can speak for you three or four times a week, unless it be just before I come to Music Hall. I should like to have one or two days quiet previous to that."

The Rhode Island speeches added to Anna's reputation. In Providence "the youthful Anna E. Dickinson of Philadelphia," as one local paper put it, "provided a rich treat to all who heard her.... People were amazed that one so young as nineteen years only should show such a matured and disciplined mind, so well acquainted with facts of recent and remote history, and was able to speak with such fluency. ... Thankful should we all be for such an advocate of human rights."

"We are at a loss to conceive when sprung this new champion in petticoats of an anti-slavery war," the *Providence Press* declared on its second hearing of Anna, "but in sending her forth, her coadjutors have made a wise selection—for, with the tongue of a dozen women, she combines the boldness of forty men, and presuming upon her sex, will boldly utter sentiments in condemnation of men and measures, the utterance of which by one of the sterner sex might at times, and in some places, subject him to some little inconvenience. Nevertheless, it is a treat to listen to the woman, so bewitching (if we may apply the term) is the eloquence of her tongue and the significance of her gesture." The "sending forth of this modern Joan of Arc to preach the crusade against slavery," the *Press* concluded, "is a stroke of policy on the party of the Emancipationists."

From Pawtucket, Rhode Island, where she was scheduled to make a speech before going to Boston for her major address, Anna wrote to Susan playfully, describing her thrilling experiences:

April 18, 1862

My Dear Sister,

Here I is; at the house of a Mrs. Chase, very comfortable, thinking about speaking in this town tonight.

Third-day morn, reached the cars in safety, bought my ticket, checked my baggage, and came safely to New York. Went through to the Fall River boat, secured my stateroom and sat down to read. The boat leaves at five, and should reach F.R by four next morning, but the night was very stormy, the sea high and we did not arrive there till the next afternoon; I was very glad of this as it gave us almost the whole voyage by daylight and nothing could be more delightful than the scenery along the "Sound." Spoke at Fall River to a very large and very enthusiastic audience. It is a city of some 20,000 inhabitants; a great manufacturing place. From there I went to Newport, and had a splendid house, and fine success; stayed at Mrs. Murray's, an English lady, who has lived all over the world and who is now camped down with her two daughters at the great watering place, where she had resided for years. It is a country town of some 10,000 people, the streets are narrow and crooked, the sidewalks principally made of sand, the place generally one-horse. Summer time exhausts them for the rest of the year. Ellen and Harriet Murray and myself went to the beach first and then to the rocks. Were there from 9 in the morning till 5 in the afternoon, and then I was even more reluctant to go than I had been at first. There is no use trying to say anything about the ocean, or its voice, or to describe its wonderful fascination. I thought I knew something of it from descriptions, but the reality speedily dispelled that illusion—

How are you all—is mother any better, and has thy cold departed— With much love to Mother and Sam, and with the hope that I shall hear from thee in Boston, I am

Affectionately Thine

Anna

P.S. I am well, my throat strong, my voice excellent.

When Anna reached Boston she learned that the committee wanted her to speak on Sunday, April 20, the day originally assigned to Wendell Phillips. Phillips had just returned from the West so worn out and exhausted that he was unable to appear, and so came to Anna to ask that she take his place that day. "Think of that, mum—this small snip—acting as Wendell Phillipses substitute and at his own request at that," Anna wrote Susan. But Anna's flippant report was written after the ordeal had been endured, not before. Actually Anna was terrified by the prospect of facing the four or five thousand people that jammed Music Hall to hear her. Phillips was there, as well as other distinguished leaders of the anti-slavery and women's rights movements. Anna did not sleep at all the night before the speech nor could she take any breakfast the next morning. And all day long she was in a state of almost complete depression. Garrison tried to reassure her and give her confidence, as did other friends, but she seemed beyond such comforting. She was in an absolute agony of suspense and she was most lacking in that quality of self-confidence for which her audience so esteemed her.

The tendency to suffer great emotional depressions during which she was practically inconsolable seemed to be a significant aspect of Anna's personality—indeed, she seemed to be two different people. Left to herself she was certain of failure and weighted down by an immeasurable sense of despair and doubt; facing an audience from the platform, with all eyes on her, she was the very epitome of success and certainty and inspired such confidence that listeners often were borne past the bounds of rational behavior. Her mind and heart never seemed to work better than when they were under the great strain of public performance; her command of words and clarity of expression were never achieved more expertly than when the greatest demand was made upon them. The private Anna Dickinson and the public Anna Dickinson were two distinct individuals, and discerning friends like Samuel May, Jr., who arranged her talks at Fall River and elsewhere, expressed his fears to Elizabeth Buffum Chace. "It must be a great trial and even danger, to so young a person, to be the object of so much interest, to receive so much public applause, and to possess so great and happy a talent for holding and swaying the minds of large audiences," he wrote. Garrison had told him of Anna's not sleeping or eating before the speech and he himself had noted her depression. "I could wish she might be much with you," May wrote Mrs. Chace, "for the kind, motherly interest you feel in her would surely be for her benefit."

Anna's Boston speech was a success like all the other speeches before it. Wendell Phillips told her the next day that he had never been so gratified and so deeply moved by a speech. "Actually my dear Anna brought tears into my eyes—they had almost forgotten the sensation," he said. "I see him almost every day—as well as a great many other splendid people and indeed they have almost devoured me," an exuberant Anna wrote Susan. "One would suppose that 'no sich' had ever been seen in these quarters. Mr. Garrison says he has been overrun with thanks for finding me. However, I will stop blowing my own trumpet, being somewhat out of breath and will send you a paper or two, if I can find any about the house."

"I do not expect to be very rich—in pocket wealth this time," she went on. "Shall have *some,* but I am making my way and name now." She planned to return the next winter and then she could command her own price. Garrison had treated her like a father, and she found his wife and children delightful. "Willie is decidedly my favorite—talented as he can be, witty and gifted, and as splendid a specimen of simple, natural, dignified, attractive manhood as I ever met. Don't be alarmed now—there is not the slightest danger of falling in love."

Susan evidently was very pleased to hear of her sister's success, but like Mary Dickinson, no little concerned that Anna might become immodest of her own accomplishments. "Beware my dear child of being carried away by the voice of adulation," Mary Dickinson gently advised Anna. Susan wrote cautiously: "The newspaper writers appear to think thee is succeeding remarkably." Of Anna's pleasant description of the Garrison boys, Susan commented in jest, "Such a conglomeration of adjectives about Willie are de-cid-ed-ly suspicious. I shall begin to take the matter of consent into consideration if thee keeps on." And then, ever practical in her concern for money, Susan reported: "Mother wants to know whether, if she gets the parlor chairs done up, a matting for our floor, and one or two little matters done up in the furniture line, thee can spare her money enough when thee comes home to pay the bill, which she says will be from five to ten dollars."

A week after the Music Hall triumph, Garrison took Anna with him to New York to attend the annual convention of the New York Anti-Slavery Society at Cooper Institute. In that great and famous hall, he introduced her to the members of the Society and Anna made a half-hour speech that won favor from her fellow abolitionists. Anticipating Lincoln's Emancipation Proclamation by five months, Anna called for immediate liberation of the black men.

"Slavery," she said, "is the cause of the war. The war will not be fought with cause unless slavery is abolished. Proclaim its abolition immediately and the end will be achieved." Emancipation was simply a question of time. "I think the signs of the time point clearly to that," she said with an air of confidence that hardly befitted her years, "but it rests with you to say whether this time shall be shortened." Then, in a powerful emotional climax to her speech, she compared the warriors for emancipation with the courageous soldiers of General Grant, who stormed Fort Donelson, and painted a thrilling analogy that brought her listeners to a fever pitch of enthusiasm.

"Are you ready," she asked, "when the order comes, to send up word to our general in Washington, not merely that you desire it, but, as those men said to Grant, 'We will have it!' and step forward in the advance to take it? Are you ready to respond to the President, when you hear him ask, 'Are you ready?' to answer, as those men did, 'Aye, aye, sir, ready!' Are you ready to march straight up against the ramparts of slavery, mount them with one determined bound, and plant, on the ruins of the shattered and fallen system, the Stars and Stripes, bearing upon them the declaration, in characters of living light, 'Liberty proclaimed throughout all the land, to all the inhabitants thereof'?"

After the meeting Anna returned to Massachusetts to complete four weeks of talks. Out of this, her first New England adventure, there came one substantial reward: an invitation to address the Boston Fraternity of the 28th Congregational Society in the fall. It was to be Anna's first lyceum engagement; she would speak in a course of weekly lectures that included Henry Ward Beecher, George William Curtis, Wendell Phillips, Ralph Waldo Emerson, and Owen Lovejoy. Anna was the only woman on the schedule and though she was young and comparatively unknown, she would get $100, the same fee accorded the more distinguished luminaries in the series.

By turns inspirational, selfless, and, from force of circumstances, intensely practical, Anna briefed Susan in late May on the latest developments in her career:

Boston
May 27, 1862

Dear Susie—
I have not been silent because of sickness, or lack of desire but simply that I had not time. I have been changing my abode so continually since I left New York; have had so many claims on my time that I actually could not write nor indeed do scarce anything for myself. And this morning I can write not more than a

word. I shall tell you all that I have seen and heard, when I come home, for if I write again it will be not more than a line. I shall when my expenses are paid, and my debts carried out of the way, have next to no money at all, cannot indeed afford to buy myself a summer silk. However I am satisfied—I have made an opening which will be worth hundreds to me next winter and probably thousands afterwards. I already have an engagement to speak in the Fraternity Course—the highest honor that could be given to any lecturer with the price of $100. Satisfied? I hope that mother and thee are quite well again.

Love to Mother and Sam, and believe me

Very Affectionately Thine

Anna E.

Anna returned home for the summer and spent most of her time visiting wounded soldiers in crowded Army hospitals. It was common for respectable young ladies to contribute their services to the hospital—nursing and feeding the convalescing men, writing letters for them, and sometimes adopting one or two soldiers as their individual responsibility. "If thee chooses to keep that farina and cornstarch till I come up," Susan wrote Anna one day when she was out of the city, "I will cook it then, and thee can take it round and distribute it by cups-full—that is, if thee don't choose to do it thyself." The summer of 1862 was especially bloody for both North and South, with the Federal armies suffering a succession of defeats, casualty lists mounting steadily, and the war seeming no nearer its conclusion than the year before. Anna spent many hours talking with the soldiers recently returned from the battlefields. She learned their personal histories and their hardships, the motives that prompted them to enter service, what they had seen in battle and what they thought of the war. From these conversations she acquired an insight into the soldiers' life and feelings that supplied a firm foundation for the speeches she later made to men in uniform and their families at home.

To her benefactor, Elizabeth Buffum Chace, Anna wrote a pleasant letter describing her summer's activities and her state of mind. "My visit to New England taught me many things," Anna wrote. "Chief among them was a fuller appreciation of the great cause in which we are all interested, and the need for earnest, unselfish labor. And with this a better understanding of my own lack of knowledge, and general unfitness; and an earnest determination to strive after that which would make my work better and more effective, in the future." And to another new friend, Susan B. Anthony, the vigorous campaigner for women's rights who was Anna's senior by twenty years, Anna sent a letter that began a warm correspondence:

> The sunniest of sunny mornings to you, how are you today? Well and happy, I hope. To tell you the truth I want to see you very much indeed, to hold your hand in mine, to hear your voice, in a word, I want *you*—I can't have you? Well, I will at least put down a little fragment of my foolish self and send it to look up at you....
> I work closely and happily at my preparation for next winter— no, for the future—nine hours a day, generally; but I never felt better, exercise, morning and evening, and never touch a book or paper after gaslight this warm weather; so all those talks of yours were not thrown away upon me.
> What think you of the "signs of the times?" I am sad always, under all my folly;—this cruel tide of war, sweeping off the fresh, young, brave life to be dashed out utterly or thrown back shattered and ruined; I know we all have been implicated in the "great wrong," yet I think the comparatively innocent suffer today more than the guilty. And the result—will the people save the country they love so well, or will the rulers dig the nation's grave?
> Will you not write to me, please, soon? I want to see a touch of you very much.
>
> Very affectionately yours,
Anna E. Dickinson

In September, Lincoln issued the preliminary Emancipation Proclamation to take effect January 1, 1863. Lincoln knew that the Northern people did not support the abolitionist drive to turn the war into a crusade to free the slaves, and he, himself, had no marked enthusiasm for the cause of liberation. But the President felt that some gesture was necessary to placate the abolitionists. The proclamation was essentially meaningless: it freed the slaves only where the Federal government had no power to free them and left them in bondage in states that were still loyal to the Union. As one English newspaper commented, "The principle is not that a human being cannot justly own another, but that he cannot own him unless he is loyal to the United States." Almost six months after "emancipation" took effect, a reader of the *Baltimore Sun* in the loyal state of Maryland, sent to Anna an item printed in the classified advertising columns:

> TO BE SOLD A BARGAIN—A lady leaving for Europe wishes to dispose of her COLORED GIRL, in her ninth year, a slave for life. Also her 6 octave PIANOFORTE, in Mahogany case, with metalic plate and extension bar. Apply at the Sun office.

The abolitionists nevertheless greeted the proclamation triumphantly, feeling that it marked a turn in the war. Many, if not most, Northern voters did not favor the proclamation, however, and in the November elections, the Democrats capitalized on the popular discontent and war weariness, picking up such large blocs of seats that control of the Congress almost passed into the hands of the party that wanted a compromise or peace with the South.

In Boston to deliver her Lyceum lecture, Anna met some of the Republican political stalwarts. She was introduced to both Massachusetts senators, Charles Sumner and Henry Wilson, leaders in the antislavery fight. Susan wrote: "And so thee has really met Charles Sumner, and I suppose it put thee into quite an ecstasy of delight. Of course thee liked him exceedingly but is he just what thee expected from what thee has heard of him, or different. Give us a crum of information, will thee?" And then, later, "Glad thee liked Sumner. Why specially don't thee admire Wilson?"

In her lecture, Anna spoke on "Hospital Life." She related many touching incidents of the summer and drew vivid pictures of the horrors of both war and slavery. Though the lecture was a success, the hoped-for invitations to deliver similar talks throughout New England did not materialize. She did receive an invitation to deliver several talks at soldier benefits in New Hampshire in late December for $15 or $20 each, plus expenses, and having no other work to hold her, she accepted the engagements, though they would barely sustain her through the month. Her lecturing career, which in the spring seemed to have such a brilliant future, now seemed to be running out. Anna was again in a state of depression.

"I don't think since reading thy letter that lecturing prospects are very bright," Susan wrote to Anna in early December. "I hope, however, both for thy sake and ours that thee will be pretty well paid for what thee gets to do. What a weight would be taken off if we were only fairly out of debt."

Susan had been teaching in a small town called Mannington, but did not expect to continue when the term ended two weeks later. "I have had to fight my way through just the obstacles thee had in that school up river," Susan wrote. "If I were to stay it would be through various discomforts, and then I should come out in the spring without a cent left to buy clothing, no matter how closely I might try to economize." She was thinking of studying color painting for two months, in the hope that might prove a more profitable occupation. "As John has been urging on his sisters to learn something they can make more at, I shall tell him my plans by this next mail," Susan wrote Anna, "and tell him he must send on in next March the money for that quarter's rent, as a loan to me." From Anna she asked for a loan of $11.75 to buy a badly needed all-wool delaine dress.

As 1862 drew to an end and a new year beckoned, the fortunes of the Dickinson family approached the nadir. Susan abandoned the painting scheme upon learning that it paid but four to six dollars a week, and Anna, stranded in New Hampshire without any speaking engagements, besought Susan to make inquiries in Philadelphia in her behalf. No money had come from either John or Edwin who felt that their sisters should be able to care for themselves, and both daughters and Mary Dickinson were on the verge of penury. The weeks went by and still no hope brightened the horizon. Anna was now desperate for some means to sustain herself. She wanted to go home where she knew that at least she would have a roof over her head, but Susan bid her stay in New England "as long as thee can find anything to do, as there is no prospect of anything in the lecturing line here."

And then Susan offered Anna a suggestion. "I have been thinking lately whether it would not be well for thee to give poetical readings after the fashion of Mrs. Kimberly, Murdoch, &c. Thee has voice enough, and has had it trained enough to succeed, and it is likely to pay a great deal better than lecturing at present," she wrote. "I commend it to thy serious attention. Also while things are stagnant in the lecturing line and we are so in need of devising ways and means to make money would thee not do well after thee comes home to have a private class or classes in reading for a while." She knew Anna's feelings on the subject. "I know thee does not like teaching, but this would be very different from any teaching thee has ever undertaken, and it does not follow that thee need follow it always if thee should not like it."

Anna wondered whether she should abandon lecturing and attempt a career on the dramatic stage, though she knew that to do so would run contrary to all Quaker teaching and custom. She had been to the theater with the Garrisons and was fascinated by the actors and the costumes. So many fine things had been said of her voice and her emotional powers; why not transfer them to the theater? She confided her thoughts and intentions to Susan who was horror-struck: "I don't want thee to go on the stage, and hope thee will succeed otherwise in some way or other. Thee knows I don't like it.... I do get very discouraged sometimes," Susan noted sadly, "but I do my best not to, and hope we may both succeed in finding what may bring in more than we've been able to yet."

Thus, more than a year after she left the mint, and with two important lectures behind her as well as innumerable unimportant ones, Anna found herself once again without income and without prospect of any. She was all the more unhappy with her fate because success had been dangled so tantalizingly before her. Twice she had tasted it and now she wanted the experience of public adulation again and again. But her success depended foremost upon public interest and support, and these she could not manufacture of her own will. These time and events determined, and she could only await the conditioning of the public mind until there might be a public disposed, even anxious, to hear her call to arms in the war against slavery. The world looked very dull and gray to a depressed Anna Dickinson in January, 1863, because she forgot, or did not know, that events often move with dramatic suddenness, and careers can be made overnight, as it were, if the time suddenly ripens and opportunity presents itself.

CHAPTER 4

"SHE HAS NO EQUAL IN CONNECTICUT!"

WITHIN a month Anna's fortunes had completely changed and she was up to her neck in a bitterly contested gubernatorial campaign in New Hampshire, speaking night after night to immense gatherings.

The dawn of 1863 saw Republican political prospects at their lowest ebb. There was real danger that the Copperhead Peace Democrats would gain sufficient political support to block vigorous prosecution of the war and the North would be forced to negotiate a settlement with the South. The fall elections had come as a heavy blow to the party of Lincoln. In New York a fifty-thousand-Republican majority in 1860 was transformed into a Democratic majority of eleven thousand in 1862; Pennsylvania, Ohio, Indiana, and even Illinois, Lincoln's home state, went Democratic. And in states that remained Republican there was a marked decline in majorities. The issues of the election were the conduct of the war, the emancipation of the Negro, Lincoln's arbitrary arrests of suspected Confederate sympathizers, and military conscription. The verdict showed clearly that the people of the North were opposed to the Republican record on each point.

New Hampshire was the first state to hold a major election in 1863 and the whole country watched the campaign closely to see whether the trend away from the Republicans would continue. The optimistic Democrats nominated a Copperhead who opposed the Emancipation Proclamation while the despondent Republicans chose an ambitious but colorless candidate who stood for abolition and condemned slavery as the cause of the war. A third candidate was put into the field by a group of "Union" Democrats who supported the war and hoped to attract the votes of moderate Republicans and Democrats.

"The conflict was sharp, and the result in the utmost doubt," wrote the *Concord Statesman* on March 13, after the votes were in. "Had the vote been taken in the beginning of February, the State would have been lost to the Administration." Both parties threw their major resources into the battle and waged furious campaigns, bringing into the state congressmen, governors, and prominent orators from all over the country.

It was this New Hampshire election campaign that roused Anna from the slough of despond and first cast her into the public limelight in the role of a popular heroine. Anna entered the fray through the astute offices of one Benjamin Franklin Prescott, a thirty-year-old Dartmouth graduate who was secretary of the Republican State Committee and who later became governor of New Hampshire. Prescott had heard Anna's lecture on "Hospital Life" in November and reportedly said to a friend, "If we can get this girl to make that speech all through New Hampshire, we can carry the Republican ticket in the coming election." On his invitation, Anna went to New Hampshire in December, and for the next several weeks, she spoke in various small towns as Prescott tried to persuade the state committee to hire her as a campaign speaker. The notion that a twenty-year-old girl should be sent out on the stump at first struck seasoned politicians as slightly ridiculous, but many changed their minds when they observed the enthusiasm that greeted Anna at her fifteen and twenty dollar talks. They began to think they might make use of her much as a tribe of elephants, forced to cross an untried bridge, first sends over a "little white elephant," knowing that if it goes over without the bridge shaking they can go over without its breaking. Anna was to test out audiences and arguments for the main speakers. But not all committee members felt that she was qualified. "Don't send that damn woman down here to defeat my election," wrote one member to Prescott. Later, when he saw the furor Anna created he changed his mind and implored Prescott to send her to his district, but Prescott replied, "It is too late; the program is arranged and published throughout the state; you would not have her when you could, and now you can not have her when you will."

Prescott became Anna's personal adviser and political mentor. With her he impatiently awaited the committee's decision. When he learned that she was thinking of abandoning the platform for the stage, he did his best to dissuade her. Then, when the committee finally decided to sponsor her, he booked speeches for Anna throughout New Hampshire and advised her what to say, though he knew better than to tamper with her speaking style. He felt that Anna could do the most good in small towns and, after opening the campaign at Concord, he engaged her to speak at Dover, Somersworth, Rochester, Milton, Fannington, Conway, Alton, and Laconia. "Show up the disloyalty of the Democratic party and their sympathy with the rebels and take their acts to prove it," Prescott told Anna in a letter. "The women in this State who have sons in the war are considerably nervous and want the war closed (and you know the women are not always right) at almost any sacrifice. Please encourage them in all possible ways, and this way you can do much good," he wrote. "I will risk you anywhere. I think you will get good audiences wherever you go.... If you want any money, please write me and also direct me where to send it, and in whose care," he added. "I will pay all your postage, telegraphing, etc."

Delivering essentially the same speech she had been making since October, Anna swept through the state. When she spoke at Concord's Phoenix Hall, every seat on the main floor and in the gallery was occupied and hundreds were standing in the rear of the hall and in the side aisles. "Her audiences are held as though they were electrified," wrote a Concord paper. In Claremont the two local papers joined in praise of her. "It is only once in a great while that a Claremont audience are permitted to listen to such a flow of patriotic eloquence, to such noble, chaste, inspiring words from the lips of a noble and refined lady," stated the *Northern Advocate*. "What else than the living truth, demanding witnesses against traitors, could have inspired the delicate young girl, of twenty years, modest and unassuming in private deportment as any other mother's daughter in the land, to stand unabashed in the presence of thousands and electrify them by her thrilling sentences!" asked the *National Eagle*. "Miss Dickinson, the lady in question, is a very remarkable person. To the true woman's natural wit and readiness, she adds a masculine vigor of thought and generalization, a memory never at fault, a voice of much sweetness but of a great volume, earnestness, pathos, and a spice of Irish invective that renders her a formidable foe to Copperheads."

Anna was saying nothing new, but what she said she said vigorously and impellingly, and the people were now disposed to listen to what before they had ignored. She defended Lincoln's administration of the war and called upon her audiences to come to its support at the ballot box. She went beyond the Emancipation Proclamation and argued that the North should allow Negroes to enlist and fight as soldiers on an equal basis with white men, and justified Lincoln's arbitrary arrests of suspected traitors on the ground that nothing should be permitted to hinder the government from maintaining its authority in time of great national peril. Wrote one reporter: "She showered grape and canister on the heads of inefficient tenderfooted military leaders, and rattled thunder in the ears of traitors who stay at home crying Peace." She called upon the young men to enlist valiantly in the war of liberation and thus spare themselves and the state from the workings of the widely detested draft at the same time as they won glory for themselves. "For a combination of statistics, historical allusion, thrilling narrative and true pathos, the lecture of this truly accomplished lady is rarely excelled," wrote one listener. "A guerrilla speech, utterly regardless of headquarters and red tape," noted another. "No speaker in the State merits more honorable mention than Miss Dickinson," wrote the *Concord Independent Democrat*. "It is sufficient to say that wherever she has been, and she has spoken about 20 times, her audiences have been the fullest of any during the campaign; and in no instance have they failed to urge her to speak a second time. . . ."

As the campaign drew toward its close, the Republican leader in Sandwich, New Hampshire, wrote to Prescott. "We must have Miss Dickinson in our town if possible, for it may be the means of saving us. Such men as we want to hear a lecture will not turn out to hear a man. A few of our Copperheads heard her at Moultonboro[?] and they are completely shelled out. Now, cannot the matter be so arranged that we can have her services some evening or P.M.? Our people say they must have her, or we are 'stuck in the mud.'"

The election was close. The five thousand votes polled by the third candidate prevented either of the main candidates from winning an outright majority and the election was thrown into the Republican-controlled state legislature, which gave the governorship to the Republican. The party was jubilant and heaped praise on its "little white elephant" who had campaigned so vigorously for the party's cause. The governor-elect swore that Anna's speeches had made his election possible, and Republican papers unanimously insisted that if Anna had spoken in every town in the state, the victory would have been more decisive.

The *Granite State Free Press* wrote: "Although our political triumph is all we could expect with the opposition we had to overcome, yet we are confident that had Miss Dickinson spoken in every town in the State, the result would have been more gratifying...." As Anna was about to take the train from Lebanon to Concord, the local citizens presented her with a purse of $18 as "a light token of their esteem" and a crowd assembled at the depot to bid her good-by with six rousing cheers as the cars moved away.

The public image of Anna Dickinson as a heroine was rapidly taking shape, swept along by an accelerating momentum of feelings and events. Inwardly Anna was still very much the same girl, and for a considerable time she resisted the seemingly inevitable tendency toward a ruinous vainglory that so often entraps one who has the misfortune of being praised too much. It was inspiriting to know that she was wanted and was doing good for a cause she so passionately believed in, and her moments of depression now came less frequently. She gave thought to her own welfare and that of her family. The New Hampshire race had brought Anna very little by way of money. Susan, acknowledging receipt of a postal money order, wrote that she would use it to pay for Anna's coat and her dentist's bill, and "a couple of dollars for home," and that "Mother says she will be glad to see thee safe housed at home again." But the campaign established her as a political power the Democrats would have to reckon with and Anna shrewdly suspected that she would be able to make some personal capital out of the situation. She had shown that her impassioned addresses could swing votes and, in crucial contests, possibly turn the electoral tide. Republican politicians in Maine faced municipal elections in a fortnight and invited Anna to tour the state in their behalf. Her career continued to pick up speed in its advancement.

In three weeks voters in the state of Connecticut would be casting their ballots in a gubernatorial election. In the first two years of the war Connecticut, under a Republican governor, had given Lincoln staunch support. But popular dissatisfaction with the war was undermining Republican strength in the state. Desertions from the floundering armies averaged two hundred a day and battle casualties were high. To maintain the armies at battle strength the Congress, on March 3, passed the first national conscription act, which authorized the drafting of men by federal officers and provided exemptions to those who paid $300 or supplied a substitute. The act was distinctly unpopular and the Democrats denounced it as unconstitutional. The enrollment officers often met armed resistance outside homes and factories. Resentment against the draft found its natural political outlet in a feeling against the Republicans who had enacted it in the closing days of the session. Mothers of Connecticut soldiers longed for the return of their sons and could find little warmth in their hearts for a party that brought neither victory nor peace. Many manufacturers, like the New Haven carriage makers, who before the war had sold three fourths of their products in the South, were eager to end the war and restore their trade, and the numerous Irish and German immigrants showed no enthusiasm for the new emancipation policy that freed Negroes to compete with them in the labor market. All in all, it was a poor time for the Republicans to face an election: a Republican defeat would effectually withdraw Connecticut from the Administration fold, cut off further support for the Union forces, and pressure Lincoln and Congress into calling off the war. Connecticut Republicans, mindful of the November town elections, which had brought sorrows to the party and presaged an even more sorrowful state-wide election—Milford had gone Democrat for the first time in nearly fifty years and Hartford and New Haven and other large cities had also registered clear-cut majorities for the Democrats—were fairly resigned to defeat in April. They renominated the incumbent, but privately conceded that the Democrats would carry the state by at least four thousand.

Confident of victory, the Democrats put up as their candidate the leading "Peace Democrat" of the state—Thomas H. Seymour, a former governor, who called upon the people to rally under the banner of "No more war!" Seymour urged the people "to abandon the monstrous fallacy" that the war could restore the Union and proposed withdrawing the Northern army from the field.

With the issues clear cut and the eyes of the nation upon the outcome, the campaign was launched in an atmosphere of virulence and antagonism, which often flared into violence. "We are having the most bitter campaign I have ever known in this state," wrote Calvin Day to Secretary of the Navy Gideon Welles, "and in the absence of so many of our brave men in the field I have great fears of the result. Men who have sent their sons to fight Jeff Davis at Vicksburg and on the Potomac are doing all one can here to support the rebellion by electing Tom Seymour."

In an effort to overcome their own desperation, the Republicans imported a galaxy of governors from Wisconsin, Indiana, and Texas, and a generous collection of congressmen and generals. It was perhaps the *New Haven Register,* a Democratic organ, that set the tone for the campaign when it proclaimed: "A vote for the Republican ticket is a vote to mortgage every dollar's worth of property in this State for the Abolitionist Disunionists to carry on this negro war and flood the whole North and South with lazy, thieving negroes to be supported by the charity and taxes of our people."

This was the situation in Connecticut when Anna entered the campaign belatedly, on March 25, with only two weeks remaining before election day. But the story of her success in the next twelve days soon became a subject for conversation and wonderment throughout New England and, indeed, throughout the North.

It was Prescott once again who engineered Anna's entrance into the Connecticut campaign. He wrote to a Hartford friend who sounded out the Republican state leaders about hiring the girl who had made such a splendid success in New Hampshire. The friend reported a surprisingly warm reaction from one of the chief politicos: "Though always opposed to ladies taking so conspicuous a position, as that of speaker to promiscuous assemblies, he thought there might be an exception in this case, that it seemed as if she were raised up for this present crisis, like Joan of Arc, and advocated her coming." On March 23, Prescott received a telegram from J. G. Batterson, chairman of the Republican State Committee, asking Anna to come to Connecticut to deliver a speech at Hartford two days later. The Connecticut Republicans, it was clear, were ready to experiment with "the young Quakeress."

"A new volunteer Champion for the Union, 'Miss Maria E. Dickinson,' has come to speak for it, and will make her appearance at Touro Hall this Tuesday evening at 7½ o'clock," announced the *Hartford Daily Post* on March 24. "She is a very strange prodigy that came into the canvass in New Hampshire at their recent election; not a woman, but a girl 20 years of age, a Joan of Arc that God sent into the field, as many half believed, to maintain the cause of the country at this dreadful and last crisis."

The Democratic press, anticipating no danger in Anna's arrival on the scene, made no comment. Within forty-eight hours the situation changed.

When Anna finished her first speech in Hartford, the overjoyed chairman of the Republican State Committee wired Prescott: MISS DICKINSON SPOKE TO A CROWDED HOUSE LAST NIGHT. SHE HAS NO EQUAL IN CONNECTICUT. PEOPLE WILD WITH ENTHUSIASM. BATTERSON

Hartford for once has been astonished [reported Charles Dudley Warner's *Press* the next morning]. With some curiosity to hear what a woman could say about politics, people went last night to Touro Hall. The speaker, Miss Anna E. Dickinson of Philadelphia, was almost unknown to most who went, except by a vague rumor, unheralded, except that just at night her positive coming was announced in the *Press*. Yet the Hall, which was comfortably filled at the beginning of the address, was packed as we never saw it as the evening went on. And the audience, which began to listen in a quiet, half-critical manner, soon lost control of itself under the witchery of such a spell as a Hartford audience was never under before....

She spoke rapidly, her ideas evidently outrunning even her lightning-like utterance, memory and imagination both crowding her. We shall attempt no hint even of her lecture. It was at once a rapid, masterly sketch of the war in its inception, continuance and prospective end, exhibiting a knowledge and careful estimate of men and measures which constantly astonished her listeners. And as she went on mingling argument, invective, pathos, sarcasm, irresistible appeal, we felt that she had the passion of the South and the brain of the North on fire with inspiration. It was Portia making a statement, it was a Pythia prophesying, it was better than either, an American Woman, cultivated, trained, endowed, devoted to the noblest cause since the Christian era began.

Do we exaggerate? Everyone who heard her will say that what we have written above is cold and inadequate. In certain powers as a speaker we have never heard her excelled. Only one man, whom we have heard, George Thompson, at all equals her in the ability to carry a climax successfully to the dizzy heights where born orators alone walk with step firm and eye serene. Her peroration we have never heard equalled. With figure dilating, face impassioned, eye flashing, she poured forth that wonderful illustration and appeal, and the audience, breathless, almost translated, hung upon her words, and, when her voice ceased but slowly regained their self-possession and broke forth into cheering and the most extravagant demonstrations of delight, which continued several minutes.

If every voter could hear her there would be no doubt of the general expression of opinion which was heard last night—this woman is sent as from on high to save the state.

The Republicans were beside themselves with delight at Anna's overwhelming success in her first Connecticut speech and immediately scheduled her to speak every night throughout the state. The Democrats now felt that Anna could not be safely ignored and proceeded to deride her publicly and to plant hecklers to upset her meetings. But if they expected Anna to fall under the weight of calculated disturbances and rowdyism, they misjudged their quarry. The *Hartford Times,* a Democratic organ, responded to Anna's first speech by denouncing her as a "spirit medium" or a "spiritualist" and charged accurately that she was a female abolitionist only "48 hours from the presence of W. Lloyd Garrison." The *Hartford Courant* came to Anna's defense and called for an apology, which the *Times* refused to tender, and the two papers waged an editorial war over Anna's role in the campaign. "Nothing so popularizes any cause as a petticoat," snorted the Democratic *New Haven Register* with sarcastic gallantry, "and the Democrats, having been assailed in their affection, must surrender at discretion."

Meanwhile, night after night, Anna addressed audiences all over the state and took on the Copperhead hecklers in a manner that made her speeches pure drama. In Middletown, Anna had been speaking for about half an hour to an audience of two thousand people when the Copperheads put on a demonstration. In the midst of her speech, the gaslights suddenly grew dim and then went out, leaving the hall in absolute darkness. It was not immediately realized that some local Democrats had turned off the lights by cutting off the fuel supply at the local gasworks. The audience remained quiet, waiting anxiously for the lights to be restored, but several rowdies near the door, planted there for a purpose, began to shout and whistle and catcall and created a general disturbance.

"I see," said Anna calmly, "that there are those here who evidently love darkness better than light, because their deeds are evil." As the lights reappeared in two or three minutes when the sabotage was discovered and the gas turned on again, Anna said, "I read my Bible. I read of the Prince of Darkness, and judging from the present display, some of his children are present!"

The laughter of the audience induced Anna to continue in the same vein: "I read natural history, too," she said. "I read of a creature that loves caves and dens and holes in the earth, dank and *dark* places—and I suppose from the last fact that some of them are in this hall. Copperheads, I believe they are called."

"Good! Good!" cheered the audience.

But the Copperheads were still determined to break up the meeting. Cries of "Fire! Fire!" were soon heard from the street; a fire engine rattled down the pavement and stopped near the hall. In the auditorium suspicious Republicans cried out: "A Copperhead trick!" A woman screamed "Fire!" at the top of her voice. There was some excitement as the firemen were called for, but the audience refused to budge. When it was learned that a barn had been set on fire in another part of the city and the trickery exposed, Anna went on with her speech.

She had hardly resumed when the cry "Fire!" was repeated out in the street and in the corridors of the hall, and a large bell began to ring violently, drowning out the speaking and spreading a sense of alarm. On the platform behind Anna sat Congressman Jenckes of Rhode Island, a Republican representative who had been elected the day before by a large majority. As the bell continued to ring, Anna said simply: "I have been wondering why that bell was ringing. I suddenly bethink me. They are rejoicing over the glorious victory in our sister state of Rhode Island, and showing due respect to the man, elected by over two thousand majority, who honors us by his presence tonight."

The audience rose to its feet and cheered again and again for Rhode Island.

The Democrats, not wishing to lend further endorsement to the Republican victory in Rhode Island, stopped ringing the bell and Anna went on. But not many minutes had elapsed when the cry of "Fire!" was again raised at the door. Anna paused, with an expression on her face that bespoke her anger at this rowdyism, and with a flushed face and flashing eyes, she stepped forward toward the audience and cried out in resounding tones: "Yes, there *is* a fire—by God's grace we have kindled a fire, which these people by their acts are assisting, that will never go out, till naught is left of the principles they profess, or of their party—save ashes!"

That was enough. The Copperheads slunk down abashed, the house cheered till the roof rang. Without further interruption Anna went on to complete her speech. It was a remarkable demonstration by a girl who, six weeks before, was being urged to resort to the teaching of poetry reading.

In Waterbury, on the night Anna was announced to speak, long before the doors were opened, the street in front of the auditorium was literally blockaded with men and women waiting to enter. It was the largest audience ever assembled in the city and Anna created the same unbounded enthusiasm she aroused wherever she went in the state. Anna knew that most of her listeners were Irish immigrants who had voted Democrat the year before and who came to hear her mainly out of curiosity. She directed her whole speech toward winning over the immigrant laborers to the Republican party's position on the war. In doing so, she made one of the very few speeches of the whole campaign that touched on the protective tariff policies of the Republicans.

Anna asked her listeners why they came to this country if it was not to avoid starvation and to obtain decent standards of living. "In the old country you worked for ten cents a day, and Mr. Buchanan, the late Democratic president, said that was enough for you," she said.

"That's all we get now!" cried an Irishman in the back of the house.

"What was that?" Anna asked, her eyes seeking out the challenger.

The assertion was repeated.

"Then, my friend," said Anna deftly, "you must be working for a Democrat!"

Shouts of "Brown Brothers!" rang all over the house as the audience turned its laughter against the Irishman. As all Waterbury workers knew, every large company in the city had increased wages except Brown Brothers, the only Democratic factory in Waterbury. Anna's clever reply may have struck home as a pure coincidence or else Anna was making use of information she picked up the day of the speech.

"You have nothing to gain," she told the laborers, "by voting for slavery. Give the slaves their liberty in the South, and they will stay there. Refuse it, and they will come to the North, and slave labor will be in competition with your own. Which do you prefer?"

Turning to the Irish immigrants, she asked: "Shall it be said of you who have come from foreign shores—you who have fled from despotism at home—that you have come to this country to crush out the four million human beings whose fate is infinitely worse than yours ever was?"

Anna's reputation grew with each speech. "If forty iron-clads had made their appearance in the Connecticut river any fine morning unannounced, they would not have excited the Copperheads to a more violent fury," noted a local paper on Anna's arrival in the city for a speech. "The organ of this disloyal set burst into a foaming torrent of epithets on her arrival, such as with all its practice it has not used toward any *man* in New England. The welcome thus given to her, turned to the fair speaker's advantage, as she is now addressing friendly audiences whose enthusiasm runs wild in her favor. In nearly all sections of the state the cause looks more promising than it has at any time since the campaign began....A few more days will decide the battle against them." The *Norwalk Weekly Gazette* noted in an editorial titled "The Modern Joan of Arc," that "For the past ten days the loyal press in the vicinity of Hartford have gone *wild* over a new sensation—a Miss Dickinson, a young Quakeress, who was stumping the state for the cause of the Union." By the end of March Anna's name was already familiar to top Republican leaders in Washington. Joseph Allyn, a Connecticut politician, wrote to Secretary of the Navy Gideon Welles on March 30, "The little Quakeress is stirring the popular heart..." and wrote all about Anna to the Secretary's wife. Prescott wrote to Philadelphia to tell Mary and Susan Dickinson of Anna's huge success, but Anna had little time to write herself. She had become the toast of the Republicans. She was the object of adulation from all sides, but she seemed to maintain a firm hold on herself. Before the campaign was over she wrote to Susan to look for a better house for the Dickinsons to live in. With the earnings she expected from the campaign and from anticipated lecture bookings guaranteed by her new prestige, she would be able to afford more luxurious quarters for the family. Certainly the toast of New England could not expect to entertain her important friends in shabby rooms. Anna now moved in a circle of the most influential liberal journalists of the day. Acidulous Sam Bowles, editor of the *Springfield Republican,* became her warm friend, as did Charles Dudley Warner, of the *Hartford Press,* Isabella Beecher Hooker, and numerous congressmen with whom she campaigned, including her own Philadelphia representative

Judge William D. Kelley, a kindly six-foot-three congressman who took a very close interest in Anna's prospective career.

By the end of her two weeks of stump speaking, Anna had so established her popularity that the Republicans singled her out from their whole list of speakers to deliver the closing speech of the campaign at Allyn Hall in Hartford. They were willing to rest their case upon her efforts. It proved to be an occasion long remembered by those whose good fortune it was to attend.

Allyn Hall was packed as never before. The aisles were full of men who stood patiently for more than three hours; the window sills had their occupants, every foot of standing room was taken, and in the rear of the galleries men seemed to hang in swarms like bees. Ladies were told not to come, but about three hundred came just the same. A special train from Bristol, Terryville, and New Britain brought several carloads of irrepressible ladies who were permitted to sit on the stage behind the speaker. "People who used to be afraid Allyn Hall would tumble down must have been satisfied with the test applied Saturday evening," noted a Hartford paper. "We do not see where a dozen more people could be 'accommodated' in the hall, except by stringing them up on the strips of red, white and blue, so gracefully extending in festoons from the center of the ceiling."

A heavy cold had kept Anna in bed throughout the day, but it seemed to disappear at the sight of the audience. Once she began she did not stop for two hours. "Her power over that audience was marvellous," observed the *Hartford Courant*. "She seemed to have that absolute mastery of it which Joan of Arc is reported to have had of the French troops. They followed her with that deep attention which is unwilling to lose a word, greeting her ever and anon with bursts of applause."

> She reminded me of a lioness or tigress pacing back and forth in her cage, [wrote one observer] as she herself paced back and forth on the stage; if anything, her look was more fierce, her bearing more majestic, and her wrath more terrific. To some insulting remarks by a Copperhead, she roused herself like a tigress about to spring upon her prey—her whole manner fierce and imposing—her eyes almost literally flashing coals of fire. The audience were disposed to put the man out. She said, "No, I want him to stay and hear me." He did hear her, and I would almost bet my life against

his, that he felt so infinitely small that it would not have been a difficult matter to have squeezed him into a grain of mustard seed.

I never heard such terrible, yet polite invective from any one; it was scathing. . . .

I think I hear you say I am excited. I admit it, I am; it seems as if I was on fire, and everyone else that heard her are about as bad off. Editor —— says that, as old as he is, he never heard anything that would begin to equal it. Edward Everett is nowhere in my humble opinion. I will now stop, or you will no doubt think I am crazy.

The *Hartford Post* confirmed this listener's account. The speaker "was frequently interrupted by perfect storms of applause that fairly shook the hall, and sometimes prevented her from being heard for five minutes at a time," the *Post* declared. *THE GREATEST RALLY OF THE CAMPAIGN! A SPLENDID SPEECH FROM THE MOST REMARKABLE WOMAN OF THE AGE,* headlined the *Courant.* When the address was over, the audience gave Anna nine rousing cheers.

When the ballots were counted, the Republican governor edged through to victory by almost three thousand votes and Connecticut was saved for the war. The victory that had been in the Democrats' grasp throughout the campaign had suddenly slipped away at the end. Both parties agreed there was only one explanation of the surprising result: a last-hour reaction in favor of the Republicans was the principal cause of their victory. To Anna Dickinson was assigned primary responsibility for influencing the final turn. Had the President himself entered the lists in behalf of the Republicans and swung the election, the demonstration of his power over public opinion would have been impressive. But for a young girl, only two weeks before without position in politics and unknown in the state, the achievement was nothing less than monumental. The joy and gratitude of the Republicans knew no bounds. Some of the leading members of the party, flush with victory, presented Anna with a gold watch and chain, $100 for every night she had spoken, and $400 for the closing speech at Hartford. Popular sentiment toward the heroine was suggested by a letter writer to a Hartford paper who asked where Anna would work next for the Union. "If it were submitted to the popular vote in Hartford, doubtless she might within a week have a

Major-Generalship," wrote the anonymous enthusiast. "She could easily have enlisted a small army from Allyn Hall on Saturday night who should have been glad to fight under her leadership. But she may not like this—and as there are no more elections to carry just now—the question is, what *shall* she do. She is of course public property—to go wherever the public directs." The writer suggested that Anna be sent to England to enlighten the British about the war. "God makes only one such woman in an age—and no one who has witnessed the wonderful power of this modern Joan of Arc, can doubt that she has been raised up for some great purpose."

Soon invitations poured in asking Anna to speak in different cities. There were no elections, but people were intrigued by the sensational newspaper reports and wanted to see "the young Quakeress" for themselves. She returned to Boston to address the 28th Congregational Society and then New York beckoned. Anna was invited to speak at Cooper Union. Her way was paved by a letter Batterson, the Connecticut Republican leader, wrote to a political friend in New York:

> Office, Republican State Central Committee
> Hartford, Conn., 15th April, 1863
>
> Dear Sir:
> I desire to say a few words to you in behalf of Miss Anna E. Dickinson of Philadelphia, who has been speaking in Connecticut during the political campaign which has just closed so triumphantly for the cause of truth and justice.
> Prejudiced against her at the start, we had great misgivings as to the propriety of inviting her to take a part in our campaign. She had not spoken ten minues before all prejudices were dispelled; thirty minutes, and not a man could be found who would admit that he ever had prejudices; sixty minutes, and she held 1500 people breathless with admiration and astonishment; two hours, and she had raised her entire audience to a pitch of enthusiasm which was perfectly irresistible. She is really a wonderful woman, and you ought to invite her to speak in New York. Her voice is clear and of sufficient power for any audience you can get, and yet not masculine. She speaks rapidly, but her enunciation is so complete and perfect that not a word is lost.

Possessing a remarkably logical and argumentative mind, she is not wanting, nevertheless, in that brilliancy of thought and expression which gives life and zest to a public speaker.

With a fund of facts and information which would be a fortune for an editor or a politician, she makes her own mark, and needs no endorsement after she has once spoken.

I trust you will not deny yourself the pleasure of hearing the most eloquent woman of the century in the largest hall you can command in New York.

> Yours very truly,
> J. W. Batterson,
> Chairman

In New York Anna received one of the greatest ovations ever given a woman in that city. Five thousand people crammed into Cooper Union and hundreds were turned away, unable to find standing places in the lobbies and outer halls. Anna was led into the hall by Charles Gould, head of the Loyal League of Union Citizens, and on the platform sat former Governor Morgan of New York, Horace Greeley, of the *Tribune,* Theodore Tilton, of the *Independent,* Senator Wilson, and numerous political and literary figures of the city. Henry Ward Beecher introduced her. "With a single turn of her bright dark eyes around the immense assemblage," a reporter noted, "she uttered one emphatic sentence that reached the farthest person in the vast room and silenced the house so that you could almost hear the rustle of a handkerchief." No war speech "so full of shot and shell as hers have we heard since the contest began," wrote another. Anna cried out: "Here stands the North and liberty; yonder stands the South and slavery; and one straight line of gore that reaches from one to the other is the only pathway that we dare to tread until the Union and Freedom are triumphant!"

She reviewed the unhappy history of the war with the succession of Union defeats, and placed the blame squarely on the generals who were either too timid or unwilling to do battle with the enemy. On McClellan she unleashed another merciless attack, but older and less impetuous now, she did not renew her charge of outright treason: "Finally they gave us a man who, if he is not a traitor, is unfortunate in his selection of friends, who waited month after month with the country looking on in concern, while his army was dying at the rate of 4,000 men a month from disease alone, and at last, when the feeling of the country drove him down to Manassas, at the close of the campaign, he found it defended by empty entrenchments with wooden guns."

Derisive laughter and long continued cheering broke out at this savage onslaught on the nation's military leadership. A man in the rear of the hall took exception and proposed a cheer for McClellan, producing loud cries of "Put him out!"

Anna stepped to the front of the platform and said, "Ladies and gentlemen, there is to be but one speech here tonight, and that is from the platform." Cheers drowned out the objections from the rear.

Anna went on: "Today the South is fighting for a government which shall recognize not a resemblance of free institutions, that will tolerate no independent middle class, permit no system of free education, allow no hours to labor, countenance no progress to the mechanical arts, encourage no development of the resources that tend to the improvement of the great middle classes."

She summed up her argument and called upon her followers to enlist in the crusade: "If this is a war for ideas, what is left us but to marshal the democracy and liberty against their serried hosts and fight, for the freedom of the world is at stake. Men on one side belie the contest, and cry out that it is a war for the nigger, men on the other hand belie it, and say it is a war simply for the black man. It is neither. It is the people's war for free government!"

"Last Tuesday night, New York, for the first time, met and recognized its living priestess," wrote a Connecticut correspondent to his home paper. "You, in Hartford, perhaps thought you were enthusiastic at Allyn Hall. You didn't begin to be. The audience at Cooper Union went crazy. Applause came often and in long-continued storms, hats were swung and handkerchiefs waved and at times the whole house was like a moving, tumultuous sea, flecked with white caps. Never have I seen in New York any speaker achieve such a triumph. At the close of the speech the audience almost overwhelmed her with congratulations, and she was nearly crushed by the eager throng which for three-quarters of an hour impeded her passage from the hall."

"This lady will be much better entitled to a statue than any of the Ministry or any of the Generals," wrote the correspondent for the

British Standard. "She is worth a hundred thousand men to the government."

The *New York Times,* like the other metropolitan papers, gave Anna's speech an extended account:

> Miss Dickinson must undoubtedly henceforth take rank among the leading, if not at the head of American female orators, and the sterner sex will be fortunate if she don't [*sic*] rank it too. . . .
>
> She sways the audience from the first moment of her electric utterance down to the last syllable of the ten thousand words which she must have spoken in one short hour. She is a walking encyclopedia of the events of the war, with all the pages open to you at a glance. She heaps history, fact, proverb, warning, story, appeal, and exhortation in convincing array, sweeping all before her in an avalanche of intellectual force. She has her hearers alternately laughing, crying, cheering, applauding, and listening with breathless suspense. 'The Charge of the Light Brigade,' as a battle picture, must fall into insignificance before her vivid and life-like description of the capture of Fort Donelson. No reporter's pencil is dexterous enough to follow the magical rapidity of her vocalization. As a faint specimen of her style, witness this imperfect extract of a sentence from her peroration:
>
> "The President asks you; the government of the United States asks you; the 200,000 graves and trenches, crowded with the best loved of the land, offered up for your sakes, ask you; the hundreds of thousands of brave fellows on the battlefield, facing death with gallant and undaunted front, ask you; the millions of the oppressed in all climes and of all countries, looking across the waters and praying with uplifted faces to God, ask you; four million of outraged, oppressed people, loaded with manacles, with hands held up with imploring supplications to God, ask you; the hope, the liberty, the truth, the justice of five hundred years at stake, ask you; this mighty nation struggling on step by step, almost to the grave, asks you. Loyal people of the North, *how will you respond?*"

Thunders of applause rang out at the climax of the sweeping conclusion as Anna lifted her arms, and the assembly, amid waving hats and handkerchiefs, rose to its feet and responded with one tumultuous cheer.

Flushed in face, but apparently unwearied, Anna took her seat. Henry Ward Beecher came to the front of the platform. "Let no man open his lips here tonight," he said. "Music is the only fitting accompaniment to the eloquent utterances we have heard." The evening closed with the singing of a ballad and the audience streamed out of Cooper Union with "John Brown's Body" on their lips.

CHAPTER 5

AMERICA'S JOAN OF ARC

"THEY do mistake who think we want all argument in our public speeches now," wrote a Hartford journalist after hearing Anna at Cooper Union. "We want Peter the Hermit, to preach crusades."

At places of business in New York the next day little was discussed save the public's new heroine. Delegations pursued her, to have her speak for one cause or another. "New York has taken her up and will not be refused," wrote the Hartford correspondent to his Connecticut readers. "Perhaps I tell you an open secret, but some hundreds of the leading men in New York will invite her to speak at the Academy of Music next week, and she will receive for it a sum so large that you would hardly believe me if I should tell you. And you, who take an interest in her, will be glad to know that she was handsomely remunerated for Tuesday night. I mention this gross matter not because she speaks for such considerations, or is moved by anything but the highest patriotism in her wonderful mission, but to show you the high favor New York is determined to lavish on her."

The address at Cooper Union brought Anna $1,000 plus an invitation to deliver a second talk two weeks later. She was besieged to repeat the lecture in Philadelphia: "Having heard with pleasure of the success that has attended your patriotic labors in New England and New York, and desiring to testify our high appreciation of your services," ran the invitation from thirty leading Union League Republicans of Philadelphia. Seven hundred people were crowded on the stage of the Philadelphia Academy when Anna spoke there and every seat was taken. When Mary Dickinson arrived and saw the thousands gathered for the sole purpose of hearing her daughter, she was almost beside herself.

"That child can never do it," she whispered to Susan.

"Why, mother, thee knows she has been speaking before just such houses for six months," Susan replied.

Connecticut invited Anna to be an honored guest at the inauguration of Governor Buckingham and the convening of the state legislature. Susan B. Anthony asked Anna to speak at the May anniversary meeting of the Women's Right Central Committee. "I see what wonders you are doing in slaying the Copperheads," the suffrage leader wrote. "Well, go ahead, it is a glorious work."

For Anna it *was* a glorious work, and those were glorious days. She had tapped a rich vein in public sentiment and the rewards of fame and fortune were flowing in. The moment called for a popular leader in the cause of war, and Anna was chosen for the role. She was chosen because she spoke the language of the people, appealing to feelings of pride, honor, self-sacrifice, and even self-interest, and thus could stimulate her audiences to do what they inwardly knew was their duty. She was a platform pamphleteer. She did not voice original ideas, but gave power and persuasiveness to ideas suggested by others. And so, Republican leaders sought her counsel. Senator Pomeroy of Kansas asked Anna if she would serve with him on a small vigilance committee to supervise Lincoln's administration of the war. In a few months an obscure Philadelphia maid was transformed into a figure of political importance and the metamorphosis was revealed not only outwardly in the popular image of a Joan of Arc, but inwardly in progressive changes of her own mind and heart. Anna developed new tastes and new desires. Accepting the lofty position assigned her by the public, she prepared to play the role of heroine to the fullest. Yet even in these moments of triumph she was beset by a confusion of desires and purposes, and she alternated between feelings of personal futility and exaggerated acknowledgments of her true status, one moment acting out of a genuine spirit of sacrifice and generosity and the next out of sheer self-interest. She was unpredictable not only to others, but to herself. But at all times she retained a sense of mission that carried her through moments of despair and excited those who heard her speak.

Soon she began to break away from her orthodox Quaker ties, though in doing so she necessarily ran counter to the counsel of Mary Dickinson. But Anna had seen the world outside Quaker circles and she wanted some of the beauty Quaker traditions proscribed. She bought a new wardrobe for the day when she would cast aside her religious habit. She rented a large house in Philadelphia, at 1710 Locust Street, for the Dickinson family. It was an expensive house; the rent amounted to $500 a year at first and later $1,000, which was a huge sum at the time. She furnished the house and paid the rent plus an additional $250 a month to cover household expenses. (Susan hired a colored girl at two dollars a week. "The few best girls who are to be had now are asking that," she explained to Anna.) She bestowed lavish gifts on friends and family and responded generously to charitable appeals. She seemed to have no sense whatever of the value of money and in her zeal to give to others she often gave more than she could afford, overlooking the more pressing needs of self and home. Two weeks after she donated $200 to the Western Provident Society and Children's Home in West Philadelphia, Susan was appealing to Anna to mail her some money to pay the grocer and butcher. "I shall have to go out this evening to borrow money," the sister of America's Joan of Arc wrote in desperation. "I hate to do it— it is very mortifying, but it cannot be helped."

After the speeches that spring, Anna settled down to rest in her new home, to assess her new prominence, and to prepare herself for a busy fall schedule of lectures. To the home on Locust Street streamed Anna's new friends—important people from the world of politics and journalism. Prominent widowers were especially attracted to Anna and paid court. "Ah, the poor Judge!" wrote Susan one day when Anna was away from home. "Mother says thee'll be like other women, settle sometime, and she don't believe thee'll ever have a better offer than the one thee's been putting by. What does thee think of that, my lady?" Anna thought poorly of the proposal; she was in no mood for marriage; she enjoyed the life of a heroine too much.

One day in June, a young man came to call on the Dickinsons in the company of Judge Kelley, the Philadelphia Congressman with whom Anna had campaigned in New England. The Judge's companion was only twenty-six, but he had already made a name for himself as one of the more promising young journalists in the country. He hailed from Xenia, Ohio, and was a war correspondent for the *Cincinnati Gazette*. His shrewd reports of front-line activity and his critical comments on McClellan's generalship had made him a favorite of the abolitionists. His lucid, restrained, and well-balanced style also won him a reputation as a reliable and perceptive reporter, and he had acquired many important political friends. A few months before, he was given a part-time post as librarian of the House of Representatives; he continued his journalistic duties on the side.

When Whitelaw Reid called in mid-June at 1710 Locust Street, he was a rising young man, not yet of great importance, but the eye of fortune was on him. He made a clean-cut appearance: a broad forehead, full mustache, well-shaped nose, and a small cluster of hair under his lower lip in the fashion of the day. His wide-set eyes were quick and missed no detail as he wired back to the *Gazette* a report on his first meeting with the young lady he was to know very well in the months and years ahead.

Judge Kelley and Whitelaw Reid were led into the parlor by the maid and busied themselves looking at the pictures of Napoleon on the wall. Presently Susan came in, "a petite little figure in blue," to entertain them while they waited for Anna. They discoursed most pleasantly of pictures, books, Philadelphia people, and Quaker ways. Judge Kelley began to get impatient and looked at his watch nervously. Suddenly they heard a rustling in the hall and a gay reply to an unheard question. A door was thrown open and, with her face flushed from exercise and her curls disordered, a young lady entered, exclaiming in a voice so rich, so steep, so mellow that one could not help envying its possessor: "It wasn't my fault, Judge. I'd have been back long ago if I'd had my way."

So Reid recorded the scene for his readers. He saw "a plump, round, supple figure, of about medium height, with graceful outlines half-concealed by the neatly fitting dress, glossy black hair, but tolerably short, and falling in luxuriant profusion about the neck and curling away from a low, broad forehead; deep eyes, of a dark hue you can hardly define, contracting and dilating in the excitement of the animated talk; a broad, rich mouth, with ripe lips that curve into a score of expressions in an instant; a square (not masculine) but still firmly set chin, that gives a hint of the persistent purpose that has brought this girl up through all manner of difficulties to a position almost as proud in its way as that of Mrs. Harriet Beecher Stowe."

It was a delightful visit, Reid told his readers. Indeed it must have been: Reid seemed quite taken by Anna and called frequently at the Dickinson home. She kept his calling cards with their brief, handwritten notes: "Will call here afterwards, if agreeable. Say Yes or No, on a card, please. W. R." And on the back Anna's reply: "Am just dressing for a lecture. Can I see you afterwards?" To which young Reid rejoined: "Who fails to keep engagements now? Shall try to come in between six and seven. W.R."

And another: "If Miss Dickinson won't consider me as fickle as—a woman—I'll beg to change my plan, and call this evening, at eight. If the charge of fickleness is withdrawn, I'll explain—not otherwise, why the change. W. R."

By nature Reid was cool, reserved, and undemonstrative, but his attitude toward Anna was one of great warmth and affection and the two would surely have seen more of each other that summer if their occupations did not call them in different directions.

The summer of 1863 proved the bloodiest of the war. That summer of Gettysburg Anna made only two public appearances. The first was at the National Hall in Philadelphia the very week of Gettysburg when mass meetings were called to raise three Negro regiments under authority recently granted by the Secretary of War. Judge Kelley, Frederick Douglass, the famous Negro freedman, and Anna were the featured speakers. Under the enlistment program Negro soldiers were to be paid less than whites and to receive no bounties. To overcome the resentment bred by this discrimination, Anna admitted the patent injustice of the ruling, but appealed to her Negro listeners to volunteer for nobler reasons than personal self-interest. "We need you," she said, "yet it is not because of this need that I ask you to go into the ranks of the regiments forming to fight in this war. My cheeks would crimson with shame, while my lips put the request that could be answered, 'Your soldiers? Why don't you give us the same bounty, and the same pay as the rest?' I have no answer to *that*. But for yourselves; because, after ages of watching and agony, your day is breaking; because your hour is come; because you hold the hammer which, upheld or falling, decides your destiny for woe or weal."

She continued: "The slave will be freed with or without you. The conscience and heart of the people have decreed that.... But the black man will be a *citizen* only by stamping his right to it in his blood!" She concluded with a call to arms: "You have not homes? Gain them! You have not liberty? Gain it! You have not a flag? Gain it! You have not a country? Be written down in history as the race who made one for themselves and saved one for another!"

The second speech Anna made that summer occurred on short

notice some weeks later and in rather dramatic circumstances. A field day was announced at Camp William Penn, not far from Philadelphia, for a public review of the Sixth Colored Regiment of U.S. troops. Many of the men were to leave for battle before the day was out. A vast crowd of friends and relatives came from Philadelphia to witness the review. Many of the soldiers who marched in the dress parade were men who had responded to Anna's call at the mass meeting the month before. They demonstrated the manual of arms and then formed in square formations before the commanding general. At this point in the proceedings word spread among the people that Anna was present on the field. Cries were heard on all sides for Anna to speak, and she came forward, mounted the platform atop a gun wagon, and stood with the general and his staff. The troops gathered round with bristling bayonets and flags flying, and the band was hushed. It was late afternoon, and the setting sun cast a soft light over the whole scene.

Anna's speech was short. She recalled the story of a huge chasm in ancient Rome, which the gods would not close until Rome had cast its most precious possessions into it, how all the treasures of the city were sacrificed in vain, until at last Quintus Curtius, declaring that Rome's most valued possession was her young manhood, rode full armed into the gaping chasm, which closed upon his grave, and gave to Rome solid ground and security once more.

"You go perhaps to your own graves," Anna said, "but I fear not that you will falter in your glorious mission. And when the solid ground once more closes in peace over our country, now so rent and torn, you shall never be forgotten, but they who come after shall say, 'Tread lightly! Tread lightly! For the ground whereon ye stand is the grace of martyrs, and is holy ground.'"

In August, Anna took the first real vacation she ever had in her life. First she persuaded Susan and Mary Dickinson to go to Cape May, New Jersey, for a few weeks and gave them the money for their seaside rest. Then she took off by herself for the White Mountains of New Hampshire, where she enjoyed the vigorous country air and built up her strength by climbing the highest peaks. She was a surprisingly athletic girl and she loved physical sport. Elizabeth Buffam Chace, who was also vacationing in the White Mountains, tells how she encountered Anna "making a tour of the mountains without a chaperon and also without fear and without reproach." Mrs. Chace asked her: "Has thy family become reconciled to thy public work?"

"Oh, yes!" Anna answered. "What I am doing was all wrong at first. It is all right now. Success, like charity, covers a multitude of sins."

Anna returned to Philadelphia in September and prepared for a lecture tour of New England cities. But instead of beginning her tour as scheduled, she found herself embroiled in political campaigning once again. The states of Pennsylvania and Ohio faced gubernatorial elections the next month; their loss would cost the Republican party state control and virtually insure the election of a Democratic president to succeed Lincoln the next year. In Ohio, Clement Vallandigham, banished to the Confederacy for hindering the prosecution of the war, was campaigning for governor on the Democratic ticket from his hide-out in Canada. In Pennsylvania, George W. Woodward, Chief Justice of the State Supreme Court and an outspoken apologist for secession, who had declared the draft act illegal, opposed Republican governor Andrew Curtin, one of Lincoln's strongest supporters. Judge Kelley feared that Curtin would lose unless a strong fight was made in his behalf; he pleaded with Anna to make herself available for the campaign. With invitations from the Ohio and Pennsylvania Republicans, Anna chose to campaign in her home state. Undoubtedly she was swayed by the offer made by the Pennsylvania Republican State Committee: $1,000 a day for twelve days of speaking. A host of distinguished men were invited to campaign for the party: Chauncey M. Depew, Henry J. Raymond, John W. Forney, Orestes A. Brownson, and numerous governors, senators, generals, and congressmen, but Anna's fee was by far the largest. The reason for the fee went beyond her unique capacity to win votes; no man dared to campaign for the Republicans in the back mining counties where the party intended to use Anna. Opposition to the draft and the war itself was so intense among Pennsylvania coal miners, many of whom were Irish-born members of the secret Molly Maguire society, that violence broke out when federal officers tried to enforce the conscription law. The year before, the officers had attempted to get lists of workers from the mine owners, but the employers refused to co-operate, fearing retaliation from the miners. Anyone connected with the draft stood in peril of murder by the Molly Maguires. More than five hundred miners forcibly prevented a trainload of draftees from leaving Potts-ville, and many draft evaders took advantage of the anti-conscription sentiment to hide away in the back counties. One day that summer a large body of armed Mollies entered Mauch Chunk, overwhelmed the citizens, seized the jail, and released the prisoners. A local surveyor who was suspected of co-operating with federal draft officials was murdered in his own home by a band of Mollies. The antislavery Republican orators of Anna's stripe were so repugnant to most miners that even the party's name was dropped for the campaign, the "People's Party" being substituted in its place.

Fears for Anna's safety in such a campaign were voiced by many of her political supporters. One friend wrote: "Apprehensions are ex-pressed that you will meet with a rough reception at Shamokin and I have been asked to urge you to avoid that place." But he thought Anna could safely run that risk. "Your sex will gain for you an at-tentive audience and your genius will do the rest." Anna seemed anxious to get into the back country and one may wonder to what extent she was motivated by a desire for martyrdom in so exposing herself. She began her speeches at Easton, Pennsylvania, and spoke daily in some of the roughest cities of the state: Allentown, Mauch Chunk, Wilkes Barre, Danville, Shamokin, Pottsville, Lebanon, Carlisle, Gettysburg, York, and Chester.

The miners' reaction was mixed. Many turned up out of curiosity, anxious to hear a speech from "petticoats." Others were rebellious and tried to cause trouble. In one of the towns, a group of rowdies gathered to prevent Anna from speaking. As she stepped upon the platform she was greeted with hisses and shouts of derision, and as she ad-vanced to the front the tumult increased. She stood there with an undaunted air, her head thrown back, her eyes blazing, one arm behind her, in an attitude all her admirers knew to be typical of her under fire, and stood waiting for the tumult to cease. Suddenly one man, more reckless or more inflamed than the others, drew a pistol from his pocket and fired at her. The bullet sheared off a lock of her hair. Anna held her ground. The look of contempt on her face deepened and her lips closed tightly. For a moment there was dead silence. Then a voice cried out: "Ah, but she's a brave girl, boys; let's hear what she has to say."

The tide was turned. There was a responsive cheer, as heartily voiced as the hisses of before.

Emboldened by this experience, Anna took the offensive when she was greeted with hisses at her next speech in Wilkes Barre. "I know of but two animals that use that mode of expressing themselves, the goose and the snake," she said. "If you, sir," turning in the direction of the sound, "can sit and listen to falsehoods in a Democratic meeting, and cannot listen to plain facts now, use the mode of locomotion designed by nature for your kind, and *get down and wriggle out!*" Reported the *Pottsville Miner's Journal:* "The effect was awful and the reptile was effectually scotched, if not killed outright, and not another hiss was heard."

The Pennsylvania speeches seemed to stir up a semireligious fervor wherever Anna went. Local comment reported in the press, referred to "crashing bolts of truth from Heaven-inspired lips." "We are told," went another report, "that Heaven is peopled with angels, and could anyone doubt that earth also has its angels, as he gazed upon that moving form, and listened to those enchanting tones, all heightened by the appeals in the cause of a true freedom, of a nation wounded almost to death, calling upon her children to rescue her from the poisonous fangs and boa-constrictor folds of the serpent 'rebellion' which even yet threatens to crush her existence!"

At Shamokin, Anna spoke for two hours in the local Methodist church and miners attended in considerable numbers. The *Philadelphia Press* reported that several fervent Copperheads openly expressed themselves as highly delighted with her oratory. One old gentleman who had never heard a lady speak in public or on the stage and whose prejudices against female orators were deeply rooted, was taunted by his friends for venturing to listen to Anna. "Well, I am of the same opinion still. A woman's place is at the fireside of the heart, to feed its flame," he replied, "but I verily believe Miss Dickinson has a special mission from Heaven for the conversion of Copperheads, and I am proud to acknowledge myself as one of her converts."

The Republicans swept through to victory and Anna accompanied the re-elected governor to Buffalo. There both joined in a plea for a Republican success in New York where the election of a Secretary of State and legislators took on national importance because of the prestige of Horatio Seymour, Democratic Governor of New York.

Anna addressed two mass rallies in Buffalo on a Saturday night, speaking first at St. James Hall and then at the Opera House. "It was oratory unparalleled in our experience," the *Buffalo Morning Express* said, "and we have no words with which to characterize it. The audience was fairly crazed with enthusiasm, and when this wonderful girl had retired from the stage, to pass over to the Opera House, the whole meeting would have followed her had not the Chairman announced that every inch of room in the latter place was already filled." After the meetings Anna was presented with a magnificent set of jewels, including a breastpin and earrings, by the Republican leaders. The Pennsylvania State Republican Committee, however, did not carry out its financial commitments to Anna. The $12,000 was never paid Anna, for reasons never publicly explained, and she never forgot or forgave the fraud perpetrated on her by her political friends. This was not to be the last instance of chicanery in business matters of which Anna was to be the victim, and in time such shocking experiences would shatter her ingenuous attitude toward business and political relationships. She was to learn to insist on written contracts and to have them observed to the letter.

Anna's fame was now unequalled by that of any other woman spokesman for the war. She had spoken in most states of the Northeast, and people clamored to hear her again. Where she had not yet spoken, the stories of her triumphs reached the unbelieving ears of men and women who wanted to see her in person. With the campaigns behind her, Anna was ready to return to the lecture platform. She was booked for ten talks in New England at $100 a night, the same fee earned by Henry Ward Beecher, the top lecturer in the country. But before she could leave for New England, she was besieged with an urgent request to address the huge gathering assembled at the Northwest Soldiers' Sanitary Fair in Chicago. The Fair was held to raise money for soldier benefits. It was Anna's first trip West. Chicago in 1863 was a small cattle city with unpaved streets. Anna stayed there only long enough to deliver two addresses, collect $300 for each (by far the largest fee paid any speaker at the Fair), and return East to complete her engagements. The size of her Chicago audiences can be judged by the fact that the Fair netted $1,140 on the two talks with tickets selling at a minimum price.

The cup was full and soon it must run over. There seemed to be no end of homage and fortune America would pay to a heroine. When Anna returned to Philadelphia, she found awaiting her an invitation to her most glorious triumph. She was to go to Washington to address the Congress of the United States.

Washington had had its eyes on Anna ever since the Connecticut campaign. As early as May, 1863, Senator Pomeroy of Kansas had raised the possibility of Anna's addressing the assembled bodies of Congress. Republican congressmen accepted her as an unofficial if somewhat unpredictable spokesman of the abolitionist wing of their party. She was their best vote getter and her command over public opinion grew with the months. It was Judge Kelley now who suggested that a good purpose might perhaps be served by inviting Anna to Washington for a talk. He thought she might be able to work her wonders on some of his Democratic antagonists. The reaction of his colleagues was favorable, and it was agreed to ask Anna to deliver an address in one of the Washington theaters where congressmen and senators might hear her.

Such an invitation, tendered through a congressman, might have impressed a person of even more than normal self-assertiveness. But not Anna. She was now fully aware of her own importance, undoubtedly too much so for the preservation of her humility. She set her own terms: she would not speak in Washington unless formally invited by the members of Congress and the place of her speech must be the Hall of Representatives itself. Judge Kelley protested; there was no precedent for such use of the Congressional chamber; no woman had ever been invited to deliver a political speech within its walls. But Anna would not budge from her determination. Those were her terms and they were not subject to compromise.

Kelley returned to Washington. There was some debate. The desire to have Anna in Washington was by now too great to be denied. The terms were accepted, and a formal invitation was drawn up by the Librarian of the House inviting Anna to the national capital. Over the signatures of more than one hundred senators and congressmen, including the Vice-President and Speaker, Charles Sumner, Thaddeus Stevens, James Garfield, James G. Blaine, Pomeroy, and William B. Allison, Whitelaw Reid, the Librarian of the House, wrote in clear letters on a long sheet of parchment:

To/ Miss Anna E. Dickinson
     Philadelphia, Penn.

Miss Dickinson:—
              Heartily appreciating
the value of your services in the campaigns
in New Hampshire, Connecticut, Pennsylvania & New York, & the qualities that
have combined to give you the deservedly
high reputation you enjoy; & desiring
as well to testify that appreciation as to
secure ourselves the pleasure of hearing
you, we unite in cordially inviting
you to deliver one or more addresses
this winter, at the Capital, at some
time suited to your own convenience.
Washington, D.C.
16th Dec. 1863

H. Hamlin.
Schuyler Colfax   J. H. Lane
A. C. Miller   James Dixon
Thaddeus S.   Chas. Sumner
Henry C. Deming   A. B. Stribling
Wm. D. Kelley   H. Wilson
Wm. B. Allison   S. C. Pomeroy
J. W. Patterson   John Sherman
Robt. C. Schenck   Lm. Morrill
J. A. Garfield   Edgar Cowan
Isaac N. Arnet.   H. S. Lane

First page of the invitation to Anna Dickinson to address Congress

Heartily appreciating the value of your services in the campaigns in New Hampshire, Connecticut, Pennsylvania, and New York, and the qualities that have combined to give you the deservedly high reputation you enjoy; and desiring as well to testify to that appreciation as to secure ourselves the pleasure of hearing you, we unite in cordially inviting you to deliver one or more addresses this winter, at the Capital, at some time suited to your own convenience.

Anna accepted and set the date for Saturday evening, January 16, 1864. The House of Representatives, over the opposition of some Copperhead Democrats, passed a resolution granting the use of the House to Anna for the speech. The proceeds from the talk (the congressmen would be charged admission to enter their own chamber!) were to be turned over to the National Freedmen's Relief Bureau, an organization designed to help emancipated slaves. The invitation itself was formally delivered to Anna in Philadelphia by Judge Kelley, representing the members of Congress, and with him came John Nicolay, secretary to the President, evidently representing Mr. Lincoln. The President, it appeared, was interested in Anna and most anxious to hear her speak. "The world belongs to those who take it," Anna often said. She was taking a firm grasp.

When Anna went to Washington in January, she was set to make a speech that would be long remembered by those who heard it. She chose for her targets the Rebel secessionists, the Northern Democrats, the Supreme Court, which had backed slavery in the Dred Scott decision, and the President himself. She would criticize Mr. Lincoln for his declaration of amnesty, issued the month before to all Confederate soldiers who were willing to swear allegiance to the Union. Anna felt that those who warred against the Union in violation of their obligations as citizens to the United States could not be trusted to honor a new oath with any greater fidelity. She feared that the end of the war would see a return to power of the very slave holders who had been instrumental in bringing about secession, and that the war would have been fought in vain. She was not so ready as Lincoln to forgive and forget while men still waged war in the field.

When the evening of the speech arrived and Anna entered the spacious chamber on the arm of the Vice-President and greeted the throng of dignitaries, she was well aware of the explosive possibilities of her speech.

She may very well have discussed it with the Speaker of the House, Schuyler Colfax, at whose public reception the night before she had been guest of honor. Yet the speech Anna delivered was a curious blend of wisdom and folly, of impudence and respect. In the presence of the President, she proceeded to denounce his policy of amnesty, but before the speech was out she about-faced and endorsed his administration, concluding with a wholly unexpected and dramatic call for his re-election. Since the abolitionists had not yet decided on their candidate, and were at best only lukewarm if not actually hostile toward Lincoln, Anna's endorsement was politically embarrassing, and she was chided by friends like Reid who would have no part of Lincoln. Susan B. Anthony had lost all confidence in the President, charging him with uttering "canting lies" when he said he was powerless to free the slaves. "The pity is that the mass of the people really believe the man honest," she wrote Anna.

Why did Anna come out for Lincoln in the same speech that bitterly criticized him? She never explained her motives, at least not in the letters that are still available to us today. It may have been that she was advised to do so by one of the President's associates. It may have been that she was unnerved by the sight of Lincoln entering the chamber at the very moment she was attacking him. Or it may have been that she was carried away with herself and the occasion, her sense of the dramatic demanding a great climax to the speech. And when she saw the electrified audience rise to its feet to cheer her declaration, she could hardly have thought she had acted in error or might someday regret her impetuosity. Nor had she reason to feel otherwise the next Monday when, accompanied by her brother and Judge Kelley, she called on President Lincoln to pay her respects.

The Washington address put the name of Anna Dickinson on the front page of newspapers throughout the country. Invitations descended on the Locust Street home, or were posted simply to "Miss Anna Dickinson, Philadelphia," requesting her to lecture in one city after another. Sixty-four members of the Ohio General Assembly invited her to speak in Columbus. The Pennsylvania legislature invited her to Harrisburg. New York State asked for a talk in Albany. Cincinnati and St. Louis followed suit with similar requests, and Philadelphia asked to be graced with another lecture from its favorite daughter. Anna was caught in a whirlwind of activity and traveled about from one eager throng of admirers to another. She was enjoying the adulation of the masses such as no girl in the history of her country had ever known. The President was quoted (though not necessarily accurately) as saying, "Miss Dickinson has in her keeping the hearts and consciences of tens of thousands of her countrymen who will vote as she speaks," and that "no other one person in the country can do so much toward securing my re-election as this young girl if she will speak; that no one else can hurt my prospects so much by silence."

In all the months that followed, Anna did not know what it was like to be at home with her family. As she traveled about, greeted everywhere with praise and applause, she left further and further behind her the simple Quaker lass of eighteen months before. The *Portland Transcript,* covering one of Anna's Maine speeches, gives us a glimpse of the changes that had come over her. "She wore a rich drab silk," the *Transcript* reported, "cut high in the neck and trimmed with black lace. She carried herself with aplomb, and moved about the platform with the air of a stage queen." But to most of her admirers she was still the same Anna. "God bless Anna Dickinson, the brave, earnest, and eloquent worker in the cause of freedom and human progress," said the *Rochester Evening Express* in an editorial commending Anna's speech in the city. "This young girl, so thoroughly earnest and decided in her hatred of oppression and injustice is yet withal thoroughly womanly in her love for, and championship of the poor, the weak and the oppressed, and for them she is day by day doing a greater work than perhaps any other single human agency now at work in moulding public opinion, and in which she makes the poor and the outcast, now and in all future time, her debtors."

But the editors were much disturbed by fears for Anna's physical well-being. "This brave, strong heart is encased in a frail, slender body, seemingly too weak to endure the extraordinary labors to which it has been devoted. Those who saw Miss Dickinson last night almost feared they noticed that she was not so strong, not so full of exuberant life as a few months before; and thinking what would be the loss to the cause of freedom and humanity, they could not refrain from inaudible prayers for her health and continued labors."

Indeed Anna's health showed the strain of unrelenting work, of long nights in poorly heated trains, of food often badly prepared and irregularly served. She fell victim to chest colds with great frequency, and sorely felt the need for some rest. But she thoroughly enjoyed her life; she was important, she was the envy of most young girls and the desire of many young men; the life of a Joan of Arc paid well, although lecture fees seemed to disappear in personal and household expenses even before the receipts were signed.

"I have barely enough money to hold out for this present week," wrote Susan that spring of 1864 as Anna rode in triumph, "so I wish thee could send me some as soon as possible after receiving this." Susan was never able to master the role of manager of a fashionable house, but she delighted in entertaining Anna's friends. Anna mailed her regular monthly drafts, but they never proved adequate for Susan's needs. "I can scarcely understand how the money vanishes," Susan wrote her younger sister, "till I go to my book and add up the amount for it. The prices of so many things are perfectly outlandish."

"I see you're persisting in your wickedness about the renomination," Whitelaw Reid wrote Anna early in February, 1864. He had booked some of Anna's Midwestern engagements before state legislatures, but he could not go along with Anna's endorsement of Lincoln. "Never mind," he added, "the other side will have its day." Reid favored Secretary of the Treasury Chase, though he recognized Lincoln's popularity and knew there was only the slightest chance of replacing him with another candidate. By March, Anna was ready to agree with Reid; in her speeches she omitted her call for the renomination and substituted in its place an attack on Lincoln's policy of reconstruction for the postwar South, a policy she characterized as "nothing but a miserable compromise which would restore the Union as it was."

"I told you long ago I knew the apology would come," Reid wrote Anna, welcoming her repentance, "but I don't mean to exult. Too many others have made the same mistake and I very much fear we shall yet have bitter fruits from it." He cautioned Anna against "making efforts to set herself straight," either in Washington or elsewhere. "It can do no good now for you to get tangled in the strifes of personal politics," he advised Anna, "and it may do much harm." He suggested a more cautious approach, in the hope that Lincoln might not be renominated at the Republican convention scheduled for Baltimore in late spring. "I'm sorry to read in the papers of your continued indisposition," he added. "Some old fellow once discovered that Rome wasn't built in a day. Before long you'll be making a similar discovery—that a career need not necessarily be run and finished in the winter of 1863-4."

In April, Anna secured an interview at the White House with Lincoln. No formal record exists of what went on in the private talk between the tall, careworn President and the determined young woman. Anna was anxious to discuss the President's politics with him in the hope that she might persuade him to abandon or modify them, or else to come to an understanding, which would make it possible for her to support Lincoln in the coming campaign.

The interview was unsuccessful and the two parted with divergent views. Anna referred to the conversation in some of her subsequent speeches. The President, it appeared from her account, was most cordial and gallant. He would rather have her on his side, he said, than any twenty men in the field, and he would rather have any twenty men in the field against him than her. Anna was deeply touched. When they came to discuss policy, no agreement could be found. Lincoln went over all his lengthy papers dealing with reconstruction and stated his policy in detail. Anna remarked that she thought his plan was "all wrong, as radically bad as can be." Lincoln ended the conversation by remarking, "All I can say is, if the abolitionists want me to lead, let them get out of the way and let me lead." On that note the conference ended, and when Anna came out of the White House, she remarked to a friend, "I have spoken my last word to President Lincoln."

After that, Anna attacked Lincoln publicly in her speeches. In Boston she went beyond respectful bounds, and in relating the interview she ridiculed the Presidential person. She talked about Lincoln's figure, "his dress, his old coat, out at the elbows which look as if he had worn it three years and used it as a pen wiper—his stocking limp and soiled." During the interview, the President had said, "That reminds me of a little story." "I didn't come to hear stories," Anna had replied. "I can read better ones in the papers any day than you can tell me." And she mimicked Lincoln from the platform.

This was an overconfident Anna—overconfident of her personal influence and intolerant of views that disagreed with hers. The result was unpleasant, and she lost many of her most ardent followers who were taken aback by the poor taste of her statements and felt that perhaps this young woman was not really prepared to accept the responsibilities of mature discussion.

"You are so incurably wrong-headed on the Lincoln question," Whitelaw Reid wrote to Anna. "Pardon me but you know I am nothing if not rude." Reid did not support Lincoln either, but he knew the abolitionists could not at this late date prevent Lincoln's renomination and he felt that the kind of fight Anna was making would cause her only trouble. He closed with a personal note: "Please to remember that you're engaged for a little shopping expedition with me next week."

Throughout the summer, the prospects of the North were on the decline. Grant's armies made no headway, the casualty lists mounted alarmingly, and a feeling of futility pervaded the North. Apathy and pessimism reached throughout the party, into the upper circles, and penetrated the White House where Lincoln prepared himself for defeat. Running against Lincoln on the Democratic ticket was a familiar figure: General George B. McClellan. The national canvass had brought together in one ring Anna's foremost antagonists. Which one would she support?

To abolitionists like Wendell Phillips, the choice was so outrageous that he refused to vote for either candidate. Susan B. Anthony counseled Anna: "Of two evils, choose neither. Do the right and trust the consequences with God." But Anna was willing to swallow her pride, and she made what she felt was the best choice possible in the situation. When reports appeared in the press that she intended to oppose Lincoln's election, Anna wrote a public denial that appeared in the *Independent* and was widely reprinted. She remarked that she had received "letters of warning, entreaty, advice, denunciation, abuse, upbraiding," from all over the country, "for having deserted a good cause, for refusing to work with 'my party' to swell its triumphs next November."

Her reply was simple: "I have no 'party' save that which strives with sword and pen, with blood and treasure, and precious lives, to save this country." If the Republicans sought her support, she would give it. "When I conclude to desert my post," she wrote, "I shall travel straight to Richmond, and not stop at any half-way station." Yes, she had said that there were men in the country who would make better Presidents than Lincoln. "Whatever words I then spoke, I believed to be in the best interests of the country. Personally I had everything to lose and nothing to gain by the course pursued. I was laughed at, ridiculed, ostracized by people who up to that time had given me nought save most generous help and overliberal praise." But that was history. Nothing remained now save "the most determined support of the party represented by Abraham Lincoln, from this moment till election morning."

Anna's letter cleared the air on her position, but by twice reversing her attitude toward Lincoln, she succeeded in alienating still more of her friends. Reid congratulated Anna on the effective way she scotched the ugly rumors about herself, but he would not join in support of Lincoln. "I know one young person who does not mean to get on the stool of repentance, and who will vote for Mr. Lincoln, if at all, very much as he has swallowed pills," he wrote to Anna.

Anna entered the Presidential campaign for the Republicans and delivered a speech entitled "Chicago and the Last Ditch" at Cooper Union before a capacity crowd. She delivered a blistering attack on the platform and candidate chosen at the Democratic convention in Chicago. In accepting the Democratic nomination McClellan had said "he was glad that in his nomination his record had been kept in view." Anna retorted that she agreed with the dear old lady who said, "Why will the people keep attacking poor, dear, little George McClellan? I'm sure *he* never attacked anybody." The correspondent of the *Philadelphia Press,* noting Anna's effectiveness, thought the Pennsylvania Republicans had made a great mistake in not hiring Anna at the beginning of the campaign. He did not know that Anna, having been defrauded once by the committee, would not again put herself in their hands. That Anna's speaking had lost none of its power was made clear by the report of the New York correspondent for a San Francisco paper who heard her for the first time at Cooper Union. He wrote: "Her strong feelings throw a radiance over words and sentences, and so completely magnetize her language that few can resist its spell. I have seen no grander tributes to the power of oratorical excellence than those manifested by the immense audience which heard Miss Dickinson's last address on public affairs in this city. Hats, handkerchiefs, and voice bore frequent testimony to the intense sympathy of the audience."

With the election over and Lincoln safely returned to the White House, Anna turned about once again and resumed her criticisms of the President. Everywhere she spoke she demanded a rigid prosecution of the war: "No amnesty, but absolute, unrelenting war until the foe lies under our feet, when we will give them wise, generous terms of peace, terms good for the enemy, good for us, and good for the world, but terms of unconditional surrender!" As it became clear in the winter of 1864-1865 that the Confederacy would soon collapse after Sherman's march across Georgia and Grant's advance into Virginia, the issue of reconstruction seemed of transcendent importance. What should be the policy of the Union toward the defeated South? To those who felt that the war had its cause in slavery, the victory would be empty unless slavery and all its trappings were removed without possibility of resurrection. The Negro must not only be freed, but he must be made a citizen with full rights of suffrage. Anna wanted confiscation of slave holders' properties, she wanted the plantations to be parceled out among the former slaves, she favored no amnesty for Jefferson Davis and lesser Confederate leaders.

In April, 1865, the war came to a grand close at Appomatox, and less than a week later, in Ford's Theater, the President was felled by an assassin's bullet. The nation was stunned, and the sense of military victory after long and bitter war was dulled by the loss of the national leader. Throughout the country meetings were called to pay homage to the memory of the dead President. Though Anna had so often opposed Lincoln and had spoken about him so vituperatively, she was nevertheless invited to address some of these meetings. In Philadelphia she was the first to suggest that a monument be erected to the late President and she made the largest subscription to the building fund. In New York three thousand people gathered at Cooper Union on May 10, 1865, to hear Anna pay tribute to Lincoln. Theodore Tilton presided and on the stage sat Senator Wilson and George Thompson, the famous English preacher. Anna said:

"No words of mine, though in the past I have said hard things of him when I thought hard things were needed, can justly tell the story of this man's life or fitly praise him.... And yet, let us not deceive ourselves. It is not simply the death of a man, however high his station, however great his attributes, however foully murdered, that tortures us today. It is liberty that was assailed in the person of our Chief—it is the country that bleeds and put it how we will, it is slavery that inflicts the blow; it is we, the freedom loving, who are the victims aimed at."

The war was over and the nation knew peace once again. Battle cries and impassioned crusades must cease with the war that gave them birth. The end of the war found Anna twenty-two years old, a veteran of innumerable political battles, not unscarred from her many encounters, with a national reputation for unmatched oratory and for stubborn independence, of immaturity of thought and action. At twenty-two she had known enough excitement for a life three times her years, but, like the soldiers returning from the fields she still had a life to live. Many of her admirers wondered what the future would hold for her. What happens to Peter the Hermit who can no longer preach crusades? Where in a land at peace does a wartime heroine find a place for herself? Was she quickly to become a faded memory? Two years before, a reporter for Sam Bowles's *Springfield Republican,* had pondered this question with keen prescience: "Here is a Joan of Arc," he wrote, "as good as she of France, a woman made by the occasion, and," he added suggestively, "who possibly will sink with it. She said nothing new, only spoke with the spirit that makes all things new."

What awaited America's Joan of Arc in the quiet years of peace? All who knew Anna Dickinson wondered what the answer would be.

CHAPTER 6

QUEEN OF THE LYCEUM

THE question of Anna's future was soon answered. She took to the lecture platform, and for the next ten years she traveled up and down the country, twice invaded the South, ventured across the lawless prairie to the rough towns of California riding the caboose of the first transcontinental train, traipsed through the new Mormon encampments of Utah, periodically revisited New England, New York, Washington, and Philadelphia, and took time out to write a novel, reject three suitors, and scale the highest mountain peaks of Colorado.

The war had left a legacy of unresolved issues that required public discussion. There was no means yet of mass communication besides the press—no radios, or television, or films—and the public, in almost every city and hamlet, turned out to attend the local lyceums that booked nationally prominent speakers. Lyceum lecturing had been common in the United States for at least two decades before the war, but it reached its peak of popularity in the first eight or ten *post-bellum* years when, under the management of such agencies as Redpath and Fall's Boston Lyceum Bureau and the American Literary Bureau in New York, a host of outstanding orators traversed the country from October to May of each year, talking on serious or light topics to thousands of people able and willing to pay anywhere from fifty cents to five dollars for the privilege of listening. In the quiet world of provincial America, the visiting luminaries were the high points of the social and intellectual season. Speaking five or six times a week, each time in a different city, the lecturers might earn anywhere from $100 to $1,000 a night less their expenses and the agent's fee. Among the more prominent lyceum orators were Henry Ward Beecher, Edward Everett, Charles Sumner, George William Curtis, Wendell Phillips, Ralph Waldo Emerson, John B. Gough, Susan B. Anthony, and a dozen other famous names. Anna formally entered the world of the lyceum when she was twenty-three and was immediately recognized as the most successful woman in the field, rivaled by only one or two men. By 1872 Anna was grossing $23,090 a year from her lectures. (The President then was paid only $25,000, and there were no income taxes!) James B. Pond, a leading lyceum manager who wrote a history of the movement a generation later, confirmed Anna's position at the top of the ladder. "Anna E. Dickinson, for many years, indeed from her first appearance until she retired from the lecture field," Pond wrote, "was without question of a rival, the 'Queen of the Lyceum.'"

The role of lyceum queen continued though, as subsequent events proved, did not complete the transformation of the simple Quaker girl. Anna never left the public eye; her peregrinations were noted with envy by thousands of admirers and disparaged by a growing circle of critics. Twenty years after Victoria ascended the throne of England, an American girl was essaying a life of freedom and independence. Anna was rich on her own earnings; she was beholden to no man; she would not be shackled by Victorian rectitude or the vestments of tradition. In an era when propriety seemingly was the foremost of virtues, she recognized no master save her impulses and her means. She was blatantly and self-consciously nonconformist, and seemed to take delight only in asserting her individuality and refusing to accept without question or protest the code of behavior that shaped the lives of her contemporaries. She dressed as she desired; she traveled where and how she willed; she delivered lectures on subjects many people felt should not even be mentioned in the presence of unmarried young ladies. As a result, she antagonized many of her former friends and supporters. Conservative newspapers now began to find fault with her and even to ridicule some of her habits and beliefs. But Anna was not to be swayed from her new life by such criticism. She bought a sleek black horse named Topsy and maintained it in Boston for the occasional visits she paid that city when she might find relaxation on the bridle paths, at the same time shocking passers-by by riding the horse astraddle. Summers she vacationed by herself or with friends at Swampscott, Massachusetts, or at a Long Island beach resort. She met most of the important people of her time and many of them became her friends. In politics Senators Sumner, Wilson, Pomeroy, and Allison and Congressman Ben Butler were close friends. In journalism she associated with Samuel Bowles, Charles Dudley Warner, Theodore Tilton, Noah Brooks, Whitelaw Reid, and a host of other leading men. She met and liked Bret Harte and Joaquin Miller, while Mark Twain and Moses Coit Tyler were personal acquaintances. By virtue of her war record Anna was almost a legendary figure in her own right and her position on the lyceum kept the spotlight of public attention firmly trained on her for almost a decade after the end of the war. Thousands of women looked up to her with mingled envy and admiration while other thousands became increasingly critical. Favorable or unfavorable, almost everyone had an opinion about Anna Dickinson.

The queen of the lyceum looked the part, too. Describing her appearance at a lecture in 1867, the *Boston Post* noted that "Anna wore an elaborate toilet, a dress of black silk cut in the prevailing style, with gilt buttons on the waist and the sleeves puffed at the shoulder and down the arm to the waist, where a snowy lace was folded back upon the sleeve. A rich lace collar graced her neck, with wide flowing ends, fastened with a costly brooch. Her hair was cut short as before, unconfined, with no ornament or artificial decoration on it. But diamond rings glistened upon her taper fingers in profusion."

"I often mourn thy strong attachments to the trivial pleasures of the world, more especially dress and theatricals," wrote Mary Dickinson, plainly distressed by her daughter's new ways, "but I pray the loving Shepherd of Israel, our blessed Saviour, will yet find and enclose thee in His happy sheepfold." Though Mary Dickinson and her devout sons were almost wholly dependent upon Anna's lecture earnings, they could not bring themselves to approve of her departure from the fold. Susan, however, reveled in the reflected glory of Anna's fame and friends, and used Anna's monthly checks to run the modestly fashionable home on Locust Street.

As Anna traveled about the country, she attracted an enthusiastic coterie of supporters who admired her personal fortitude, independence, and advanced opinions. "In these days when women seem to have gone insane on all matters concerned with the appareling of their persons," wrote one reader to the *Boston Commonwealth,* "it is singularly refreshing to see a woman who entirely understands the art of dress. And that woman is Anna Dickinson." The queen of the lyceum had demonstrated that "corsets, crinoline, and trailing skirts" were not necessary for a woman to be beautifully arrayed. She would have no part of the "multitudinous hardware beads, gimp, velvet, cord, ribbon, and scallop" that bedecked the "festooned and flowing draperies" of the day. "At a time when the female head is systematically tortured and disfigured, and divested of every grace of contour," Anna Dickinson "wears her hair in thick, wavy masses, cut short like a school girl."

"This girl," wrote the admiring reader, "slips quietly out of all the weary coil, and stands serenely resplendent in some rich, plain fabric, without one atom of so-called 'trimming' visible from the crown of her queenly head to the sole of her dainty foot.... You may describe her costume in three lines; but if you have an artistic eye you are not likely to forget it. You remember, if you saw her, sweeping the platform of Music Hall in a pearl-colored moire silk; or again in vivid ruby color or green; or in simple black or gray, with a single bright ribbon for contrast; or in clear corn-color, only relieved by a few loops of black lace and a faint mist of ruche at the throat and wrists. No more."

To those who criticized Anna for the costliness of her array, who felt that "a nun-like severity, a Quaker-like meagreness, would more benefit the earnestness of her mission," Anna's admirer, speaking as it were for Anna herself, made reply: "No narrow, stinted colorless life will suffice her; and she certainly earns the right to live her own life with whatever of grace of form and warmth of coloring she may choose to put into it. She earns her own money in doing a work that no other woman in either hemisphere can perform so well; she spends it generously for others and freely for herself, to gratify the woman and the artist in her own nature; and for this," the reader added with a show of contempt, "there are plenty to pronounce her unwomanly. If she would but spend other people's money instead of her own; if she only lavished the substance of her male relatives in velvets, diamonds, and camel's hair shawls; if she only exhibited herself under the lusters of drawing rooms, and if she only lisped pretty inanities to pretty young men ... she would be 'womanly past question.'"

Not all newspaper comments were so friendly. "Miss Dickinson is a good specimen of a very useless sort of woman," editorialized the *Providence Daily Post.* "We commend to her attention the answer of the first Napoleon, to Madame De Staël, who, having asked him, 'Who, sire, is the most worthy woman,' replied, 'She madame, who bears the most children.' "

"We wonder how many young men who have just completed their 27th year have accomplished as much as this often-ridiculed woman," said the *Newark Morning Register,* coming to Anna's defense. "We may differ with her on political questions, we may even get angry at her 'unwomanly ways,' but we cannot but admire the energy she has displayed in the work she has undertaken, and grow enthusiastic over the results she has already accomplished."

Each year meant a new season to Anna—one or two new lectures to prepare and a new itinerary. Her lyceum tours called for her to lecture in anywhere from one hundred to 150 different cities a season at fees ranging from $150 to $400 a night. Some seasons the lecture routes were limited to New York, New England, and Pennsylvania, and these seasons were the best, for they reduced the number of long and lonely train rides that her occupation so often required. Other years took Anna into the Midwest, and these seasons she found most trying and exhausting. Everywhere she went she was greeted eagerly. People crowded into the local assembly halls to see the famous Anna Dickinson and to applaud or reject her sentiments. No doubt many came to the lyceum because it provided a break in the monotony of small city social life. Some of the prominent lecturers made it their business to entertain such people, but Anna was more concerned with public enlightenment, not popular entertainment, and her audiences expected highly informative, if strongly opinionated, discussions of important social and political questions of the day. And though she had to repeat her talks night after night, week after week, Anna always gave each set of listeners the impression that she had composed and was delivering the lecture especially for them. She was extremely sensitive to audience reaction and knew how to adapt her speaking accordingly.

"I made I believe the best speech of my whole life last night," Anna wrote to her mother in 1870 after delivering a lecture called "To the Rescue" in Chicago. "I don't know when I have felt as I did—half a dozen times, it seemed to me I would fly apart, and as for the audience,

I never saw such an one. Not noisy, but so solemn and earnest that it was wonderful to look at them. I couldn't make such speeches as that every night, however. Not for long or I'd make none at all."

"Well! I have put 'What's to Hinder?' in battle array and made it tonight," Anna wrote Susan in 1872. "The way people listened, and laughed, and wept, and sniveled, and howled is quite beyond description. So that's off my mind. Now for something else. John and Martha both say that Marmee must not get Edwin any clothes. That he won't wear them and that they will just grow rusty and old. I think they are right, and I will send him enough money to get what he needs, when he needs it...."

Several years later Anna put together her thoughts about lyceum lecturing and made some interesting observations about the kinds of audiences she had faced in her speaking career. "Some audiences are stone," she said. "You strike against them and rebound—angered by their hardness. Some are sponge—absorb and absorb and absorb, and give nothing back, till you feel as though you had enjoyed six hours of the Turkish bath and then been put under an exhausted receiver; and some are like champagne, or vigorous tea, or clear cognac, or aggressive coffee, or whatever it may that the most quickly and enchantingly stimulates your brain and nerves.... I have faced a crowd ready to talk, full of enthusiasm, well and strong, and in ten minutes have grown so tired I could scarce stand; and I have crawled off the cars after a twenty-hours ride, shaken to a jelly, banged black and blue, asphyxiated with coal gas and the perfumes of burnt iron and dirty humanity, and been spirited to the hall without rest, food, or a clean face, so tired that I wanted to prop against some convenient table or wall, and have felt, long before I finished, as though I could never be sick nor weary, nor disgusted, and having ended wanted to begin and do it all over again."

On Sundays some of the lyceum lecturers would get together at a good hotel in a large city to rest and feast and talk over their long journeys, the hard fare at the country hotels, and their more unusual experiences. In these conversations, Anna supplied her full share of episodes that enlivened otherwise dull lecture tours.

There was the local banker in the small Illinois town who, called upon to introduce her, besieged the audience to pay heed to the words of a young woman whose name was known wherever the English language was spoken. "Listen to her then, and I know, fellow citizens, you will listen to her," he said, "since she always addresses herself to the poor, the maimed, the halt, and the blind! You will listen to her since she always addresses herself to the ignorant, the downtrodden, and the oppressed of every color, clime, and tongue!"

There was the president of the students' lecture association in a New England college town who, in place of an introduction, offered a twenty-seven-minute prayer in the course of which he besought that "this woman might be brought to see that no temporal prosperity, nor even the accomplishment of seeming good, justified her in an open defiance of the ordinances of God, and the divinely appointed sphere of her sex."

There was the chairman who said, "Ladies and gentlemen, I have the pleasure of presenting to you Anna Dickens, who, I am informed, is a sister of Charles Dickens, the celebrated poet."

Then there was the chap on the train who learned that the young lady seated toward the rear was the famous Anna Dickinson. Introducing himself, he sat down opposite Anna and tried to make conversation, only to be greeted by monosyllabic replies. "Well, now look here," he said finally, eying Anna quizzically. "You'll never lecture in our town. It's too derned small. But I'd like to hear what you can do when your steam's up. How about making a speech for me right now?" By now Anna was annoyed and tried to dismiss him. He made one final appeal: "I thought I'd get a free blow out, but I reckon you weren't born yesterday." He reached into his pocket. "There's a dollar," he said, extending Anna the bill much as if he were making a purchase in the village emporium. "Will that pay you for a good square talk and all the fixens?"

One of Anna's favorite stories told of speaking in a stifling hall. There was no means of ventilation except the windows at the back of the gallery which, because it was raining outside, were closed. A low ceiling, a raging furnace, and flaring gas jets devoured what little oxygen filtered into the hall. Finding the air unbearable, Anna lost her temper and said testily: "This is a horrible hall."

"Horrible hall?" echoed an indignant voice. A red-faced, perspiring man rose to view. "Horrible hall! This is *my* hall, and I should like to know what you mean by calling it such a name."

"Because the name defines it," Anna replied. "It is a deathtrap.

Fresh air is as essential to life as a pair of lungs. This is a grave—without ventilators."

"No ventilators?" the man exclaimed. "What do you call those?" He waved his cane wildly at what looked like an unbroken expanse of smooth ceiling.

"Those?" Anna asked. "I call that a ceiling."

"*In* the ceiling," the man shouted.

"I see nothing in the ceiling."

"There and there," he repeated heatedly, pointing his stick upward. "Can't you see?"

"Where and where?" Anna asked, making a telescope of her left hand. "No, I can't see." She stooped to one of the ladies on the front bench and borrowed her opera glass. "Permit me," she said. "Oh," peering through the glass, "I beg your pardon. Did you mean those gimlet holes?"

"Gimlet holes!" stammered the outraged proprietor, as a thousand voices laughed. "Gimlet holes! They are ventilators!"

"Into what do they open?" Anna asked blandly.

"Why—into a loft."

"And what may be above the loft by chance?"

"A double-action, patent-waterproof, airtight roof," shouted a boy from the gallery, whereupon the audience roared.

The irate owner muttered, "The Lord save her husband, if she ever has one."

"Amen," said Anna, anxious to reply to friendly wishes, "and may He be mercifully disposed toward your wife."

Though Anna's lyceum lectures bore many different titles ("Idiots and Women," "Men's Rights," "For Your Own Sake," "To the Rescue," "What's to Hinder?" "Whited Sepulchres," etc.) and varied from year to year, they always dealt with one or another aspect of the same topic—"universal freedom, universal suffrage, and universal justice." Her addresses were really fighting talks in behalf of fundamental social and political principles and their application in contemporary life. The war had been fought for the principle of human freedom, to Anna's way of thinking, and not until that principle was firmly established in both North and South would the battle end. The black man was legally emancipated, but he was not in fact free: his ballot was in jeopardy. When thirty-nine lawfully elected Negroes were expelled from the Georgia legislature, Anna delivered a fiery speech, typical of her lyceum talks, which set forth a program to complete the battle for freedom by stamping out racial discrimination in voting altogether.

"Nelson was once asked by a theorist to plan a battle on scientific principles," she said. "His reply was, 'Get as near your enemy as you can and then fight him.'

"Today the United States has an enemy more bitter, more active and relentless, more subtle and determined than Nelson ever found the Frenchman; an enemy which opposes cunning to power and prejudice to argument; an enemy which saps the vitals and undermines the foundations of the Republic....

"The name of this enemy is Caste."

The crime of prejudice was all the greater because it occurred in a democracy where all men were held free and equal. "Liberty brings obligations," Anna said. "A wrong under a republic is more infamous than a wrong under an empire and is so regarded by humanity. The larger our professions the closer scrutiny will be made into our practices; the greater our advantages, the stricter regard of our deeds; the nobler our heritage, the meaner will seem our exactions from others." She asked her listeners two questions that could be answered only one way. "Can it be anything else than a farce to call a government democratic wherein one-eighth of all its people are ostracized because of physical peculiarity? Can the liberties of the nation be thought secure, when we have beaten down the only sure basis of freedom—a belief in the minds of the people that these liberties are the gifts of God? ... Let the spirit of government be that of injustice to even the smallest class, let but one human being be robbed of his rights without a protest, and it will not be long before the rights of every human being will be jeopardized. One cause will suffice just as well as another, if the only sure barrier to despotism, an inherent spirit of justice in the hearts of the people, be broken down. It is not necessary to inculcate the whole human body with virus to produce death; a drop of poison on a needle's point, if inserted once, will cause the destruction of beauty and life."

Anna's solution to the problem of caste was free public education and political equality for all literate citizens. "Give to every child in America a spelling book and a free schoolroom, and to every intelligent and respectable person, black and white, man and woman, a ballot and freedom of government, and you will see that this country will stand stronger and stronger amidst the ruins of dissolving empires and falling thrones. . . . Let us, then, that justice may be done by the American people, introduce into Congress and pass a bill, of not more than ten lines in length, which shall assert that suffrage in the United States shall be impartial and universal wherever its flag floats and liberty has a name."

Anna carried her proposal beyond the realm of ideas into the field of practical action itself. In September, 1866, at the National Loyalists' Convention in Philadelphia, Theodore Tilton, editor of the *Independent*; Frederick Douglass, the renowned Negro leader; and Anna formulated the idea of a fifteenth amendment to the Constitution to prohibit disfranchisement of any person on account of race, sex, color, or previous condition of servitude. Not long thereafter the proposal was accepted in slightly modified form by the Republican party and a forty-six word amendment was added to the Constitution of the United States. The word "sex" was omitted, however, despite the vigorous protests of the women's rights advocates. "To Anna Dickinson belongs the honor of suggesting the 15th Amendment," wrote Elizabeth Cady Stanton and Susan B. Anthony when they wrote a history of women's suffrage some years later. Frederick Douglass confirmed Anna's role when he wrote to Mrs. Stanton: "To dear Anna E. Dickinson and brave Theodore Tilton belongs the credit of forcing that amendment upon the attention of the nation at the right moment and in the right way to make it successful."

When Anna was not speaking or acting against racial prejudice, she was speaking in behalf of women's rights and against a double standard of morality for the sexes. She called for a change of attitude toward women who worked. "It is not respect for a woman to express admiration for her beauty, person, and acts, and show contempt for her mind," she said. "It is not respect to call a woman an angel and treat her like a fool. It is not respect to train a young girl for the matrimonial market, and strike her down to the highest bidder." Anna spoke for the right of women to enter the professions, to participate in government, to live full, well-rounded lives free from domination of father or husband. Her philosophy was simple and to later generations it would doubtless seem banal, but in the age of Victoria it was certainly unorthodox: "Do each what you like, at any and all times; follow your own will, live for yourself, without regard to what others may say or think, guided and controlled only by God." She urged parents to permit their children to follow their individual bents, and not to be discouraged because such a course would shock the proprieties or run counter to public opinion. "It is not that we should do some great thing, but that each should live his own life. It is not the amount of the thing done; it is the amount of life, of determination put into it." To many of the newspapers that commented on Anna's talks, these were shocking, fallacious, and even dangerous statements, and editors took great delight in poking fun at her.

Reporting one of Anna's lectures on women's rights, the *Spirit of the Times, The American Gentlemen's Newspaper,* paid Anna faint praise in an editorial comment. Anna Dickinson is "the only pretty, well-shaped, and womanly-looking advocate that progressive ideas have ever had for an oratorical champion in this country," said the gentlemen editors. "Miss Dickinson is a lady whose beauty and wit entitle her to aspire to the highest position within the gift of men who most truly reverence women: that is, of course, the domestic throne at the head of the cradle and the tea table—a rolling pin her shining scepter, the cook her prime minister, and her sweet sway despotic. The lecture was a very clever presentation of untenable propositions."

Though she was an ardent spokesman for women's rights, Anna was slow to warm up to the women's suffrage movement. This was probably due to her inability to subordinate herself to the work of a group. It may also have been the result of the belief that women's suffrage, in and of itself, was inadequate as a working political program. Anna knew Susan B. Anthony and Mrs. Elizabeth Cady Stanton, and the other leading suffrage figures on a warm and friendly basis, but in the early sixties she worked from outside their movement. In 1866 she signified her willingness to join it by delivering a speech for the Women's Equal Rights Association. From that moment on, she was continually pursued by the suffragettes who desperately hoped she would assume leadership. When Mrs. Stanton heard that Susan B. Anthony wanted to give up the editorship of the *Revolution,* the women's rights journal to which Anna had once donated $1,000, she suggested that Anna be asked to take the job. "If Anna Dickinson will be sole editor," Mrs. Stanton wrote, "I say, glory to God! ... Tell our glorious little Anna if she only will nail her colors to that mast and make the dear old proprietor free once more, I will sing her praises to the end of time." But Anna decided she was not suited for this kind of editorial work and her friend, Laura Bullard, of New York, took it over instead. When Miss Anthony celebrated her fiftieth birthday Anna sent her a silk gown and a check for $200. Miss Anthony affectionately signed her letters to Anna, "Your grandmother Susan."

"I passed one night in Philadelphia with Miss Anthony, at Anna Dickinson's home—a neat, three-story brick home on Locust Street," wrote Mrs. Stanton many years later. "This haven of rest where the world-famous little woman came, ever and anon, to recruit her overtaxed energies, was very tastefully furnished, adorned with engravings, books, and statuary. Her mother, sister and brother made up the household—a pleasing, cultivated trio. The brother [Edwin] was a handsome youth of good judgment, and given to sage remarks; the sister, witty, intuitive, and incisive in speech; the mother, dressed in rich Quaker costume, and though nearly seventy, still possessed of great personal beauty. She was intelligent and refined, and, in manner and appearance, reminded me of Angelina Grimké as she looked in her younger days. Everything about the house and its appointments indicated that it was the abode of genius and cultivation, and although Anna was absent, the hospitalities were gracefully dispensed by the family. Napoleon and Shakespeare seemed to be Anna's patron saints, looking down, on all sides from the wall. The mother amused us with the sore trials her little orator had inflicted on the members of the household by her vagaries in the world of fame."

In 1869 Anna made her first trip to the Far West. That year saw the opening of transcontinental railroad traffic in the United States. The last spike of the western trunk line was driven near Ogden, Utah, in May, 1869, and that summer a group of congressmen made the first cross-country journey. The prospect of pioneering rail traffic through Indian country and over the Rockies into California was an exciting one, and Anna, ever eager for adventure, decided to make the voyage with her brother John. The cost of the journey was to be covered in part by lectures Anna arranged to give in San Francisco and other California cities.

Anna and John boarded the transcontinental train in early June. As the train ventured farther and farther west through the frontier country, Anna wrote long letters to Mary and Susan Dickinson, describing what she had seen. The trip was evidently very inspirational for some of Anna's letters ran over one hundred handwritten pages.

"The most disagreeable feature of these men is whiskey," Anna wrote from Leavenworth, Kansas. "It's awful to contemplate the amount of liquor drunk in this region. Downtown every other shop is a 'saloon,' and eight-tenths of the men you meet, even so early as eight or nine in the morning, smell of this atrocious stuff." Anna was no prohibitionist. Her objection was not to liquor, but to the consumption of it in overlarge quantities or in poor quality and she was apparently well equipped by knowledge and experience to distinguish one bouquet from another. "It kills them off fast, too, the stuff they drink, and no wonder," she wrote. "In Omaha, I sent to the best chemist in town for pure brandy and rose water, and the best even he could give me was adulterated whiskey. What then must the stuff be that the saloons sell? However, it's as well, perhaps, if these men are to kill themselves, that they do so as speedily as possible."

As the train continued west, Anna felt a growing exhilaration. For a good part of the time she left her compartment and went up to the caboose of the train to join the engineers, or in riding stagecoaches, she joined the driver up front. "At six o'clock in the afternoon I was in my usual seat—the driver's seat, on top of the coach, rumbling and rattling out of town—away, away towards the great mountains," she wrote from Wyoming. From Nevada, Anna wrote Mary Dickinson one of her long letters:

June 26, 1869

Dear Little Mother

I am no genius at describing nature, and indeed if I were I should be somewhat put about, at trying to make clear what we have beheld through the last week. Anyone labors under a vast disadvantage in seeing this huge country from the window or platform of a railway car. You are whirled past so rapidly that you do not have time to fix on your brain a distinct picture of each section, and at last they are all mingled and mixed in wild confusion.

One week ago, last Wednesday, we left Omaha, the platform presenting a curious crowd. Curious from its varied elements and from the noise and numbers. The lavish expenditure everywhere, yet the discomfort of newness. It was manifest we had reached the West.

The country we passed through that afternoon and evening was no novelty to me—just such rolling, open fertile prairie land as I have traveled over hundreds of times in other parts of the West— what seems from here the East. Towards sundown, we met a freight train, making its way towards Omaha, the tender and tops of the cars filled and covered with an array of Pawnees—mean, dirty, miserable looking creatures—all tatters and dirt, who laughed and called and waved their hands and rags to us as we went by.

It seemed a strange contrast, the steam wonder—cultivated growth of brains and civilization, and these red men and women being carried about by it, yet not stranger than to stand as we did, upon the rear platform, when night had shut down, and look through the flashes of lightning across the limitless space in even crossing, and recognize the combination of cars yet no houses, and telegraph wires yet no people.

The next morning we breakfasted at North Platte, still open rolling prairie, and were besought to join the Congressmen, but declined. Dined at Sidney, and went aboard the Congressmen's car, and that afternoon and evening were ones to be forever remembered. The country is green and lovely, and from this beautiful base, the Black Hills, spurs of the Rocky's shoot into the air— red sandstone and granite, big and little masses of rock torn up by the storms and beaten by wind and rain through countless ages into every shape and form. Strange, grotesque, sublime. While away off at the South, through gaps and rents in the nearer and lower range the Rocky Mountains lifted themselves shapely and grand and crowned with eternal snows, the sun blazing across them, and the evening shadows, blue and purple softening them to our gaze.

At night we went back to our own car, and in the morning opened our eyes upon the Bitter Creek country, a region which Mother would travel far to see. . . .

At Virginia City, Anna was invited to speak, and she chose to discuss the level of morality she saw about her. "I 'went in heavy,' in the elegant parlance of this place, upon the drinking and gambling every-where seen," she wrote home. "It's perfectly disgusting the state of society. You can't go into a house but they offer you liquor, and in the party to the Lake there was more poison put down the throats of the members than I ever saw drank in the same space of time. When I drink wine I choose my company, and it was not this. At the dinner table the scene was positively disgraceful, the girls as bad as the men, all of them half-drunk together, and these the *first people* of the place. I trod heavily on all their toes." She concluded: "I should be very sorry to stay in this country long. 'Tis a great land to travel through, but the people are not after my heart. All they care for is to get and spend, eat and drink, wear fine clothes and drive fast teams. . . ."

San Francisco was much more to Anna's liking. "I never wearied of tramping about the street gawking at the people and the shops rich with the spoils of the world and found ceaseless pleasure in running out of the city to any one of a score of lovely spots about it," she recalled some years later. She visited the Chinese quarter and saw the miserable conditions under which the Oriental immigrants were obliged to live. She saw white folk abuse the Chinese and heard them say over and over that the Chinese were an inferior race not deserving of elemental human rights. Anna refused to believe this and in the course of her first public talk out West she had something to say on the subject in her typically forceful way.

The day before the speech, a steamer had entered San Francisco harbor and discharged its cargo of a thousand Chinese "coolies" to, as Anna put it, "the tender mercies of American freemen." Four of the Chinese were dead on arrival, their bruised bodies bearing irrefutable testimony to the brutal treatment accorded them aboard ship. No inquest was held nor was punishment assigned. Anna's sense of justice was outraged. She abandoned the scheduled introduction to her speech and instead denounced the Californians for their treatment of the Chinese. The audience was made up almost wholly of men who were hearing a woman speak in public for the first time. They hissed her threateningly. Anna brought that to a halt quickly. "My friends," she said, "you are not used to me. Never before have I had the pleasure of facing you, and you, apparently, never before had the profit of listening to an unpleasant truth. I will then tell you, so as to save time and trouble, that as I have endured a great deal of hissing, some stick and stone throwing, diverse odorous eggings, and finally one or two re-volver bullets through political campaigns in the East, I am not to be scared by a trifle of goose breath in the West." She asked if they would kindly do all their hissing at once, get it over, and let her go on with the talk.

Then Anna made a plea for justice. She called for training the Chinese immigrants in citizenship and removing them from victimization of racial prejudice.

A man in the audience tried to upset her. "Would you marry a Chinaman?" he shouted boisterously.

Anna replied in a manner that indicated she had heard similar questions many times before. She asked him: "If you were poor and oppressed, wouldn't you like to hear me, or someone else, defend you?"

"Yes," the man agreed.

"And I would defend you," Anna said, "but oppress you by marrying you, never, not if you got down on your knees to me would I marry you!"

Anna's courage made a good impression in California. She delivered two more speeches in San Francisco and others in neighboring cities. In Stockton, the local paper recommended her lecture in its editorial columns and described Anna with unrestrained enthusiasm and egregious inaccuracy as "the most creditable living specimen of *representative* American womanhood."

On her way back East at the end of the summer Anna stopped off in Utah to look over the new Mormon colony at Salt Lake. Out of this visit developed one of her most successful lyceum lectures, "Whited Sepulchres." As one might have expected, Anna did not like what she saw there—a polygamous society in which women had little or no legal rights—though she was impressed with the tremendous industry of the people. She interviewed Mormon women and was shocked to discover their complete servility to the men. She was further shocked by the subservience of the men to their chosen leader. "Utah is the most absolute tyranny, the most unmitigated despotism, upon which the sun shines today," Anna said in her lecture. "Utah, Mormonism is Brigham Young." The Mormon leader was president of the church and head of the state and consequently an all-powerful ruler. When elections were held he was the only candidate. To Anna the Mormon society illustrated the inevitable degradation that attends the unjust sub-

ordination of women to men and of some men to others. No achievement of material wealth could compensate for the denial of human
dignity.

The following year, for the first time in her lyceum career, Anna
offered a lecture outside the realm of current political and social controversy. The temper of the people was changing as the war became
more of a memory and the lyceum was obliged to place greater emphasis on entertainment than on instruction and persuasion. Anna
compromised with this development by working up lectures that offered historical materials in a popular biographical guise. Much like
modern magazine profiles, these sketches, when prepared and delivered with skill and imagination, could be instructive as well as entertaining. Anna's first attempt at the biographical talk became her most
successful lyceum lecture and she eventually delivered it almost five
hundred times. The subject of Anna's profile was of more than passing
interest.

"Among the names to which mortals have decreed immortality," the
lecture began, "is that of Jeanne d'Arc. With reason. Consider the time
in which she lived, the needs of her day, the work she wrought, the life
she lived, the death she died. . . ." The lecture was a dramatic account
of the Maid of Orleans, setting the historical background and carrying
her from her days as a peasant girl through her sensational victories,
the crowning of the king at Rouen, and then to her capture by the
British and the burning at the stake. Delivered by a young woman
about whom the mantle of Joan had more than once been draped, the
lecture assumed a rather remarkable character. The Maid of Orleans
was traditionally regarded as an agent from God, a worker of miracles,
whose instructions from Providence came in mysterious voices audible
to her alone. Anna could scarcely be expected to go along with this
interpretation of Joan. She was too secular to subscribe to the idea of
Providential voices and, armed by her own war experiences, she was
wholly confident that an inspired young French girl, with a good head
on her shoulders, could, quite without the aid of miracles, do at least
as well as an inspired American Quaker. The story of Joan of Arc was
thus nothing but the powerful tale of inspired womanhood. Comment-
ing on Joan's military prowess, Anna pointed out that her plan of
battle was the same as Napoleon's centuries later. "Of the man," Anna

said ironically, "the world says, 'What august power! What commanding genius!' Of the woman, under precisely similar conditions, it cries, 'Why what a lucky accident it was, she should happen to hit upon that plan.'"

Three years after she first delivered the lecture, Anna was able to write to Susan from Portland, Maine, "I have had jammed houses all the week, and at Portland they were absolutely crazy over 'Joan of Arc.' I never saw an audience so wild, they cheered, and shouted 'brava, brava,' and beat the most tremendous uproar I ever saw at the Opera." The evening in January, 1871, when Paris capitulated to the invading Prussian armies, Anna delivered "Jeanne d'Arc" at a benefit performance for the friends of France in Washington before an audience of fifteen hundred who had come to the hall through a driving storm. Senator Charles Sumner introduced her and she spoke for nearly two hours. "It was really a tremendous lecture," wrote the correspondent of the *New York Tribune*. "Outside the storm roared and raved; inside the hush was hardly broken by one or two brief rounds of applause, hastily smothered in the breathless attention that feared to lose a word."

Two amusing stories went the rounds about Anna's "Joan of Arc." One told of an honorable member of the Missouri legislature who desired that the hall of the House be voted to Miss Dickinson "to give her speech on Jonah's Arc there was so much talk about." He supposed "it must be a lecture about whales, and might be interesting as well as instructive." To this proposal a fellow legislator replied that he would rather hear Miss Dickinson on "female agitation."

The other story related the painful introduction Anna had to bear one evening. "Miss Dickinson will address you tonight," said the chairman preparing the way for "Jeanne d'Arc," "on the life and adventures of John Dark, one of the greatest heroes of antiquity. We are not as familiar with antiquity as we ought to be, owing to the long time since antiquity, but one thing is certain, and that is that Miss Dickinson can tell us all about the most remarkable man of them all— John Dark."

Writing home to her mother, Anna told of still another experience. "At Whitehall, a donkey of a President announced with a satisfied smirk as tho' he thought his wit was superlative, 'We shall now one and all enjoy a pleasure that has hitherto been considered the exclusive right of the married man—a lecture from a lady.' Upon which I got up and made my solemn harangue and the brilliant fellow marched himself on to the platform when I was through, with tears in his eyes, and on his face, and said, 'I beg your pardon. That's a sermon that ought to be preached from every pulpit in the land. I wouldn't have made such an introduction if I had known, but I thought you gave humorous lectures.'!!!" She concluded with an air of resignation: "There's fame for you."

ANNA'S LECTURE SCHEDULE FOR THE 1871-1872 SEASON

Oct.	2	Mt. Holly	$150		22	Kalamazoo	$200
	3	Nyack	150		23	Grand Rapids	200
	4	Port Edward	150		24	Ionia	200
	5	Troy	200		27	Batavia	150
	6	Great Barrington	150		28	Buffalo	200
	9	Andover	150		29	Medina	150
	10	Boston	250		30	Rochester	200
	11	Roxbury	150	Dec.	1	Syracuse	200
	12	Lynn	150		2	Amsterdam	150
	13	Randolph	150		4	Cambridge	150
	16	Charlestown	150		5	Westfield	150
	17	Cambridgeport	150		6	Wakefield	150
	18	Springfield	175		7	Boston	250
	19	Home			8	Concord	150
	20	Philadelphia	400		11	Salem	150
	23	Rahway	150		12	Gloucester	150
	24	Newton	150		13	Lowell	150
	26	New York	—	Dec.	14	Portland	200
	27	Norwich	150		15	Dover	150
	30	Bloomfield	150		18	So. Boston	150
	31	Williamsburg	150		20	Hartford	200
Nov.	1	Home			21	New Britain	150
	2	Baltimore	200		22	Newark	150
	3	Washington	200		25	Christmas	
	6	Altoona	150		27	Elizabeth	150
	7	Pittsburgh	200		28	Plainfield	150
	8	Wheeling	175		29	Danbury	200
	9	Columbus	200		31	East Boston	150
	10	Dayton	150	Jan.	1	New Year's Day	
	11	Greencastle	200		2	New Bedford	150
	13	Paris	200		3	Providence	200
	14	Mattoon	175		4	Attleboro	150
	15	Decatur	200		5	New London	150
	16	Kankakee	200		8	Honesdale	200
	17	Chicago	300		9	New York	200
	20	Aurora	150		10	Brooklyn	250
	21	Chicago	300		11	New Haven	175

	12	Middleton	$150		4	Willsboro	$150
	15	Waterbury	150		5	Corning	150
	16	Ansonia	150		6	Mt. Morris	150
	17	Orange	150		7	Dansville	150
	18	Rhinebeck	150		8	Perry	150
	19	Glens Falls	150		9	Lockport	150
	22	Newburgh	150		11	Warsaw	150
	23	Hudson	150		12	Hornellsville	150
	24	Rondout	125		13	Wellsville	150
	25	Sing Sing	150		14	Friendship	150
	26	Poughkeepsie	150		15	Cuba	150
	29	Amenia	150		18	Jamestown	175
	30	Yonkers	150		19	Fredonia	150
	31	Newark	150		20	Warren	175
Feb.	1	Wilmington	150		21	Titusville	200
	2	Lancaster	175		22	Oil City	200
	5	Washington	——		25	Barnesville	150
	12	Wilkes-Barre	200		26	Xenia	150
	13	Pittston	150		27	Cincinnati	150
	14	Scranton	150		28	Louisville	250
	15	Binghampton	150		29	Indianapolis	250
	16	Auburn	150	Apr.	1	Washington	175
	19	Oswego	175		2	Pittsburgh	200
	20	Fulton	150		3	Kittanning	175
	21	Palmyra	150		4	Indiana	175
	22	Clyde	150		5	Tyrone	150
	23	Lyons	150		8	Williamsport	150
	24	Seneca Falls	150		9	Carlisle	175
	26	Watkins	150		11	Philadelphia	400
	27	Owego	150		12	West Chester	150
	28	Ithaca	150		15	Oxford	150
	29	Towanda	150		16	Avondale	150
Mar.	1	Elmira	175		30	Washington	200
	3	Bath	150	May	6	Nyack	150
					7	Honesdale	——

CHAPTER 7

THE WOMAN BEHIND THE IMAGE

The public image of Anna Dickinson, the Queen of the Lyceum, whose life was so tremendously exciting and purposeful that women all over the country envied her was, as in the case of so many popular celebrities before and since, a complete and thorough-going deception. Though Anna did her best to leave the public image unblemished, in truth she was a profoundly unhappy woman. She alternated between days of complete despair when existence seemed endlessly wearisome and devoid of purpose and she communicated with no one, and days when she perceived plan and pattern in life and a place for herself in both. Then, in an effusion of zeal, almost enraptured, she poured out her heart in those long letters home, in the impassioned lectures, in animated conversations with close friends which went late into the night. She lived in a continual and enervating fear that the rest of her life would be a protracted anticlimax to her wartime triumphs, and she could not bear to face this prospect. She must equal or surpass the past; failing this the future would be barren of hope. Were she not a woman, she could enter politics like a returned soldier and aspire to greater heights. But that way was closed. In the sphere of oratory she had achieved all that a speaker could achieve, but at too early an age, and all subsequent accomplishments must necessarily pale by comparison. She was gripped by a haunting fear that her name would inevitably diminish in public importance and her career would be marked by a steady decline from greatness. Another woman obsessed by such fears might have triumphantly closed the chapter on her public life and sought personal satisfaction in marriage and a family. But there was that about Anna—her disposition to fight, to lead—never to compromise or surrender—that came between her and this resolution of the crisis. She wanted desperately to write off the wartime Joan of Arc and to carve a new career, to prove to herself as much as to the world that she was not a woman of the past, but a woman of the future. But the way to do this was not clear, and she groped about during these years in the lyceum, seeking a new road to fame.

She tried literature. In summer months and during off hours between lectures she worked busily on a novel and in the fall of 1868 she brought out her first book. It was called *What Answer?* and was more a social tract than a polished piece of fiction. The small praise it won was directed toward the author's earnestness rather than to any artistic accomplishment. Its plot was contrived and melodramatic. A well-bred young officer marries a beautiful young girl who turns out to be a mulatto. His family is shocked by the discovery and tries to break up the marriage, but the officer refuses to desert his wife and becomes a social outcast with her. The story comes to a violent end when both lovers are killed in the draft riots of 1863.

The most favorable comment on the book came from a woman who knew how to write social tracts herself. Harriet Beecher Stowe wrote to Anna: "I lay on my sofa all alone on Saturday night and read your book all through and when I got through I rose up mentally and fell on your neck and said, Well done, good and faithful Anna—daughter of my soul. I thank you for this. Your poor old grandma in this work rejoices to find it in your brave young hands."

As an afterthought, Mrs. Stowe added discerningly: "Don't mind what anybody says about it as a work of art. Works of art be hanged! You had a braver thought than that."

The *Nation,* in a long critical review, took Mrs. Stowe to task for this endorsement. "Whatever a novel should have it lacks, and whatever a novel should not be it is," declared the *Nation.* "A thoroughly bad novel."

Anna then toyed with the idea of entering journalism and becoming a noted newspaper writer. She discussed this occasionally with Theodore Tilton and Whitelaw Reid and some plans were made, but nothing ever materialized. Her style had become too set to be changed to the journalistic métier.

After that, Anna discreetly surveyed the possibility of going on the stage. She had followed the theater with the keenest interest and admiration ever since the Garrisons first took her to a show in New York, and deep down in her heart she longed more than anything else to wear elaborate theatrical costumes, to mount the stage, and become a great actress. But for years, she was obliged to suppress her inner longings; her respectable friends looked down on the stage and orthodox Quakers would not be seen entering a theatrical house. Mary Dickinson would be grief-stricken by such a venture, and Anna feared that if she went on the stage it would be at the price of breaking with her mother and her closest friends. She had tried to broach the subject with the family once before, that winter in New Hampshire during the war when things looked so black, but Susan had quickly put a stop to it. A few years later Anna quietly discussed with some business acquaintances the possibility of a theatrical career and word somehow leaked to the press. Immediately there were repercussions at home. "May not I or someone contradict the reports out in regard to thy going on the stage?" her brother Samuel wrote her then. "I have pronounced it, so far as I know, a lie. I hope thee is growing to be more and more a child of God." And Anna, her heart aching, wrote a denial to the paper that carried the report. "I am *not* going on the stage," she said. "While there is so much to do and so many burdens to lighten in the world, I will not, God willing, leave my post, or desert work, honestly if inefficiently done, for useless play."

And so, balked at each turn, Anna went back to the lyceum every year with reduced zeal until she came to dread the long hard months from October to May when she was continually on the move through snow and rain, spending sleepless nights on rickety trains that were either overheated or freezing, but never just right. She fell ill easily and was subject to a recurrent bronchitis which often forced her to take to bed in lonely hotels for weeks at a time. The summers at Swampscott were hardly adequate to rebuild the energies she lost in each year's tour, and her moods of despair came more frequently and persisted longer. Susan B. Anthony's path crossed Anna's during the lecture season of 1870 and they spent a day and a night together. "I have found her the most weary and worn I had ever seen her," Miss Anthony wrote, "and desperately tired of the lecture field."

Then Anna played with the idea of going to England and in the spring of 1871 she went so far as to make inquiries about platform or theatrical work abroad and to work out plans for the voyage. "I was thinking how all my old enthusiasm has been worn out of me," she wrote to Whitelaw Reid who by now had become an intimate friend. "I am ready to go away, yet also ready at any moment to throw away the plan. I go, not because I want to go, but . . . because I must. . . . What with constant fatigue and suffering I think the easiest thing would be to slip out of life, and so done with it altogether."

"What new grief has come to you, that you write so despondently?" Reid hastened to reply. "I'm sincerely sorry for you, and I know how wearing is your life, but you speak as if there were something new and worse. One thing you must do. All these sudden interests in the misfortunes of your friends exhaust you utterly. You must learn moderation. Your store of vitality is not exhaustless; and you must economize it. . . . I hope you are to be here soon. You need rest; and you once thought I rested you. Health and quiet will bring back your old enthusiasm; and even the English trip will renew its attractions. But there's a comfort. If you don't go, you'll not be quiet so inaccessible to, Your Faithful Friend, W. R." In response to a request from Anna that an announcement be made in the *Tribune* of a change in her lecture schedule, Reid replied that a personal note would be "set afloat" immediately. "To make it look less official, and less as if you could have had anything to do with its suggestion, I shall couple with it a mention of the time when Kate Field sails. . . ."

A week later Anna was undecided about the European trip. "I wish one always knew just what to do and when to do it," she wrote to Reid. "What a lovely and orderly world it would be, to be sure." She seemed unable to make up her mind on any major issues, and the trip was the subject of continued indecision until finally it was too late to go. Her despondency carried over into the fall. "I wonder why people so cling to life—give everything for it, suffer ten thousand times the pangs of dying and more, rather than accept death. Canst tell?" she asked Reid. "For me, if I have not soon some other way of life than that I have known, something in which I shall be more at home, at ease, at rest, something foreign and remote from all the past, I know not what will become of me. Then, that sounds cowardly, and I am no coward. It is written, however, and it can stand."

The Dickinson family was not without its troubles, too. Mary Dickinson was a sickly old woman, and when she took to bed with a cold and diarrhea and hemorrhages followed, typhoid was suspected. But she had a good constitution and would live for yet another score of ailing years. She sorrowed greatly over the loss of Samuel, her eldest son, who died of scrofula. Soon it appeared that Edwin was a victim of the same disease and that he would have only a few more years of life. Anna, herself, was not wholly spared the miseries of bodily pain. One day Susan accidentally dropped a hot iron on her foot, and Anna was unable to place her weight on the injured limb for several years. Upon hearing of the accident John Dickinson wrote to Anna: "I was very sorry to hear of thy mishap, am thankful it was not thy head that was struck—hope that no permanent injury has been received. Let it admonish thee and me that 'the night cometh wherein no man can work.'"

Lecture fees came in regularly and an annual gross of $20,000 was a very handsome income. But the money seemed to go as quickly as it was earned. Sometimes it was spent before it arrived. Expenses of the tours and household were high, and Anna was lavish with her friends, her family, and herself. "She has no idea of the value of money," T. B. Pugh, Anna's lecture manager, once told a press interviewer in a statement that was unusually accurate. "She is liberal to a fault."

Anna did not seem to mind supporting a widowed mother and an older sister, as well as contributing to the upkeep of two brothers, their wives and children, plus countless doctor bills, but at the end of each annual tour she generally discovered that her financial position was no better than the year before and sometimes she even found herself in the embarrassment of debt. Susan's management of the household did not make matters any simpler. Anna sent the $250 monthly drafts regularly. Susan kept books and sent Anna weekly reports, but every month extra checks were necessary to cover the gap in the budget. Susan was an excellent accountant for pennies, but she could not, no matter how she tried, keep track of the dollar—a failing not unique among housekeepers. John urged Anna more than once to bring Susan into hand, but as long as lecture fees were coming in, Anna made no move. Only once does it appear that Anna herself ran into real financial trouble. She was in the Midwest in the winter of 1866 when she fell ill and was forced to halt her tour while she convalesced. Unable to lecture for several months, she was unable to send any checks. As a result Susan fell into arrears on house bills and was dunned. She urgently besought Anna, who was still confined to bed, to send "six hundred as early as thee can possibly let me have it."

In these circumstances Mrs. Dickinson often chided Anna for her generous presents to distant relatives and friends. "I want thee to use more discretion in thy expenditures in ev'ry way thee can, until thee emerges from thy present rather heavy liability and very much ahead of them," she wrote Anna. "I want thee to keep free from debt and in case of sickness or difficulties of any kind, have something to fall back on. I do not want to freeze thy generous nature; accept the suggestions of a mother that dearly loves and longs for thy happiness, both for time and eternity and remember, tomorrow, she will enter her three-score and ten years." And the aged lady added, in words that proved prophetic: "The time may come when thee can appreciate this counsel, that thee may now think it rather impertinent in me to offer it. . . ." Mrs. Dickinson asked Anna to invite no more house guests—life was simpler and cheaper without them. She preferred to sleep later in the morning, to keep a simple table with Susan, and to indulge in quiet reading. With guests she found it necessary to get up earlier or to serve two breakfasts, and a more lavish table was called for.

John Dickinson also implored Anna to take more care of her hard-earned money. "Can't you retrench—cut down house rent?" he asked. "The family is small and thee is absent three-quarters of the time. Have a fuller understanding with Sue about . . . lavish and unnoted expenditures, and try and invest at least $2,000 a year. The years are passing; health and strength are surely suffering; sickness may come. Do, my dear girl, look squarely at the matter—in making presents to relatives and friends, curtail an exuberant generosity and make them more often in the shape of necessities rather than luxuries and don't yield so much to the demands of fashionable society, but take a little better care of No. 1."

Whitelaw Reid, also concerned with Anna's future, likewise urged her to husband her earnings: "Over every platform on which you stand should be inscribed 'The night cometh'—" he wrote. "You know how the tale ends." Anna replied: "I do not need to go to the poor house this summer tho' I suppose that will be my ultimate destination unless I turn a new leaf—and that is too much trouble. Also I have not yet read to the end of the present one."

And so Anna would not heed. She had developed a passion for extravagant living that was now beyond her power or will to curb. The very month John Dickinson asked her to curtail expenses, Anna sent the family a present. Susan acknowledged the gift. "Monday came an enormous box from St. Paul, containing an elk's head entire," Susan wrote. "Did thee send it? I've sent it off to a taxidermist for further attention, for it s-m-e-l-l-s!! Well, the reverse of fragrant, and we had to keep it in the yard overnight."

During these lyceum years it was a common point of newspaper gossip to speculate on Anna's love life, to wonder whether she would marry and if so, who the lucky or unlucky man would be. Her name was linked with one important eligible after another, but, so far as we can discover, Anna never gave marriage serious thought, ostensibly preferring to center her life about her career. Certain it is that she had numerous opportunities to marry and she received plenty of advice on that score from friends and enemies, in public and in private. "I see you are 27 years old," a stranger wrote to her in 1869. "Now Anna— be happy—get married. . . . Never mind about the rights. Preach if you like, but don't go on and get old and sour. Old maids you know about. Get some splendid fellow. A man like George William Curtis— in every way lovely—and be wife and mother."

Anna was pursued by middle-aged and elderly widowers, some starry-eyed young swains, and two or three sober gentlemen of appropriate age. The older men were fascinated by her vigor and independence and bethought themselves of the joy of making her their bride. Younger men were captivated by her sparkling and dramatic manner and her great fame. But only a determined, self-reliant, and successful young man, like Whitelaw Reid, seemed able to meet her on her own level. One abortive romance followed another; several were conducted concurrently. The trip to California was marked by numerous attempts to win her hand. After returning from the West Coast Anna confided to her mother: "I have had two regular, serious, bona fide offers this summer —one from a M.C." The congressman she referred to was William Boyd Allison of Iowa, soon to become senator from that state and to serve in the upper chamber for more than thirty years. Allison, a forty-year-old widower whose wife had died about ten years before, traveled across the country on the same train as Anna. He was a sturdy man, with a bushy shock of hair, and he carried his broad frame with an air of dignity.

Allison had his eye on Anna throughout the journey; there were private meals together and long walks when the train came to a halt. Anna saved the cards he sent her, with their little notes scribbled on the back.

Private
Dear Miss Dickinson
    Your good bro. says "Miss Anna is endéshabillé" and invisible for the day. Does this mean to me. If yes, I will soothe my disappointment by taking a ride. If not, when, where and how shall I see you. If I came from above to see you is to return. If from t'other place, why should I not on this day at least have a momentary realization of what Heaven is?

Faithfully &c
Wm B A

Answer Please

Or another card:

When Miss Anna is alone and disengaged, I will come with her permission.

Wm B A

Answer
Faithfully &c.

Anna evidently kept Allison dangling and refused to bring the matter to a head either way. The next year Allison pursued his quarry to New York. He invited Anna to vacation that summer with him, but Anna turned down the offer and the congressman eventually turned his attentions elsewhere.

The second of Anna's suitors was a gallant figure of considerably greater national prominence than Allison then commanded. General Benjamin Franklin Butler, a widower in his early fifties, had led a colorful and exciting life. He had been a famous wartime figure, a political general who commanded an army. One of the first and loudest to rush to arms, he had led the Massachusetts troops to the defense of the Union and had made himself a favorite of the abolitionists by announcing that fugitive slaves taking refuge behind Northern lines would be received as contraband of war. Anna first met Butler in the New England political campaigns and was greatly impressed by him. Even the scandals that followed Butler's administration of New Orleans, such as the million dollars his brother allegedly made from notorious transactions with the Army, failed to shake her admiration. After the war Butler was elected to Congress and soon became one of the most influential members of the House, serving as one of the managers of the impeachment trial of Andrew Johnson. The General's physical make-up hardly matched one's expectations. He was short, heavy-set, squint-eyed, and almost completely bald, with a full mustache. But he was a courtier at heart, smooth and adroit, and his charming manner had won over most of the leading matrons of Washington society. Butler maintained lucrative law practices in Boston and Washington and evidently possessed substantial wealth for he sported a private yacht. He was an ambitious man and looked forward to new and greater achievements for himself.

Butler had a great fondness for Anna and to provide an excuse for seeing her often he became a friend and adviser to the Dickinson family. When Anna asked him to use his influence to get a government job for Edwin, Butler obliged by securing an appointment for Edwin in the Pensions Bureau. The Dickinsons seemed to look with much amusement on the spectacle of the portly man courting their Anna, but they did nothing to discourage him. When Edwin reported for work in Washington, Butler dropped in to ask of Anna's whereabouts and Edwin wrote to Anna, "He asked for thy address, so I suppose thee'll have a love letter the day before or after this reaches thee." Anna found it useful to remain on good personal terms with Butler, and their relationship continued pleasant for some years.

Then there were two younger men, Elias Hicks Irish, a successful young Pittsburgh attorney who served in the Pennsylvania state legislature, and Ralph Meeker, evidently the son of Nathan Meeker, the *New York Tribune's* agricultural editor who established the new community of Greeley, Colorado. Anna had met Irish when she visited Pittsburgh during the war in connection with one of her speeches. Irish fell deeply in love with her. His letters bear witness to the intensity of his desire. "It would be very weak and very silly to confess how much I miss thee, how strongly I am impelled to go where thou art, and to be with and pursue thee, like thine own shadow," Irish wrote. "Write thy worst, and I will press it to my lips. Strike and I will kiss the rod." Irish's untimely death brought the relationship to a sudden end. It is difficult to say precisely what Anna's feelings were toward him, but it is clear that she thought favorably of Irish and kept up a correspondence with him.

With Ralph Meeker the story was quite different. Meeker was an eccentric young man who saw in Anna the personification of all his dreams of perfect womanhood. Anna was never more than amused by his ardor. Meeker was passionate in his love for her. He came East from Colorado to be near her, and called at the Dickinson home. Susan was unimpressed. Meeker extended to Anna a formal proposal and wrote of the earnestness of his love. "I have something in my love for you that the words 'Divine Passion' (as they are commonly defined) fail to express. It is adoration," Meeker wrote, revealing more earthly passion than one might have expected from a devout prohibitionist. "You are the Fifth Symphony of women. Oh, for the time when I can behold the approaching of this miracle before me. When may I come nearer? All that I can say is that I love you, and always shall.... When I enter or leave the room I kiss your picture.... I want to make you feel that I am living for your sake, and that your happiness is my own."

"Did I tell about Ralph Meeker?" Anna wrote Susan from Minnesota. "He turned up in Chicago. Had come all the way from Colorado to hear the St. Louis hoot which he thought was to be made in Chicago, and *did* hear Joan of Arc which has before been made in his queer, enthusiastic presence."

The man with whose name Anna's was most often linked in matrimonial gossip was Whitelaw Reid. That two such fundamentally different personalities should have found so much in common was surprising to many of their mutual friends. Anna—unpredictable, unorthodox, highly emotional; Reid—older by five years and a day, determined, coldly ambitious, brilliant, formal, correct. Perhaps each had to offer what the other needed so much: the woman, torn by inner emotions, seeking someone to whom she could confide her hopes and fears, who could offer direction; the man, outwardly in absolute self-control, but inwardly seeking some means of emotional expression.

After the war Reid temporarily forsook journalism to try his hand at plantation farming in Mississippi and Alabama. A year or so of farm life satisfied him that he belonged elsewhere; he returned home to Xenia, Ohio, and then accepted an offer from Horace Greeley to join the editorial staff of the *New York Tribune,* at that time the most influential newspaper in America. It was a wonderful opportunity, and Reid was well along on his way toward becoming one of the nation's most prominent men. Before coming North, Reid wrote to Anna to comment on a note he had seen in the press saying that Anna had declined marriage to one of her many suitors.

"Every day I read that she has been 'rejecting' (rejects, to throw back, to throw away) an elderly New York bachelor journalist," Reid wrote in a playful mood. "I felt thankful for that word New York. I once had the honor of figuring in a little (far Western) paper as having been 'accepted' by a young Quaker orator-ess. I was 29 years old the other day, which may surely be called elderly; was a bachelor and a journalist (i.e., a hack writer) so once more, be the fates forever praised for that word, New York."

When Reid decided to sell his plantation he wrote to Anna to say that he was returning North and "would call at 1710 Locust St. where I shall doubtless learn that my friend is out among the Yahoos just this side the Rocky Mountains making speeches and fulfilling her destiny." Anna replied that she had been horseback riding. "So you've been riding," he wrote. "I wish I had been with you. I'm a famous rider—no grace, but any amount of stick-on-ativeness and *go*." He heard that Anna was writing a novel and urged her to conserve her energies for lecturing, instead of trying to excel in all fields. "Reserve your strength. Your reputation is made," he advised. "Devote yourself now to profiting by it and strengthening it." Anna confided her theatrical aspirations to Reid, hoping to receive some encouragement, but she was disappointed. Reid counseled against the stage in the strongest terms. He warned her of the condemnation she would receive from the very people who were now her sincerest admirers. "You would sacrifice a fame already won—and a brighter fame still in store for you—for a very doubtful experiment on a plane far below the one on which your position now is pre-eminent," he wrote. Instead of having people like Wendell Phillips, Mrs. Stowe, and Lucretia Mott as her co-workers, she would be in the same company with Edwin Forrest, Edwin Booth, Maggie Mitchell, and Matilda Herron. "And you would have, as the highest triumph the century has given your sex, always before you, the spotted fame of Rachel. Consider whether that, or the present fame of Anna Dickinson, is more desirable." But whatever she decided, Reid concluded, she could always count on his "hearty respect and warm regard."

After Reid went to New York and joined the *Tribune,* relations between the two were temporarily strained. Reid seemed to lose himself in his new work as Greeley's right-hand man and cut himself off from many of his previous associations. Anna was peeved because the *Tribune,* which had always treated her with consideration if not kindness in its columns, suddenly began to treat her with ridicule and contempt for her women's rights speeches. Reid denied that he was in any way responsible for this change and, from time to time, he inserted in the paper passing items about Anna that served as good publicity. But Anna was embarrassed and annoyed. "Are you so rich in friends that you can afford to throw them away?" she chided Reid in November, 1869. "Such has not been my experience in life. You know that you have in the woman who writes you this, a friend faithful and honest. I thought I had the same in you. You have said and done too many kind things for me to consent to the thought that they came from a feeling, here today, gone tomorrow." Then she put the question directly to him. "Have I done aught to displease you? If yes, I will beg your pardon as well as I know how, tho' I'm not great at that sort of thing. If you think my friendship is not worth the keeping, tell me so. At least let us have an understanding after so many years of kindly feelings shown through a multitude of harsh words."

By December friendship was restored in full and Reid took Christmas dinner with the Dickinsons in Philadelphia. Newspaper gossip reported that the rising young editor and the famous young lady of the platform would any day be joining hands in wedlock. "I have a letter from Vice-President (V.P.) Colfax, congratulating me on my impending marriage to 'that brilliant girl, Miss D.' besides any number of other letters, and newspaper paragraphs without number," Reid wrote to Susan in January, 1870. "I hope she bears it as stoically as I do!"

The public game over Anna's marriage plans continued. Reid sent a letter to Anna in March enclosing a press clipping he had come across. It read: "Anna Dickinson announces in Cincinnati that this is her last lecture season, as she is going to retire from public life. The name of the gentleman was not ascertained nor when it is to come off."

"Are my congratulations in order?" Reid asked Anna in a show of amusement. "And shall I send congratulations or condolences to the gentleman from Boston [Butler]?" He added: "Have you seen the latest about *me?* My physicians have forbidden me to marry; and so I am making the *Tribune* my bride! Bye-bye, be a good girl and save your money!"

Through the rest of 1870 Anna and Reid corresponded frequently. "Please to take some little care of yourself," Anna wrote him, "if it is only for the sake of not depriving me of the delightful privilege of innumerable fights." They saw each other again that December when Anna came home from her tour, and they spent a quiet evening together. Anna spoke of a new book she was planning. They discussed its merits. The next morning Anna sent Reid a note thanking him for the pleasure of the evening. "How good you are, how gentle, and how kind," she wrote. "You have seemingly always been afraid to give me anything save hardness and yet, God knows, I am sore enough and worn enough to have a little fragment of coolness and softness bestowed on me.... Bah, what am I talking. I am what nature made me, and I live the life this nature ordains. I do not wish aught else: but I am glad that I know you somewhat better than I did, and that you have learned a little more of me, for I do not think it was just a book wherein you were interested." She extended Reid an invitation to join the Dickinsons for Christmas dinner again, that year. "We all want to see you, that you know," she said, "and for myself—after that long talk with you I do not need to tell you how glad I shall be to see your face, and take your hand under my own roof."

Reid hesitated to accept, pleading other commitments, but Anna insisted. "I don't doubt you want to go to some very fine, elegant, *proper* state dinner Christmas Day. Very good. I shall interfere, and ask you to come to one that has no merit under the sun save that it is a home dinner, and you shall be one of it." Then, as a sudden afterthought, she wrote: "Considering that last sentence I have concluded that the nation would be shocked thereby, so I go back and say in due shape, *we* will *all* be happy to see you on Christmas Day, and since our dinner hours are as disorderly as the mistress of the household, you will have to come in the afternoon, and quarrel till you get an appetite.... I forgot, I promised not to fight—if I could help it."

Came Reid's reply: "If I spend Christmas in Philadelphia you'll come back the next day with me?" And after the holidays he wrote to Anna as she prepared to resume her lecture tour, "You must not go West without seeing me. Please write at once whether it shall be in Philadelphia or New York." Anna sent him a picture for which she had recently posed and Reid acknowledged the gift. "My dear Anna," he wrote, "When you come to breakfast with me, on the occasion of your speech here, you shall see the picture in the place of honor; and if your Boston friend [Butler] comes with you, you shall also see a thunderstorm. Good Bye and God bless you."

What was it that drew Anna and Reid together, moved them to make appointments and write letters, quarrel and conciliate, pain and comfort each other? A gossipy public pondered the enigma and asked what it was that usually motivated a man and a woman, both in the full vigor of youth, so to act toward each other? But the public knew only the public image. Where knowledge ended, speculation began, and one guess was as good as another. The Anna Dickinson the public did not know seemed ever unable to give herself to a man; there was a point beyond which all further union was contemplated with revulsion. And there was that about the cool and correct Whitelaw Reid that satisfied him not to be faced with consummate demands or expectations that were beyond fulfillment. But this was conjecture; who could speak from knowledge? The real Anna Dickinson and public's image of her were poles apart. Standing on the platform of Steinway Hall in New York City one wintry evening, the Anna Dickinson the public knew spoke of love and marriage. For some days before, the papers had been full of a sensational murder trial—the Richardson-McFarland case—in which a divorced man murdered in cold blood his former wife's new lover. An all-male jury acquitted the murderer and the newspapers roundly condemned the dead man as a marriage breaker. Anna denounced the verdict and came to the dead man's defense. "Once in a while God blesses the world with a great lover," she said. "This man was such a one." Hisses were heard in the gallery. She addressed the men in the audience directly. "You have no right to love, you have no right to a wife, in the best sense of the term, if you are not, in the truest sense of the word, a husband in return," she said. "Love signifies companionship, friendship, understanding, some similarity of sentiment, of pursuits, of interests. It is not a mere passing fancy or a pleasing hour, it is not an episode." She advised them what to expect in the future. "I stand here to warn you, sirs, that the woman of the present is not the woman of the past, that she will mete to you as you mete to her. I give you fair warning that the law of the time to come, whatever the law of the past has been, will be equality, justice, evenness between what you give and what you receive." Thus spoke the Anna Dickinson of the public image.

The next day the voice of Whitelaw Reid spoke through the *New York Tribune*: "Miss Dickinson has appeared before New York audiences in better condition for speaking than last night," read the account, "but never before one which she carried more heartily with her, and never before one to which she made a braver speech."

CHAPTER 8

GREELEY VS. GRANT

ONE day in July, 1872, there was a knock on the door of 1710 Locust Street. Mary and Susan Dickinson had gone to the mountains to escape the blistering Philadelphia heat and Anna was resting at home with her maid, Louise, in attendance. She answered the door herself. It was a messenger with a telegram. She opened the envelope and read the carefully penned dispatch: MR. GREELEY INVITES YOU TO COME TO NEW YORK THIS AFTERNOON SO AS TO ACCOMPANY US TO CHAPPAQUA TOMORROW. WILL YOU DO IT? TELEGRAPH ME. THEODORE TILTON. Horace Greeley was running for the Presidency of the United States against Ulysses S. Grant and wanted Anna to spend the week end with him at his Westchester farm. Greeley hoped Anna could be persuaded to take to the stump for him in the campaign soon to get under way. Tilton was managing Greeley's campaign.

Anna was tired and perplexed. Her health was better than it had been for some time before, but she was looking forward to a quiet week end and was not in a mood for political discussions, even with a presidential candidate. Politics had become too deeply mired in the quicksands of corruption and ineptitude—the independent observer found himself trapped in a painful dilemma: to support the re-election of a general-president whose administration was morally bankrupt, or to encourage the seemingly hopeless candidacy of Horace Greeley and the newly formed Liberal Republican party. If Anna was to enter the campaign, she felt it must be on her own terms. PROFOUNDLY SORRY, BUT CANNOT COME, Anna wired Tilton. She was not yet ready to grapple with the dilemma.

Sunday morning there was another knock on the door. This time it was Senator Henry Wilson, Grant's vice-presidential running mate on the regular Republican ticket. Wilson was leaving for North Carolina that night and would like to stop in for tea with Anna later in the day. There was something he wanted to talk over with her privately. "By avoiding one I fell into the claws of the other," Anna wrote her mother two days later. "By saying no to the would-be President, I *had* to say yes to the would-be ('tother) Vice-President. By not accepting Mr. Greeley's invitation to spend Sunday at his house, I had the pleasure of entertaining Mr. Wilson at my own."

When the Senator returned in the evening he explained his mission. Wilson was a man of sixty; he was self-educated and lacking in the polish one might expect from a man who for eighteen years had represented Massachusetts in the United States Senate. The son of a New Hampshire farm laborer, he had pioneered in the formation of the Republican party and had been one of the senators who signed the invitation to Anna to address the Congress. "Anna," he said as he blew on his tea to cool it, "we want you to campaign for us as you did ten years ago. We need you."

Anna demurred. "I have not decided what I shall do in this campaign," she said lowering her cup to the saucer. "Perhaps I shall stay out of it altogether. I am tired, my family urges me to avoid any political campaigning, and you know what I think of President Grant. I have no heart for it. I need not tell you, Mr. Wilson, what you know better than I, that this administration has been a thoroughly corrupt and immoral one. I can think of nothing to say in its behalf other than that it will, I hope, shortly be coming to an end."

Wilson set aside his tea and came to the point of his visit. "If you will campaign for us, Anna, you will not regret it. The party is prepared to pay you $20,000."

"Mr. Wilson, the party in Pennsylvania nine years ago was prepared to pay me $12,000 for twelve days of speaking, and begged me to do it, and I did it, but I never saw a cent of the $12,000," Anna replied. "How different can I expect my treatment to be this time?"

"The party has not done right by you, Anna," Wilson admitted sadly. But, he continued, this time it would be different. He would stake his personal honor on it. Anna shook her head.

"I cannot do it, Mr. Wilson, much as I would like to return the many good things you have said and done for me. But I cannot. And it is not simply a matter of money, though an unmarried woman who must live by her labors and can expect no political office needs look to matters of money. It is more than that. I deplore the present administration, I think it is evil, I have already spoken out against it, and I cannot and will not speak now in its behalf." She paused and stared pensively. "Yet I do not know that I shall publicly oppose it and come out for Mr. Greeley. I cannot decide now." She handed Wilson the telegram from Tilton. "You see, they want me in the other camp, too."

Wilson studied the wire thoughtfully. "Anna," he said at last, "I can't urge you to go into the campaign against your conscience and I haven't the face to beg you to do it for me. Yet I will beg and pray, and pray again that you do not campaign for Greeley."

Anna's eyes sparkled. The pensiveness was gone and she was all play. "If I move men to prayer, Mr. Wilson, surely I am in the service of the Lord." The Senator laughed good-naturedly and agreeably changed the subject. After he left the house, Anna wrote to her mother: "I had a really delightful time with him, but I do wish he wouldn't saucer his tea and would use his napkin."

Though Anna had for a decade been closely identified with the Republican party she had remained aloof from party politics since the election of Grant in 1868. In the first postwar years Anna had allied herself with the radical wing of the Republican party that called for a vindictive policy toward the South. Indeed she had been one of the architects of that policy, and when Andrew Johnson broke with the radically controlled Congress after first endorsing its program, Anna presaged his impeachment in 1866 with a tremendous indictment of Johnson's record and character.

Anna had called for vigorous action by the Federal government to extend the ballot to Negroes and to guard their civil liberties against mistreatment by former Confederate leaders who had been pardoned by Johnson and once again were in control of many southern states. When Johnson vetoed the Freedman's Bureau and the Civil Rights Bill, both calling for the use of Federal power to protect the Negro in the South, Anna had turned upon the President all the invective she could command. She charged Johnson, "this man" she called him, "with the betrayal of every trust, the nonfulfillment of every pledge, the falsifying of every oath he made before his assumption of power, with drunkenness, with aiding and comforting the enemies of the Republic, with disgracing us in the eyes of all the world by his action and his speaking, with refusing to obey the laws of Congress or to see that they were executed in the spirit with which they were made, with betrayal of trust, with degradation of office, with desecration of power—alike the enemy of his party, his country, and his God."

When the Senate failed by one vote to find Johnson guilty as charged, Anna was naturally disappointed, but Johnson's term was soon to come to an end anyway, and she looked forward to the 1868 election with the hope that one of the Congressional leaders like Speaker Schuyler Colfax would be entrusted with the Republican nomination. She was, it seems, in no way attracted to the most popular figure of the day, the military hero of the war, General Ulysses S. Grant, whose name was being boomed for the Presidency and whose stature seemed to assure certain political victory. Anna displayed her customary independence by publicizing her lack of enthusiasm for the much-honored Republican candidate-to-be and in doing so disappointed many of her best political friends. She told her audiences she had heard only two reasons advanced on behalf of Grant's candidacy: First, that he was "free of isms," his opinions on the fundamental issues of the day not being known to anyone, and second, that he was a soldier. She was far from certain that the first was a virtue; as for the second, "if soldiership is a thing to be recognized, why not nominate some private?"

But the public wanted its military hero in the political saddle, and Anna, ever suspicious, quietly kept tabs on the Grant regime. And what an administration it proved to be! The wartime General made a miserable chief executive. Appointments to high office were doled out to friends and favorites with little thought to qualifications. Corruption was rife and financiers with contacts in the government were able to amass plunder on an enormous scale. The Secretary of the Navy took questionable favors from men who had business to do with the Navy. The Secretary of War resigned his office and was immediately thereafter impeached and tried on the charge of receiving bribes from a trader at an Indian post. The Whiskey Ring, a conspiracy involving hundreds of distillers in collusion with Treasury officials, defrauded the government of tax money. When Grant's own private secretary was shown to be badly involved in the Ring, the President came to his support and saved him from punishment by the law. In the South many states were subjected to corrupt carpetbag governments made possible by the abuse of Federal powers originally granted to effect enlightened state governments. Grant himself was bent on annexing Santo Domingo to the United States, but an enraged Congress refused to sanction his pet project.

After three years of Grant, many of his early supporters were soured by the corruption and immorality of his leadership. Others were disgusted with the progress of Reconstruction in the South. Anna, who had been biding her time politically, wrote letters to important friends in Congress asking their judgment of Grant's administration and their views on the next year's election. Vice-President Colfax thought that one term was enough for Grant and said so to Anna. Senator Charles Sumner roundly condemned Grant, as did Senator Carl Schurz of Missouri. Senator Henry Wilson, who the following year would be joining hands with Grant, wrote Anna: "I have not great faith in the wisdom and goodness of the Republican party, but I have a sublime faith in the continued folly and wickedness of the Democratic party." He thought the chances were "rather in favor of Grant's re-nomination."

Armed with this information and her own strong opinions, Anna contemplated the wisdom of delivering a public attack on the President. She wrote to her family to sound out their attitudes. What would they think of her mounting the platform to speak out against Grant's renomination? The family was more sagacious than Anna on matters involving risks to income. Their advice was clear: to come out against the chosen leader of her party would only destroy Anna's standing with the Republicans; to join the Democrats was unthinkable; she would make a political outcast of herself and suffer great losses in lecture cancellations by lyceum committees that would disapprove of her move. John wrote to Anna early in March, 1872: "Ed thinks it hardly wise to pitch into the renomination of Grant 'all the circumstances considered' and I think so too. He says that to amount to anything such a speech should be made extensively, in many of the large cities, and early, before delegates are chosen, otherwise you simply make a fuss, get abused and knocked, lose some influence and achieve nothing." Susan, too, had discussed the question with her brother. "Ed is certain thee will only lose thy popularity for no good by making such a speech now," she wrote Anna a week later. "It is too late to do any political good, or anything but personal harm to thyself. There is not likely to be any split—the discontented will after all support Grant, to defeat the combined Democrats and 'Labor Reform' candidates."

But Anna had made up her own mind. Her decision was to pitch into Grant publicly, whatever might be the personal consequences. Susan confided Anna's plans to Whitelaw Reid. The place of the speech was to be Pittsburgh, where Anna was scheduled to lecture on April 2, 1872. On the afternoon of the speech, Anna sat down and wrote Susan her plans for the evening:

> Dear Scrubby,
> The speech is licked into shape, at last, and I make it for the first time tonight, and I half-laugh and half-chatter, as I think of the amazement and wrath it will create in Pittsburgh. *That's* one of the "regular party" strongholds—and the speech is, after all, a regular screamer, good tempered, I hope, and not dealing with any ugly personalities, but no mistaking *what* I mean by it.
> It's no use for me to walk around a subject, or rather to try to, for I always hit a blow at the centre of it ablast.
> What tickles me, is that the Pittsburgh papers, that know nothing at all about it, are lauding it as one of my "happiest efforts" and the rest of that flummery, and that they are one and all perfectly rabid on the Grant question. Serve 'em right for indulging in the sort of senseless praise and blame of which our journals are full.

To an utterly astonished audience, Anna made a speech in which she attacked the graft in Grant's administration and criticized the President for abusing the power of his office. Grant had assumed authority in time of peace, she said, that England would not tolerate in the hands of the Queen in time of war. She detailed a long list of offenses of which Grant's administration was guilty.

Anna's blast at the President drew immediate response from an infuriated press. The *Cleveland Leader* demanded that she "get married" forthwith. "Clearly the time has arrived for some husbandly hand to lead her out of those public walks where she is stumbling at every step into the flower paths of wifehood and domestic tranquillity," declared the Ohio paper, anxious to laugh off the attack. "Was there ever such impudence?" asked a Pennsylvania paper editorially and answered: "Anna Dickinson must be ruled out." Most Republican papers played down the address. The *Philadelphia Item* remarked: "It is measurably safe to recommend to this individual to commence stitching up her winding sheet as a public speaker."

The day after the speech Anna wrote to Susan:

> The audience was a very crowded one, and I never talked to one I liked better. There was some hissing, and whenever there were hisses there was instant and great applause, but for the rest of the time the most intense stillness. People listened till it was almost painful to see them.
>
> All three of the Republican papers here are bound hand and foot, not only to Grant, but to the Pa. Central—and the people, who are very earnest, sensible people, were getting some truth literally for the first time. . . .
>
> The speech such as it is, *is,* and I shall not change it. I mean that I do not *mind* the clippings. Do not discuss facts and details, but general principles in the hoot.

Samuel Bowles, of the *Springfield Republican,* wrote to Anna two days later: "I have just written Mr. Greeley about the new speech and urged him earnestly to take hold and have it brought out. I am delighted that you have raised up your voice on this side." Anna repeated the anti-Grant speech several times in the next two weeks and then came to New York to deliver it at Cooper Union. Greeley presided over the meeting and introduced Anna. The *New York Sun,* a rival of the *Tribune,* reported: "The audience was held entranced for an hour and forty-five minutes by one of the most earnest, eloquent, and effective political speeches, certainly of the campaign that has so early opened, and possibly that has ever been heard in that place." Hisses were heard among the applause. Anna replied: "Let any hiss who please, and let those applaud who choose. I will utter the truth despite censure *or* applause, and will maintain it though I stand alone." Everyone cheered.

By April, however, it was clear that a stop-Grant movement could not prevent his renomination; the President and his allies had the Republican party machinery well under control. Dissident Republicans who could not stomach the prospect of four more years of Grantism but were unable to support a Democratic party that was still under the cloud of its Civil War record, started to talk in terms of a third party. Missouri's Governor Gratz Brown and Senator Carl Schurz spearheaded a crusade. The new party took the name "Liberal Republican" and attracted public leaders like Charles Francis Adams, Horace Greeley, David Davis, David Dudley Field, William Cullen Bryant, and others. The Liberal Republicans called a convention in Cincinnati in May to formulate its program and select a ticket. Much to everyone's surprise and to the dismay of many others, the new party put forward as its Presidential nominee the erratic Greeley, whose eccentric appearance was bound to subject him to personal ridicule in any political campaign, and who, during his long tenure as editor of the *Tribune,* had made many personal enemies. But Greeley accepted the nomination with a great sense of honor, and pledged himself to an all-out campaign. He was confident of victory. And the Democratic party, at a loss for a candidate of its own, threw in its lot with the Liberal Republicans and made Greeley its standard-bearer, too.

"Hurrah for us!" Anna wrote to Reid on hearing of Greeley's nomination. "I have sat up o'nights to rejoice over Cincinnati and next autumn I propose to do the very best hooting I ever did in my life in behalf of the good man and the good cause. God speed them—and amen."

But Anna did not publicly announce her support of Greeley. Instead she maintained an unaccustomed silence and chafed privately as most of her friends in the women's rights movement like Susan B. Anthony, Mrs. Stanton, and Mrs. Stowe came out publicly for Grant. The Republicans had included in their platform a statement saying that the party was "mindful of its obligations to women"; Greeley had never been genuinely sympathetic to the feminist cause and had used his paper to oppose the extension of the ballot to women. In making their choice between candidates the women's rights leaders were willing to subordinate all other national issues to that of the ballot. Anna was not; to her the question of women's suffrage was only one of many issues affecting the welfare of the nation, and in the coming election it was of less importance than restoring integrity to the Federal government. In so asserting her independence of thought and action Anna came to a parting of the ways with Miss Anthony and Mrs. Stanton, and feelings were sorely strained. Somehow the difference in policy transcended the sphere of politics and aroused strong emotional conflict among the women. They were no longer friends.

When the lecture season ended in May Anna went home to rest and write, while Susan and Mary Dickinson left Philadelphia to visit and vacation. Anna enjoyed the quiet relaxation of simple home life. "I took my 'shocking' and my Turkish and afterwards my dinner, with equanimity," she wrote to her mother. "Lou swept the third floor and I put it in order." It was a torrid summer and on the fourth of July Anna wrote to Susan to complain of the heat. She had read in the papers that three hundred people had died of sunstroke in New York and Brooklyn in only a few days. "The physicians say it is very healthy weather," she wrote. "Well, heat may be a healthy disease of which to die, but I suspect its victims find it no more satisfactory than an unhealthy one."

Meanwhile she kept up a fairly heavy correspondence with Whitelaw Reid who was busy running the *Tribune* and assisting Greeley in preparations for the campaign. "Dear Crosspatch," began one letter from Anna to Reid. "I don't suppose you want to see nor hear from me, since you keep such obstinate silence." In a later letter Anna modified the salutation. "You are *not* a dear crosspatch," she wrote. "You are a cross without the adjective, or qualification whatever. If you had not come to see me (if it was a little bit for me) on Sunday night I don't know what I should have done—torn my hair and lost all respect for you."

Senator Wilson's visit in July was preceded by a pleasant note some weeks before. "I only regret that you can not give the grand party that saved the country... that persuasive and eloquent voice to which I have so often listened," he wrote. "But you act I know from a sense of duty. God bless and prosper you ever is the wish of your good friend." After the tea with Wilson Anna apparently took his suggestion to heart and carefully considered whether she should remain silent or come out for Greeley. She had in mind writing another book, this one on the problem of labor in industrial society. In mid-July Sam Bowles wrote Anna: "So you turn aside from Greeley and from the girls and from heroes and martyrs and attack the labor conundrum! ... I am glad to have you try another book, and yet it does seem to me your true field is the platform...." Bowles was a Greeley supporter and hoped Anna would join the ranks of the Liberal Republicans. By the end of July it appeared that Anna *would* come out for Greeley if the Liberal Republicans asked for her support and if the proper conditions could be obtained. She was too experienced in politics to consider campaigning without fee, even for a cause in which she fully believed. Furthermore, as a professional lyceum lecturer she wanted to be sure of some form of return to compensate for possible lecture cancellations. When she rejected Tilton's invitation to join Greeley at Chappaqua, she wrote her mother: "If I want to go into the campaign I will go into it and get *paid* for it. Otherwise I propose to ... 'keep shady.' "

Anna turned to Reid for advice on the role she should play in the forthcoming campaign. "Do you want me to go into it," she asked him, "and if you do what will those vampires of the Com. [Committee] pay me—the most, *very* most?" Reid was not to understand, however, that she had made up her mind to speak in Greeley's behalf, though it was true that she had delayed completing her lyceum route for the fall season pending her decision. "Mind, I don't know that I will go at all," she wrote, "but I want to know on what ground I shall tread, if I do walk abroad. And if I don't go regularly into the row, is there any special work that you want me to do?" The implication was clear that Anna very much wanted to be asked by Greeley and his committee to campaign for them as she had campaigned for the Republicans during the war; it was not so much a matter of money (though that was by no means an inconsequential consideration) but a question of purposeful effort—to be wanted to campaign, to be consulted, to be looked to for leadership, to be handsomely paid for services rendered, all this would recapture for Anna the sense of mission and achievement she had sought since the close of the war.

"I think you might be of large service in the campaign," Reid replied to Anna. "I don't see how it could hurt you, since ours is unquestionably the side that has the Future with it. And you are so committed, voluntarily, that you could not in honor do anything on the other side—even if you would keep silence on ours." If it were up to him alone, he would like her to make one or two elaborate and well-publicized speeches at focal points at any price the committee would pay or without price if necessary. "That is my idea of the political obligation of those who aspire to political leadership—obligation to the country, to their principles, to themselves. After that (and on that I'd take what I could get but not haggle about terms) I'd treat it purely as a business question, and work or not as the terms suited. But I can't reconcile it with my notions of political honesty or patriotism to make one's utterance on great national questions, on one side or the other, or even one's absolute silence depend solely on whether one got paid enough to break silence."

These sentences seemed to embarrass Reid in the writing, so he went on to explain: "You used to rate me for being unsentimental, practical, indifferent to the sentimental demands of this or that Great Cause. Well, perhaps we've changed parts, and what I now write may seem a romantic idea of public duty that has no place in the calculations for a successful season. But it has always been my way of thinking."

Reid closed on an affectionate note. Anna had said he owed her several letters, but he denied it. "You said you'd write me from Hartford, and didn't; would stop and see me (let me see you!) coming back, and didn't," he wrote. "Then you went to our friends when I couldn't; and deserve to have your ears duly pulled—for wh. debt, draw on me at sight!"

"My Dear Mentor," Anna replied facetiously. "So you will abuse me, threaten to maltreat me, misrepresent my actions, and doubt my motives. 'Tis like you." She was still undecided whether to campaign for Greeley, and if so, what her minimum terms would be. But she was quite certain she had not failed to visit Reid when she went through New York. "Have the goodness to tell me whether you were or were not in Ohio during that small transit?" she asked jocularly. "Do you know, I am seriously of the opinion that you would not know me if you should stumble over me at high noon in the open streets. It has been so long since you took any earthly interest in me and my doings.... Well, be a good boy. Be ambitious, be hard-working, be as successful as you desire, only don't kill yourself in the effort. I don't believe that heaven hankers after you yet, and there are one or two people who are by no means ready to part from you."

The exchange of correspondence continued. "Of course you need your ears pulled again," Reid replied to Anna. "But meanwhile Heaven (or other powers) speed the time when you shall know your own mind.... When *are* you coming to New York? And why are you so unreasonably perverse? By the way I've been hearing a precious mess about you. If you don't prove more reasonable, I shall be tempted to say I believe some of it. Good Bye, and do your best this season. I told you, in my last letter, the frozen truth about your duty."

"My dear badness, you can have an opportunity, probably, to 'pull my ears' some day next week," came the response from Anna a few days later. "Only pray remember that two can play at that game, and I am more given to earnest than pastime in such little efforts of skill and strength." She would pass through New York on her way to New England for some rest and recreation. She had decided not to do any campaigning for Greeley. "Know my own mind?" she mocked Reid merrily. "You wish I would know it? Do you so? Be it then understood by you that I am to write a book, and get a pot of money, some praise (I hope) and endless abuse (I am sure) for the same, and that this same book will prevent any early campaign work...."

But Reid was right; Anna did not yet know her own mind. The next day she sent him another letter. "I told you very emphatically that I would write a book, yet I have not really decided. No? say you, why not? No, I answer, and will tell you why not." She was all befuddled over which publisher she should give the book to. Charles Warner, Sam Bowles, and Mark Twain all advised her differently. "Each one tells atrocious stories about the general scampishness of every other subscription house, save his own, and *that* is the very worst of all in the estimation of the others." Which publisher did Reid advise? "I think I am growing imbecile," she wrote, "weak-minded certainly, for I was never so thoroughly at sea as I am about everything in the shape of business this summer. I can decide upon nothing. I blow hot and blow cold till I am disgusted with myself."

Then she returned to the subject of the campaign. "I wish I could feel some genuine enthusiasm or even interest in this fight," she wrote. "I can't. It may be my fault, or it may be my misfortune, but so it is. Perhaps 'tis a physical condition and I am too tired to get into a fire over anything." But at the same time as she was *not* interested, she told Reid who by now no doubt was bewildered by her inconsistency, she really *was* interested. She wanted to go into the campaign on Greeley's side because Reid and "nearly all the friends I care very much for are on that side—and then I do have a genuine liking and admiration for Papa Greeley." Anna then suffered a moment of false modesty and added parenthetically: "Fortunately it makes no earthly difference to anything living save sure myself whether I go in or stay out. But when that's said, all's said."

Anna waited impatiently for an offer from Greeley's campaign committee, but none came. The committee felt it had no great need for women speakers and though it would welcome Anna's speaking on her own in Greeley's behalf, it had no intention of hiring her or any other woman. Anna was hurt by the committee's attitude and left Philadelphia to vacation at Swampscott. "You see I was right in wishing to stay out of the campaign," she wrote to Reid peevishly. "At no time have I desired to enter it on my own account, the only thing that could have reconciled me to it would have been the certainty that I was greatly needed, and could have done great good, and since Mr. Greeley and the com's have otherwise decided I can stay at home with a perfectly clear conscience." Now that she was not going to take part in the campaign herself, she became solicitous of Reid's well-being and cautioned him against making too many personal sacrifices for the campaign. "Don't work yourself to death, and don't burn all your bridges behind you," she wrote. "I suppose you will regard me in the light of a traitor for even making such a suggestion. Good, my friend. I was your friend long before Greeley-Republican-Democracy was ever thought of, and expect to be so long after it is dead if not forgotten, so don't be cross with me."

The announcement was made in the press that Anna would resume her lyceum lectures in November immediately after the election. "It is not her intention to take any part in the political agitation now so generally prevalent," ran one newspaper story. "Politically she sympathizes with the liberal cause and Greeley and meditated taking the stump in their behalf, but has finally yielded to the earnest appeals of her friends who are on the other side and probably will not speak at all during the campaign." Another newspaper, relying on a personal letter Anna had sent to a friend, stated that "on no account is she going to take any part in the campaign, all assertions to the contrary notwithstanding."

When the Dickinsons spotted this last report in the press, they were highly pleased. Susan wrote her sister: "Mother is in a state of *extreme* felicity at hearing that thee is not going into the campaign. What of the book?" On the same day, writing from Swampscott, Anna told Susan joyously: "Hurrah for the book! Have finally agreed to write it at a guarantee of $10,000 and a royalty of 25 cents a copy, but nothing is to be said about the terms. I shall sign the contract on my way home. So Marmee can be at rest concerning the campaign. If I wanted to go into it even so *this* settles it. Also it settles that I stay at home till the 4th of Nov.—which is jolly."

But the merry-go-round of decision and indecision did not remain motionless very long. Hardly a week later Anna had changed her mind once again. Greeley's committee had reluctantly altered its attitude at the last minute when it saw the effective work being done in Grant's behalf by the women's rights spokesmen. Unless Greeley could get a woman of equal or greater reputation than Susan B. Anthony or Mrs. Stanton, the public impression would be created that *all* women stood with Grant. The most prominent woman speaker in the country available to Greeley was Anna, and the committee had declined her services only a short time before. When the committee approached her this time, it was under pressure to bargain, and it offered Anna $10,000 if she would take to the stump for Greeley. She responded coolly to the offer, but to Susan she wrote: "There are some reasons why I greatly desire to go into the campaign. . . . As to money, I can have $20,000 on the Grant side, and of course $200,000 wouldn't tempt me. I have my offer for $10,000 on the Greeley side, and Sam Bowles says they *must* give me whatever I ask." But there was still the matter of the book for which she had received excellent offers from two publishing houses, each guaranteeing a minimum of $10,000 against royalties. They crowded her for time, however, and she would not be able both to campaign and to complete the book.

For reasons that are not entirely clear, Anna finally decided to take up the Greeley offer instead of completing the book, but without the $10,000 guarantee. The explanation may be that the book offers were withdrawn. "Do you know the Grant people are saying that they are behind your publisher's offer for a book, and that the scheme was gotten up in order to keep you off the Greeley stump?" Sam Bowles wrote to Anna. "It is a very funny idea; but it comes to me directly from one of your personal friends, high up in the Grant column." The Dickinsons were greatly distressed by Anna's new decision. Less than a month before the election John Dickinson wrote Anna: "I am wavering whether to vote for Greeley or not. If I thought he would abolish Ku Kluxism, I would."

Under Reid's management it was decided that Anna would announce her support for Greeley in a single major address attended by great publicity. The last Friday in October was chosen for the date though Sam Bowles had hoped an earlier time would be arranged. The place was to be Anna's old standby—Cooper Union. The address would ostensibly be delivered in response to an invitation from leading New York businessmen who desired Anna to express her views on the coming election. Anna was very concerned about the proper publicizing of the speech for she knew that anything less than a full house would be harmful to herself as a lecturer and to the Greeley cause. Moreover, her endorsement of a losing candidate would have an injurious effect on her winter's book-ings. "If you knew just how I stand towards a great many of my busi-ness people you would understand that what I do I do with a bit, at least, of my life in my hand," Anna wrote to Reid. "If I pay such price I do it because conscience compels, and because I believe I can be made of really large service to Mr. Greeley and a great cause, but to that end I need help." Could Reid arrange to put an agent to work publicizing the Cooper Union talk? Anna showed an uncommon knowledge of twentieth-century publicity methods. "The only way to make this a suc-cess in these days," she wrote to Reid, "is to adv. directly and adv. liber-ally and thoroughly in all the papers that amount.... Also to see that notices are in—long, short, many or few, abusive or the reverse, the longer, the more frequent, the more commendatory or the more abusive the better, and every day possible." Any publicity was helpful, even crit-ical publicity, just so long as the word was spread. The public would respond to notoriety as well, if not better than to repute.

Then Reid and the campaign committee made a mistake. Anxious to attract a full house, they arranged to sell tickets at only twenty-five cents each. When Anna heard of this she was furious and was ready to cancel the talk. "It makes me look cheap," she wrote to Reid in angry protest. "It makes lecture-going people suppose I'm 'hard up' for an audience, it hurts my prestige ... and sets a bad precedent for after prices and posi-tion. I want to serve Mr. Greeley, but I don't propose to ruin myself in the serving." Her advocacy of Greeley would cost her not less than $5,000 in canceled lectures, Anna told Reid, and she enclosed a letter she had received canceling an engagement on the bare rumor of her coming out for the *Tribune* editor. At twenty-five cents a ticket she would not even earn her ordinary lecture fee in New York. "Mind you, I am not howl-ing, nor yet vaunting myself, nor yet begging, but I think among you, you might remember the fact that I am not Mrs. Stanton, no, nor yet Mr. Schurz, but, as my lecture list shows, the most sought-after speaker in the country, that I am not asking anything at your hands, but trying to serve you, in a way, that I think will be the most effective." If the committee was so thoughtless of her welfare, she had better withdraw from their plans; after all, she had patiently waited since early summer until the committee got around to inviting her to speak. "I knew and said four months ago what Grant's people would do with the woman issue," she reminded Reid, "and I knew of just what service I could be on the other side, and your nice politicians would have none of me. Now I can have naught to do with them. Furthermore, knowing perfectly well that they ought to be thankful for me as bound turkey, I don't propose to be taken, under protest, in their need, as boiled cow." She concluded her emotional outburst with a brief, but determined explanation: "I don't like to write this sort of thing," she said, "and I like still less to be compelled to write it, but I have been quiet under provocation till I think it a wise thing to keep the peace no longer."

Reid advised the committee to raise the tickets to fifty cents, and the squall blew over. Publicity men were put to work, and though it was storming the night of Anna's speech, a capacity audience assembled at Cooper Union. The crowd was unusual in make-up as well as large in size; in the rear could be spotted Susan B. Anthony and Elizabeth Cady Stanton, come to hear their old friend and protégée oppose their candidate. The platform was draped with flags. "Unannounced and unattended, and without the absurd formality of an introduction, Miss Dickinson proceeded to address the audience," reported one paper. She was dressed in black and stood on the platform alone, near the edge, holding two or three slips of paper in her hand and referring to them occasionally for figures. There was neither a stand nor a reading desk in front of her. The correspondent of the *Boston Post* recorded an exciting and unwittingly ironic account of the speech:

> There was the least suspicion of tremulousness in her tones, not from any nervous feeling of herself or her subject, but from the very intensity of her feeling. It was the same tremulousness that used to vibrate in her voice when she spoke in the times of the war, and everyone who heard knew that all the old fire and power were there, intensified and deepened for having lain dormant so long, for though as an orator Miss Dickinson is always fine, yet it is only on occasions like this, when there is some real issue at hand, when she is absolutely working for a purpose and a principle, that she rises to the full height of her genius.
>
> With her, politics are no playthings, the caprice of an hour to be toyed with and thrown lightly aside when the whim is exhausted; she is in dead earnest, and she feels and believes all she says. That is the secret of her wonderful magnetism, so earnest herself, she makes her audience in earnest also, and they follow her, almost

breathless, through her whole address, with kindling faces and flashing eyes, reflecting every mood of her own. From the time she opened her lips until she closed, she never lost her hold on the audience for a moment. As she went on her voice grew clearer and stronger, a flush came on to the bright face, and the lithe graceful figure grew taller and more dignified. Sarcasm, indignation, and pathos were blended in her address, and rung out in the tones of her voice. But she was not fully aroused by the cheers to her points, until she got the opposition from the audience on "Who won the war?", i.e., "Who saved the country?" Quick as a flash, Miss Dickinson turned and faced him, her whole face alight with indignation. "Who saved..." she said, in a voice that no one who heard will ever forget, so clear and strong and earnest it was. Eager faces had watched the slight skirmish and eager ears listened to the passage-at-arms, and at its close the tumult was deafening.

It was indeed ironic that after months of wavering indecision, confusion of purpose, and conflict of motives, Anna delivered that night one of the finest speeches of her career. She spoke from outline only, but for fluency, organization, language, and an overpowering sense of climax, it was masterful in every way. As an indictment of an administration in power, it would be difficult to find its superior. The speech was entitled "Is the War Ended?" and had three main points: first, the Grant administration was thoroughly corrupt and disreputable; second, and this point represented a complete reversal in Anna's own thinking, the policy of vindictive reconstruction, which she herself had advocated, was a failure and should be abandoned; third, Greeley's record, despite his failure to endorse the women's rights movement, justified support of his candidacy because he stood for integrity, justice, and humanity.

Anna ripped into Grant as mercilessly as she had torn into McClellan years before. She painted a picture of plunder, of corruption, of dishonesty, of criminals in public office, of collusion between the President and grafters. "Twenty-two prominent delinquents in the internal revenue department, thirty-nine prominent post-office culprits, thirty other marked thieves in other departments of the government; two million and a half of the people's money stolen unblushingly and with open hand—two million and a half admitted, and the half not told!"

"A tree is known by its fruits. What fruits has this administration borne and is it bearing today?" She repeated the accusations commonly made against the President. "Mind! It is not I who accuse him, and I don't mean to accuse him this night. He *is* accused. Of what? He is accused of seaside loiterings, of greater fondness for the smoke of a cigar and the aroma of the wine glass, than for the duties of the White House, and the responsibilities of the government of the country." She attacked in turn each of Grant's leading defenders. "The admirable sheet that supports him in this city, on the sixth of last July I think it was, saw fit to commend him, commend the President, praise him to the full—for what supreme act of self-denial?" she asked with all her power of sarcasm. "For leaving the horse-race at Long Branch to attend a cabinet meeting at Washington. He is accused of accepting gifts and placing the givers in high places. How could he do otherwise? Did he appoint no man to a place in office in this state who did not give him a gift, the state of New York would be officerless—a consummation devoutly to be wished.... He is accused of putting relatives in place, of using his great power given him for the benefit of the republic to put fat places and rich offices in the hands of his relatives. There are very few, says one. The number is variously estimated at from thirteen to forty-seven. Well, certainly the President must be very rich in parents, for the one thing constantly said, concerning these thirteen or forty-seven or the number between is, 'The President is mindful of the good old Bible law, that whoever honors his father shall be found long in the land.' The lowest point of political degradation has been reached.

"There is no deeper depth to sound when men stand before the people and admit, and the people consent to listen to their assertions so standing that these things are so; that they don't deny them, but even excuse and defend them." Anna quoted a Republican senator from New York who had recently defended Grant from the same platform on which she spoke. Suppose all the accusations against Grant were true, the senator had said, what of it? If you want a man to pilot a ship, or lead an army, or try a cause, or build a house, or run a locomotive, what do you care what manner of man he is, so long as he does his work well? All these things are aside from the real question: Has he made a good President?

In the fullness of her oratorical passion, Anna made a reply as profound as it was pointed:

"When one chooses a man to pilot a ship, if he is moving on strange waters, he wants one not alone who keeps a firm hand on the helm, who understands tides and channels and rocks; he wants a man so honorable as to make it sure he will not give over the ship into the hands of pirates.... When a nation selects a man to lead its army ... it wants not alone a general and captain able to lead it to victory, but a man of sufficient honor not to allow scamps and thieves and bummers and camp followers to destroy all we gain. When you want a judge to try a cause, you want not merely a man wise and learned in the letter of our laws; you want a judge whose ermine is without stain, and who has never accepted the shadow of a bribe. When you want an architect to build a house ... you want to make sure not only that the architect is skillful and knows how to plan, but that the man himself is honorable, and will not sublet his contract to miserable jobbers. It makes no difference of what manner of man the engineer may be who is to run the locomotive? The accidents, so-called, in nine cases out of ten, have not come from unskillful engineers, but drunken men. The honorable gentleman has forgotten, if he ever knew, that in the long run moral attributes are as essential to thorough success as professional or intellectual powers."

Anna turned to Grant's treatment of the South and discussed the carpetbag governments propped up by Federal soldiers. "The administration in these states began in usurpation," she said, "and ended in rapine." Hers was a plea for reconciliation, a recognition that the war was over, that the North would once again have to live side by side with the South. She argued that justice had been done to the Negro by freeing and enfranchising him; that now it would depend upon the black man to use the ballot to make his own government; that to use military force in peacetime to impose government on the South was a denial of republican principles; that the new South could be trusted, with its newly acquired free institutions, to make its own way to a dignified existence; that continuation of a vindictive policy would only result in an embittered postwar generation that would rightfully hate a government so brutally imposed upon it. She referred to the boys who were too young to have fought in the war and were growing up in the *post-bellum* misery of the South. "All that they see is the wrong and bitterness of the government which rules over them. This generation that fought us, fought us without excuse. If this bitterness and wrong bring on another conflict, the men who fight for justice and against wrong will not then be in the North, but in the South." Thus, in practically every argument, Anna signaled her complete reversal of position; her acknowledgment of the failure of a policy she had believed in and her readiness to call the war to an end. An undeniable air of magnanimity pervaded the speech as the champion of the wartime North now took up the cudgels on behalf of what she felt was an unjustifiably oppressed South.

Anna went on to her third point: Greeley's qualifications for the Presidency. She said she had been asked how she could support "a man who had used his newspaper and power to trample down your rights and to scoff at your desires!" She replied by turning the spotlight on Grant and asking, "What has *this* man done to deserve the gratitude of dignified American women?"

A voice cried out from the audience, "Who saved the country? General Grant!"

Anna turned in the direction of the heckler, "Who saved the country? The American people saved the country!" Great applause and cheers broke out and the same voice shouted back from the audience, "It was the soldiers!"

"Yes," Anna said, "it was the soldiers who fought under the command of General Grant, but who learned their loyalty in twenty-five years' reading of the columns of the *New York Tribune!"*

Here followed a scene of wild confusion. Cheer upon cheer rent the air as the whole audience sprang to its feet; hats were tossed up to the lofty ceiling, handkerchiefs were waved, and a tumult of applause and enthusiasm raged until Anna indicated a desire for its cessation.

"Quite enough," she said. "Let us have peace."

This pleasantry only induced the audience to laughter, but Anna was anxious to go on. "Let us try a little quiet now," she said. "I wish to come to Horace Greeley." Over the cheers that greeted the candidate's name Anna recounted Greeley's humanitarian work and told how he had used his power "to make smooth paths for weak feet to travel over."

Anna brought the speech to a close with a magnificent peroration in the rhetorical tradition of the time. Her style of speechmaking was

generally direct; only in the emotional conclusion did she make use of
the spread-eagle manner then common in American oratory. She
achieved the most intense results and the audience felt carried to new
emotional heights as the speech came to an end. Anna concluded by
taking a historical perspective on the day of election:

"The world will perish. History will write its record concerning us.
Nay, the last sentence not having yet been put down of this war record, history waits for it; waits as the sentinel, in the stillness and
darkness of the night, placed at his castle door, hearing a stealthy step
approach, cries aloud, 'Who goes there?'

"So with the final sentence of the war record to be written, history
pauses. Pausing with uplifted pen, over the blank and untouched page,
cries to America, as it advances on the fifth of November, 'Who goes
there?' 'Friend, with the countersign,' is the answer. And history,
still pausing, cries out, 'Advance, friend with the countersign,' and
America, advancing, responds, 'Liberty for all and justice for every
man!' and history, dropping her pen, writing in characters of ever-
lasting light and glory, makes answer, 'The countersign is correct;
pass on!' and sounding on through the ages and the centuries, echoing
and re-echoing, goes the cry, 'Pass on! pass on! Oh, latest and grandest
and best of nations. Pass on, America, to the throne and empire of
the world!' "

Amid tumultuous applause, Anna left the platform and the great
speech came to an end.

The next day the *Tribune* carried the full text to the entire country.
("My dear badness," Anna had written to Reid before the speech,
"After all, the hoot is to be made, and since it is to be made nowhere
but in New York do you want to publish it in full?") Anna had struck
her blow for Greeley and against Grant in typical fashion: she was
merciless and uncompromising. The Republican party would take
many years to forget this indictment. Anna was a renegade and her
heresy was the more difficult to forgive because it was so dramatic.
When could she hope again to be in the favor of the governing party
among whose inner circle she had mingled so freely for a decade?
The Liberal Republicans naturally greeted the speech enthusiastically.
Senator Schurz wrote from St. Louis to ask for a copy: "I desire very
much to read it. I have seen it so highly praised that I should be very

glad to have a full report. You did a noble thing in coming forward when Mr. Greeley's chances seemed to be almost hopeless."

Greeley's cause *was* hopeless, and when the election returns came in Grant romped through to a smashing victory. Greeley carried only six border and Southern states. The people still wanted their military hero, whatever his faults, and Anna found herself on the losing side.

The humiliating defeat came as a great personal tragedy to Greeley. He returned to the *Tribune* offices a broken man; he had lost control of the paper he had fathered for twenty-five years; Whitelaw Reid, his protégé, was now chief editor and Greeley was divested of all authority. His mind began to give way under the shock of disappointment and shame. Years later Anna described her last meeting with Greeley the evening after the election. She had gone down to the *Tribune* to leave some printing orders and was leaning out of the carriage door to observe the deserted appearance of the usually busy street when Reid emerged from the building and came to her.

"Anna, I wish you would go up and see Greeley," Reid said. "He is alone. You will find him terribly broken."

Anna hesitated momentarily about seeing Greeley in this unhappy state, but she stepped out of the carriage and accompanied Reid into the building. She saw Greeley "seated on a chair, his arms hanging across his knees, like a man spent with toil; his sad face bowed upon his breast." Anna came up to the old man and putting her arm gently about his shoulders spoke to him. As Greeley lifted his face, she could see his sadness. A sorrowful voice said, "Anna, you see before you a very heavily bowed down and sore-hearted man."

Reid stepped out of the room. Greeley and Anna were alone. "I hear, Anna, that what you have done for me has cost you dear," Greeley said.

"No greater price than I was quite willing to pay," Anna said quietly.

"I heard from Henry Wilson, your old friend and mine, that he himself had offered you $20,000 for twenty speeches and you said, 'You might make it twenty millions and I would not talk against Greeley and the cause he represents.' Whitelaw tells me that since the speech you made on the twenty-fifth of October last, you have had over $14,000 work of lyceum engagements canceled on your hand. Is that true?"

"Yes," Anna said.

Greeley brushed some tears out of his eyes and said, "Anna Dickinson, I think you are the most generous woman alive." He leaned forward and took from where it was lying on the table a piece of newspaper copy and said, "What do you think of this, my child? Does this please you?"

Anna took the clipping. It was the principal editorial paragraph of the *Tribune* of October 26, 1872, the day after Anna's speech and read as follows:

> When the handful of third-rate women speakers gathered on the Cooper Institute platform to "speak for their sex" and attempted a transfer of its political influence to Grant in return for the ridiculous bone thrown them by the Philadelphia Convention, we promised that there should speedily appear on the same platform, to refute them, the one woman orator of America—a lady with more eloquence, more power, more right to utter the wish of women, than the whole of them put together. The columns of this morning's *Tribune,* which report the speech for Horace Greeley by Miss Anna E. Dickinson, which last night thrilled a great audience in the Cooper Institute, exhibit the fulfillment of the promise. Always magnetic and inspiring, Miss Dickinson was never more so than last night.

"Does that suit you? Does that satisfy you, Anna?" Greeley asked.

"Frankly, Mr. Greeley," Anna said, "It does not altogether suit me because it is such a very unsatisfactory fling at some of the good women who spoke there; they are not third-rate women. I suppose they believed what they said."

"Well," he said, "it is Whitelaw's writing and I hoped it would please you."

Anna prepared to leave as Reid re-entered. Greeley took her hands in his and repeated his earlier statement: "Anna Dickinson, I think you are the most generous woman alive. The *Tribune* has never been generous to you."

"Oh, yes, it has," Anna protested.

"No, it has only been severely just; henceforward it is yours to command; whatever you want you are to have. Whatever you desire will be furnished to you. And if I cannot fulfill that promise," he said, putting his hand on Reid, "Whitelaw will see that it is attended to."

Anna took her leave, went downstairs and departed in her carriage. Before the month was out, Greeley was dead.

With the election over, Anna's political escapade had come to an end. It had been an exciting and revealing episode. Judged by the effect her political transgression was having on her lyceum bookings, it had been a damaging episode, too. But to friends who thought they knew Anna well the most significant aspect of the whole affair was the revelation of certain instabilities in Anna's psychological make-up that seemed to be getting progressively more difficult to control. It was clear that Anna had developed an immodest sense of her own importance which, combined with a feeling (justified to a degree by the facts) that she was not being accorded due respect, induced emotional outbursts, a querulousness of manner, and an inability to make firm decisions. She still possessed tremendous native talent and unquestioned pre-eminence in her field; at the age of thirty, she was a woman of amazingly varied experience. For the moment she felt serene and confident: all would go well. "Dear Goosey," she wrote to Whitelaw Reid just two days before the election, "I have a beautiful new gown, and you are to take it and me by and by to the opera." Was it not Reid who had spoken of the "frozen truth" of duty and discounted the risk of supporting a righteous cause? Whatever adversity the future might hold Anna knew that at least she could always turn for succor to the man who now had under his sole command the most influential newspaper in America. With the campaign behind her Anna set out from home to complete the winter's tour.

CHAPTER 9

THE NIGHT COMETH

IT WAS not many months before it became clear that Anna was headed for real trouble in resuming her lecture career. The first intimations came the winter after the election. Lyceum engagements began to fall off; there were cancellations by anti-Greeley lecture committees and failures to make good on contracts. The season before, fees had run over $20,000; now Anna wondered whether she would make enough to pay expenses and still have something left to keep the Dickinsons in food and shelter. "I couldn't send thee any money after Michigan City as I made none till Decatur," Anna wrote Susan in April, 1873. "I told them to send thee $100. Will send another $100 tomorrow. Make it cover all that it can." And ten days later, from Minnesota: "Am flourishing, but making no money. Will tell my tale of woe and indeed the tale of all the miserable hooters who are out...this season when I write."

It was not merely a matter of Anna's having antagonized her previously loyal following. The lyceum itself was showing marked signs of deterioration. A public willing to re-elect Grant was hardly interested in the serious political and social discussions that had been the mainstay of Anna and other lecturers. Fewer requests for lecture dates were sent to the booking bureaus and the local groups were often unable to drum up audiences for talks that had been scheduled and advertised. "The lecture committees think they are having a bad time of it this winter," Anna wrote Susan from Oil City, Pennsylvania, in March, 1873. "At Jamestown, out of ten lectures, but five of the people have succeeded in getting through." Old-time lyceum personalities were finding it very difficult to eke out an existence. One of them, Melinda Jones, found herself without any engagements at all. She wrote to Anna to warn her against a repetition of the same fate. "I wish I could impress you with the desire to save," wrote Melinda Jones to Anna that spring. "Your heart is so large in its sympathies— your nature so generous—added to these—your love of the luxurious makes you so indifferent. I always picture you, Quaker tho' you be, as a Creole in tastes, revelling in flowers, wines, fruits, poetry, and oriental outer coverings. . . . Such a nature as I feel you have will never bear the cruel change from plenty to the daily annoyance of petty life. . . . I have been foolish and wicked enough to allow myself to be poor—it is the greatest crime I ever committed. Now, Anna, dear, be warned by me, steel your heart, as much against your own luxurious desires, as your friends', and don't commit the unpardonable sin of poverty."

Anna's difficulties stemmed from a number of other sources, too. She had split with the Redpath and Fall lecture bureau because she thought it was taking too much of her income without providing a substantial return. Faced with a claim from the bureau for $1,600 in unpaid fees, Anna filed a counterclaim for $2,000. To strike back at Anna, the lecture managers put into anonymous circulation an announcement to the effect that she was quitting the platform and was not seeking any more engagements. Anna was out West when this happened and did not learn of it until some weeks had passed. By this time great damage was done to her bookings. She asked Reid to help her out by printing an item saying that she was still lecturing and available for bookings. Reid obliged: "I hear on all hands that the little editorial settled the Literary Bureau and puts you all right for the season. When you come, I shall scold on the necessity of not getting in such a scrape again." Anna's legal fight with Redpath was handled by General Butler. Though Butler was one of Grant's lieutenants in the House of Representatives, he did not allow politics to come between him and Anna. After the election Anna wrote her mother from Boston: "General Butler had a long, long talk with me, and today came a lovely bunch of flowers from him. He doesn't propose to be affected by my heresies. He said he was very sorry I had made the speech, but he thought it the bravest thing done through the campaign. He asked again and again for thee. . . ." Now Butler was prepared to defend Anna against the lyceum managers. "As to James Redpath and his threatenings," Anna wrote Susan, "Gen. Butler came to see me today: Says R. is under obligations, pecuniary and otherwise to him, and he will simply be informed that the whole case rests in his (Butler's) hands, to do what he pleases,—'and'—said the Gen., 'the affair is settled—dismiss all thought of it from your mind.' I went into sackcloth and ashes, for I was made to feel before he went away, that whatever he is to most people he is so thoroughly my friend as not to be alienated even by what must have seemed to him very shabby treatment. He desired to be remembered with regard to my mother and sister."

Still another cause of Anna's troubles were some lectures she had given in the '71 and '72 seasons which, like the Greeley speech, lost her important friends and much popular support. These lectures—the first was called "Demagogues and Workingmen" and the second, "Things Hoped For"—contained Anna's views on vexing economic and political problems of the new industrial America. Anna was a bitter foe of the sprawling business corporations—her letters bear repeated testimony to this. "The more I travel in Pa., the more I detest it," she wrote to Susan during one tour to complain of long delays in the train schedule. "So much for the beauty of monopoly, and the benefits of the Pa. Central. What fools and worse people are to submit to such tyranny, and help to build it up." She condemned the gigantic industrial combines that were plundering the country and running labor and the public underfoot. "I contend a dead corporation has no right to control the lives of living men," Anna said in one of the lectures. "I can see in these corporations the most terrible despotism that ever trod down the bodies and souls of men. Who governs Pennsylvania? The people? No! The Pennsylvania Railroad Company!"

But at the same time as she attacked the monopolistic corporations, Anna also voiced grave reservations about the expanding trade union movement, and she bitterly censured union practices such as restriction of membership, limitations on apprentices, and exclusion of Chinese immigrants. She argued that the labor unions were actually combinations of skilled labor against unskilled labor, instead of labor against capital, and that the control of the labor market by the unions was done at the expense of the public. Convinced of the soundness of classical economics and the effectiveness of the free market, Anna failed to recognize that some of the new problems could not be wholly solved by theories advanced a century before. In speeches to audiences of workingmen, she assailed the campaign for the eight-hour day. "If the mantle of Adam Smith has not fallen on her," noted one newspaper, "she wears her own much more becomingly." Anna's attacks on the trade unions and big business only aroused both groups against her. While the newspapers gave a good press to her attacks on the unions, they opposed her violently when she included the big corporations in the indictment. The labor groups also turned against Anna who for years they had numbered one of their own. "We had thought her a friend of the poor and the op-pressed, a battler for the rights of humanity," said one spokesman for labor. "We find her now unmistakably on the other side." The *Roch-ester Democrat* insinuated that Anna had been bribed to deliver the antiunion talks. "I have been out of the good books of Boston, and indeed most New England places ever since I made my fight against the trade unions," Anna wrote home the year after the election.

Troubles mounted. The Dickinsons bickered among themselves as the monthly checks no longer came in with regularity. On the advice of her brothers, Anna had invested most of her savings in what was then one of the more favored property speculations—unworked lots in the growing city of Chicago. In March, 1871, Edwin had expressed the hope that Anna would be able "to continue to lay by a lot in Chicago occasionally." Later that year a raging fire devastated a vast section of the budding Midwestern metropolis and Chicago land values dropped precipitously, leaving Anna in a very precarious financial position. Any hopes she had to shorten the wearisome lecture seasons had to be abandoned. She needed all the bookings she could get to meet her annual expenses. There was the three-story house on Locust Street; she saw it seldom and only Mary and Susan Dick-inson lived in it most of the year. Anxious to reduce Anna's burden so that she would not have to seek so many engagements, Mary Dick-inson repeatedly suggested cutting down overhead. "Would it not be better to contract family and other expenses and thus avoid such constant exposure to life, health and comfort," the old lady wrote. "Thee would enjoy thine own home, and give comfort to thy poor old Mother and by wise management and economy be more com-

fortable than we often are now." Mindful of the costly summers she
spent with Susan in the mountains or at Atlantic City, Mary Dickinson wrote: "How would it do to contract Susan's and my summer
spendings, as well as thy generosity to Tom, Dick and Harry, who
have no particular claims on thee and who feel but little thanks."

Edwin, too, was much concerned over financial matters. He was
tubercular and was able to work for only limited periods of time.
He was fearful of Anna's future, as well as his mother's, if they failed
to save any money. He was furious with Susan's loose management
of household funds and he urged Anna to put her older sister on a
strict accounting basis lest Susan ruin her financially. "As things are
going, thee'll be a bankrupt...if Sue continues to be thy 'confidential
clerk,'" Edwin wrote Anna. "Perhaps installing her out of office would
be a desperate remedy, but it seems to me the case is growing desperate....As thy expenses have decreased in an arithmetical, hers are
increasing in a geometrical ratio." Edwin charged Susan with
"thoughtless extravagance" and remarked disparagingly about her
housekeeping ability. "I suppose it's needless to remind thee that this
letter is fuel and fuel only," Edwin added. "If Sue should ever know
of it, I think it would be my right to know that she knew it. If thee
should write to me and *for* me, at any time which I don't expect,
to 1710, thy letter would have to be directed by someone else. We're
as usual. Sue well enough to be out day or night."

Under Edwin's urgings, Anna gave serious thought to breaking up
home and moving her mother and sister into a comfortable boardinghouse where they would have private quarters and take their meals.
Anna would then be relieved of the burden of maintaining a large and
almost empty house. She confided her plans to Reid who approved
them. "I haven't thought so well of any business operation of yours
for a long time as of the plan to 'decline housekeeping' as the elegant
advertisements put it," Reid wrote. "You can't help saving by the
operation."

Anna wrote her mother and Susan about her plan and Edwin reported back the family's reactions: Mrs. Dickinson was agreeable, but
Susan objected. "Mother seems to be quite willing of her own a/c, and
because she thinks it will benefit thee, rather anxious to try boarding....My only fear is the old one, tho' in a less degree, viz., Sue, of
course does the room hunting. Mother wants comfort; Sue, 'West

Benjamin F. Butler as a major general in the U.S. Army

Miss Dickinson in costume

End' apartments with arrangements; Mother wants a neat sitting room...Sue wants a drawing room. Mother wants quiet; Sue her pianoforte and canaries, etc., etc. I hope or rather believe that a pretty satisfactory compromise will be effected tho' at a considerably greater expense than would otherwise be necessary."

But Edwin's hopes for a move to smaller quarters were soon dashed when Susan succeeded in changing Mary Dickinson's feelings in the matter. A week later Edwin sat down at midnight to write Anna another letter: "What can I do but write my deep regret at the change which has come o'er the spirit of the dream. Sue is certainly a capital wire puller, and all the more so from the perfect naivete with which she always 'mixes' her prejudices and conscience, her thoughts and their parent wishes, her vanity and dignity, thinking them all one. Thee knows I wouldn't express myself so plainly and forcibly if I tho't myself the sufferer in anyway, for I've watched, and sometimes felt, the wires, for years and usually said little or nought, but my impatience is more aroused this winter because I expected a greater growth of healthy character, and because in the somewhat changed aspect and relation of things of late, it hurts me the more to see the annual 'deficiency appropriation.' Several thousand, at an actual benefit of about as many hundred. Mother has been quietly brought round within a few days, made to believe that *home* is *home* and boarding can't be. A pleasant Walnut St. prospect of a few days ago is now a dismal barn....$50.00 a week board was then a decided saving; it is now very extravagant, about as much as this house costs, the latter amount being got at by a calculation of what the house's legitimate running expenses ought to be, and by the supposition that now they will be brought nearly to that minimum....Sue keeps her own counsel so far as she can, evidently suspects me, since she knows I sent thee a letter the other day which she didn't see, takes pains so far as she 'carelessly' (carefully) can to see the opening address of my letters."

From Susan Anna received a direct report: "I have looked and fare no better as to room," Susan wrote, "and Mother is more set than ever against leaving her own home....She is thoroughly disgusted with the idea of boarding; and convinced that it will not lessen expenses to any appreciable degree in the course of the year." The experience of room-hunting had only ruffled family relations. "It seems

very hard with all the money spent and pains taken," Edwin wrote
Anna, "1710 is such a lonely discontented place." When Reid heard
that the Dickinsons were going to stay on at Locust Street, he wrote
to Anna: "On every account save one, I'm glad the plan of giving
up the house has been abandoned. It seems to me too great an expenditure; but for all other reasons it is immeasurably pleasanter to
have a home than a boarding-house. Yet after all, on the score of expense, and the need of saving what you can now, I do hope that in a
year or two at least you may be able to make a cheaper arrangement.
Meanwhile it's pleasant to remember that '1710' still has a home-like
sound."

Not only family and professional problems beset Anna. There was
the continuing deterioration of her health, and the physical decline
soon made itself evident in her state of mind as well as in bodily ailments. The winter of 1872-1873, after the election, was unusually
bitter and cold. Anna had gone out to the Midwest—a territory she
dreaded, for she always seemed to come down with jaundice there—
and started lecturing. In a few days she was forced to take to bed
with a chest ailment that was diagnosed as a severe bronchitis, but
was probably pneumonia. She canceled the remaining engagements
and awaited an abatement of the fever. She seemed to have run out
of energy. The world bore down so heavily that she could control
herself no longer and she vented her pent-up emotions in brief fits
of hysteria. A few days later, the fever having gone, she recovered her
equanimity and the world seemed livable once more. She returned
home from the Midwest a weak and weary woman who felt greatly
aged beyond her thirty years. When summer came, she went to
Swampscott, and though she enjoyed the fresh sea breezes, she still
felt dispirited. Then, one day, a letter came from Ralph Meeker
inviting her to come out to Colorado to restore her health with the
bracing mountain air of the Rockies. The prospect was attractive, and
Anna decided at once that she would go if she could "make it out in
any right shape." She scraped together the necessary money and in
early August, 1873, she set forth hopefully on the long journey West
with her brother John. "I have so wanted to go to the mountains that
I am sure they will do me good," she wrote to her mother as she left
Swampscott, "and I suffer here as much from sleeplessness as I did
at home."

The anticipation of new vistas did much to restore Anna's spent energies even before she saw the mountains. As on her trip to California four years before, Anna regularly wrote her mother and Susan (whom she usually addressed as Marmee and Dickey, respectively), long, enthusiastic, and affectionate letters as the train carried her farther west.

On the cars, 9:30 a.m.
August 13, near Vandalia

Dear Dickey,

We are in a very stupid country at present but are looking for better things beyond. Am flourishing but didn't have an epicure's breakfast this morning. John is dirty. So am I, and we both send much love.

August 15
Near Wallace, 8:30 p.m.

Dearest Marmee,

We are just off the front of the Engine. Hurrah! *What* a ride. If Marmee could have taken it, 'twould have made her young again. Both send dear love to all.

Denver, Col. August 16
7:30 a.m.

Dear Dickey,

Just in. Safe and well and hearty. Had a ride of 20 miles on the Engine looking out toward the "Delectable Mountains." Ralph Meeker is here at the breakfast table, and John is here, and they both send love, at least they ought to, as does Anna.

The Colorado air was good for Anna and her depressions of the winter and spring were replaced by a boundless exuberance that wore out her companions. Now she was a girl of twenty again. She developed a passion for mountain climbing. Riding astride a donkey she scaled five of the highest peaks—Long's, Pike's, Gray's, Lincoln's, and Elbert's, each more than fourteen thousand feet above sea level. The *Denver Daily Tribune* reported Anna's ascents with some amazement. "She will rank well in the annals of mountaineering," the paper declared. Anna, it was reported, was the first woman and among the first individuals to climb to the top of Mt. Elbert. The exercise improved Anna's health wonderfully. "It was the grandest pleasure I ever experienced," Anna told a friend sometime later, and added boastfully, "I believe it has been said that I have been to the summits of more great mountains in America than any other woman alive." To her brother Edwin she wrote: "If I could scare up enough money to buy a little place here, does thee think thee could live, and be content to live here? And would thee try it in the winter as well as summer. I want thee to think of the matter soberly and answer me at once...."

Anna started back from Colorado in a spirit of complete exhilaration. Her health had been greatly improved and she was brimming with refreshed energies. Before she reached home, however, disaster struck. Not only Anna, but the whole nation was brought to the verge of complete financial ruin. On September 8, 1873, the highly respectable banking house of Jay Cooke and Company announced its bankruptcy. Within two weeks the nation was held in the grip of a financial panic. The New York Stock Exchange was compelled to close its doors for ten days. Manufacturing and trade fell to about two-thirds its former level as the panic of 1873 unleashed a terrible depression that blighted the country for five years. Now there was no longer any talk about holding on to the house on Locust Street. With Anna's prospects so uncertain, a move to less pretentious quarters was imperative; Susan and Mary Dickinson broke up home and found rooms for themselves in a boardinghouse at 1122 Vine Street in Philadelphia.

The panic took its toll throughout the nation and it did not spare the world of education and entertainment. The tottering lyceum was dealt a blow from which it never fully recovered. Though Anna received a very favorable greeting when she delivered her first lecture of the 1873-1874 season in New York City ("I had a splendid reception, flowers thrown to me and baskets brought up to the value of hundreds of dollars. A superb audience and seemingly a delighted one, and I did a great deal better than I expected to do, tho' I never am satisfied with a new speech. I think it will be a great favorite.") thereafter the season was a succession of disappointments and failures. "Thee is not to think me careless," Anna wrote Susan from Bangor, Maine, "but I have had the d—— to pay with some of my work and engagements, and I actually cannot let thee have what is needed in the way of money $1,000 or $1,100 before next Thursday. I am awfully sorry, but it can't be helped." In Stamford, Connecticut, Anna arrived to discover that her talk had not even been announced to the public. She was so enraged, she wrote Susan, as to be half sick. The manager of the lecture course had left town for a week. "Evidently he found the course was not to be a success, the failure would fall on him, and he had abandoned it," Anna wrote. "As I was to be the first one this was the contemptible and infamous means he took to get rid of me. However he did not escape me. I found him the next day at his place of business in New York (he is an immensely rich man) and with unblushing effrontery declared he had no engagement with me and would pay me nothing.... I never saw such a brazen-faced, thoroughly stamped hypocrite in all my life. He looks it to the last hair. I'd like to horsewhip him, he makes me so indignant when I think of him. I had a jolly time with Mrs. Hanaford at New Haven, and a splendid house, tho' they had abandoned the course and expected nothing, and am at home and happy, as always, here."

That Christmas was a bleak holiday for the country. Anna was in Boston at the time and was certainly in no position to engage in festivities. But she could not restrain her generosity toward friends and family. She sent to Susan a list of sixteen friends and relatives designating the presents to be given each: a purple gown to her maid Louise, "but she is not to see it till I come home"; a large bottle of cologne and a pair of dark kid gloves for a Miss Constance, two silk handkerchiefs for a man named Elwood, cologne and a new twenty dollar bill to a Miss Charlotte, a bread plate and knife for a Mrs. Everest, and a box of candy for each of several children.

Anna carried on through the season, delivering such lectures for which there still could be found a waiting audience. As the winter drew on, the raw New England climate and the disappointing, disheartening response to her lectures brought on a relapse of her earlier illness. There were other ailments, too—embarrassing and bothersome. There seemed to be no end to these troubles as the body aged. She complained to Susan of a "swollen vein." After consultation with the family physician, Susan replied all knowingly, "My dear, it is hemorrhoids—in plain English, outside piles—that is the matter...," and she passed on the treatment prescribed by the doctor. At the boardinghouse Susan and Mary Dickinson were not getting along well together. Deprived of the large home in which she had for years entertained distinguished friends, Susan was unhappy and wanted to break away from the responsibility of attending to her aged and ailing mother. Mary Dickinson wrote to Anna to complain about her older daughter. Feeling that she needed rest and change, Susan had left home for several days, telling the doctor of her plans and asking him to pass the information on to her mother. She had gone to West Pittston, a small town in the Wyoming Valley of Pennsylvania, "her darling Pittston," Mary Dickinson noted with a show of petulance, "she left yesterday in the rain and by telegram this morning inform'd me of her arrival."

There was but one bright spot in Anna's work as the '73-'74 season approached its end. That was a lecture she worked up on the issue of licensed prostitution (the "social evil," as the press commonly referred to the subject), which was then up for consideration in St. Louis, Chicago, and Philadelphia. Clearly Anna was out to shock the public once again. It is not quite clear how it became known that Anna was prepared to speak on this subject, but in March and April, 1874, she received invitations from groups of ministers in the three cities to deliver a lecture on the social evil. "Between Us Be Truth" was the advertised title of the address and when word got out that Anna Dickinson was going to speak about prostitution, a great public curiosity was aroused that made it possible to fill to overflowing the McCormick Music Hall in Chicago and to warrant a second lecture on the same subject a week later. The newspapers, however, did not think well of Anna's choice of topic. Said the *Chicago Tribune:* "Miss Dickinson is a young, unmarried woman—the last person in the world to have any knowledge of the social evil, unless she has made it a special study, and this is the last study in the world which a young, unmarried woman should make a specialty." The *Philadelphia Inquirer* advised "all respectable people to remain away from this lecture. By doing so they will show that Philadelphia has no sympathy with those who would debase the morals of the community by speculating in impurity." The *Philadelphia Press* did not share these feelings: "Miss Dickinson is by no means a sensational lecturer, and she has chosen her subject with the sole view of doing good. It is unnecessary to add for those who know Miss Dickinson that she could not be guilty of saying an unclean word."

From the content of her address, it is obvious that Anna had done some field research in preparing the lecture. She related her experiences in visiting "a sink of iniquity" in New York called "Canterbury" which, Anna remarked, was no doubt well known to many men in the auditorium. She told how she had gone to a brothel on Thirty-ninth Street in New York and how she came to the conclusion that women did not embark on a life of prostitution because of its pleasures. She cited New York police records proving that in the lower walks of vice a single woman catered in one year to no less than 2,548 men. Anna asked how any woman could find pleasure in intercourse on such a scale. Prostitution could be attributed not to any natural waywardness of the practitioners, but to the social and economic conditions that forced many women into this work to earn a living. Licensing prostitution would only augment the evil.

Although surely Anna's speeches were not responsible for the development, it is interesting to note that the measures to license prostitution were withdrawn or defeated in Chicago and Philadelphia, and in St. Louis, where prostitution had already been legalized, the state legislature passed a repealer. The next year Anna was invited to deliver the talk in New York where again she received mixed, almost violent, reactions from the press. The *Brooklyn Daily Eagle,* in an editorial capped STIRRING THE DUNGHILL, wrote of Anna's lecture: "The most disgusting spectacle that humanity in its uppermost degradation affords in civilized life is a woman wholly devoid of shame." But the *Brooklyn Daily Argus* of the same date felt otherwise: "Since the days of Mary Woollstonecraft, the world has not seen a sample of female intrepidity equal to that displayed by Miss Anna E. Dickinson at Steinway Hall last night."

But the newspapers, of course, were dealing with the public image of Anna Dickinson, not the real woman who longed for what she could not have. Anna returned to Philadelphia in the spring of 1874 in a sorry state. Two or three times during the winter she had been desperately ill and the result was a complete nervous prostration that gave serious alarm to her physician as well as her friends. In May she seemed well enough to leave home for New York. Susan reported the departure to a mutual friend: "At 9:30 she was in a hysterical condition that made dressing her seem impossible. At 11 she was at the depot receiving the compliments of a Penna. R. R. high official on her 'restored health as evidenced by her blooming complexion.' " Anna went to New York to visit in the home of Laura Bullard, and there she stayed in bed every day until dinnertime. In the evening, however, she would go out to the theater and parties and foolishly, inexplicably, dissipated her strength. She returned to Philadelphia in worse condition than when she left. According to Susan, she could not control a pen in her hands for ten minutes at a time. Her nerves seemed completely shattered. Medical treatment was administered and finally the hysterical symptoms were subdued. Anna insisted on going back to the book she had been working on since the Greeley campaign, but the doctors advised complete rest from labors of body or mind for at least a year and recommended that she go abroad to recover her strength.

Anna had contemplated going abroad several times before; in 1871 she had drawn up careful plans for the voyage, but she canceled the trip when she learned that several other prominent women were headed for England that year: Anna wanted no competition from fellow Americans when she ventured overseas. Now she wrote to some of her distinguished friends for letters of introduction to prominent persons in Europe, and of those who obliged, we still have the letters written by Mark Twain, John Greenleaf Whittier, Senator Carl Schurz, Henry Ward Beecher, and Vice-President Henry Wilson. Wilson's fondness for Anna had not diminished despite the speeches she had made against the President, and when he heard that Anna was ill, he stopped in to visit her in Philadelphia. He did not find her at home, but he left for her a fulsome note of introduction:

June 25, 1874
To American Ministers and Consuls in Europe:
I take the liberty to commend to your kind notice our countrywoman, Miss Anna E. Dickinson of Philadelphia. Her name is known throughout our Land as the advocate of good causes. She goes to see the old World after having seen more of our country and its people than any other woman, and I beg you to do what you can to make her visit a joyous one.

Yours ever,
Henry Wilson
Vice-President of the U.S.A.

Beecher wrote a letter of introduction for Anna to John Bright, the English economist, whom she was particularly anxious to meet:

John Bright,
Dear Sir:

Among the women of America who have broken down the prejudice against public speaking by women none has been more eminent than Anna E. Dickinson. Not only has she been endowed with great gifts as a speaker, but she has for many years devoted her influence to reforms, and to all generous and progressive enterprises.

She visits Europe, to rest by change of work, and is particularly desirous of looking into the condition and prospects of Labor and Laborers.

Allow me to commend her to your great kindness and to express the wish that you may come to esteem her as highly as thousands upon thousands do in America.

> Very truly yours,
> Henry Ward Beecher

Anxious to liquidate her Chicago properties before she left the country, Anna asked Beecher whether he might be of some help through his many influential friends, but the noted preacher was of no assistance. The real-estate market had collapsed. No one in New York would buy lots in Chicago, except for purposes of speculation, Beecher said, and "speculation lies in a deadly swoon." It would be futile to approach his friends who were still tied up from the panic. "I have looked in every direction and am deeply sorry that my hands are tied," Beecher replied.

With all these preparations, it was discouraging to Anna's friends to see her postpone the European trip from week to week, and then month to month, as she had three years before, until it was too late in the year to go abroad. It is not clear why Anna procrastinated so much; perhaps a fear of meeting failure abroad disheartened her. Money must not have been an obstacle, for most likely General Butler would have loaned Anna the necessary funds. "What is the use of a friend except in need?" Butler wrote Anna in answering her objections to accepting aid from him. "Fair winds and favoring gales are not the test."

With the trip to England indefinitely postponed, Anna left Philadelphia in August to spend several weeks on the beach at Atlantic City with her maid, Louise. It was Anna's first sojourn at the New

Jersey seaside resort. She lay sprawled on the beach, soaking up the sun and restoring life to her exhausted body, and slowly the depression left and some of the color returned to her face. To Mary Dickinson she wrote pleasant letters detailing her days of rest and sun:

> Today has been altogether lovely, and as I sat on the sand, and prowled a little to and fro on it, and watched the great breakers rush in and break, and heard them roar, I so wished for my marmee to see her beloved ocean as to make me quite sad.
>
> I have seen no one at all thee knows, and there is no one here *I* know, and certainly I am not tempted to widen my acquaintance. The people here stare at me as if I were a circus or at least, the elephant or special wild beast.
>
> It certainly does not conduce to a good sentiment for your kind to know it well. It is one of the cases in which distance certainly does lend enchantment. I hear the inane gabble about nurses, and food, and dress, and a touch of business going on about me till I feel as though I never could speak to those people in such wise as to open conversation with them, more than with so many animals. . . .
>
> One of the idiots pranced up to me, and actually touched me with his cane, while he asked, "What are you doing here?" Perhaps I was not cooled when I turned my head. "Minding my own business," said I, "What are *you* doing?" To which, having no satisfactory reply to make, he made none but walked away.

By the time Anna returned from Atlantic City the rest of the Dickinsons had left Philadelphia temporarily. Susan had gone to West Pittston where she managed to obtain employment as a space writer for metropolitan newspapers and was enjoying the first independence she had ever known. Mrs. Dickinson was boarding with strangers and resented her situation, feeling that her children, in not keeping her with them, were conspiring against her. John and Anna were estranged over some family matter, and Edwin was working in the Pension Bureau in Washington, though his mother had strongly opposed his leaving home. Anna was able to do very little work that fall. Her new manager, O. G. Bernard, felt he could obtain thirty engagements for her for the 1874-1875 season, netting at least $6,000. But except for several lectures in Boston and New York, Anna was obliged to rest quietly through the winter. Most of the time she stayed in Elizabeth, New Jersey, with some new friends, the Chatfields. Betty Chatfield, in her thirties, was married to an aged former general, and was apparently quite bored with her lot. She was extremely fond of Anna and the friendship was reciprocated. Anna and Betty Chatfield remained warm friends for many years. Anna seemed to get a satisfaction from her relationship with Betty that she had never sensed with her numerous suitors years before.

It was during these months, when she was staying with the Chatfields, that Anna's relations with Whitelaw Reid finally approached the breaking point. They had been good friends now for some twelve years. There had been quarrels and reconciliations. There had been innumerable letters, visits, dinners. But ever since the disastrous Greeley campaign—the campaign that brought them so close together and exacted so great a price from Anna—Reid's interest in many of his old friends had noticeably cooled. At the age of thirty-five he had come into control of a great newspaper; he buried himself in his work to master his responsibilities; many of his old friends soon found they were really former friends. The change was gradual but perceptible, and Anna sensed it as early as Christmas, 1872, shortly after Grant's election, when Reid failed to write or telegraph her about an appointment he could not keep. Anna was annoyed by what she felt was an unkind affront that was especially painful to her because Reid had come into good fortune as a result of Greeley's defeat while she had earned only trouble. She sent Reid a New Year's greeting in January that bespoke an attitude of disaffection with an overly ambitious man. "I wish you a happy New Year, and hope that it, and all of the after years, may be filled to overflowing with largess, content, success, and happiness—that life may go well with you, work go well with you, feeling go well with you, that you may wish only for what will bring you good, and wishing have it all."

Susan was so upset by this rupture in friendship that she undertook to write to Reid herself in an effort to repair it. She explained Anna's feelings in a kindly way and urged Reid to make amends. "I trust your discretion and your generosity to make all straight at the first opportunity," Susan wrote him. "I don't like the shadow of a shade between you on one hand and us on the other."

Meanwhile, reports continued to appear in newspapers linking the names of Anna and Reid. Noah Brooks, one of Reid's assistants on the *Tribune* and a former associate of Lincoln, wrote to Anna about his employer in March, 1873. "Reid did not seem disturbed about the paragraph which engaged you to him," Brooks wrote. "On the contrary, he was rather tickled and took the clipping which I showed him and carefully stowed it away. You ask me what is to be done with American journalism in such circumstance; the answer is obvious: Marry it. I see no other way out of the difficulty. Lest you should think Reid the only victim yoked to your cab, I enclose an anonymous note on the subject which I received. By what right do you go about spoiling young men's chances in the market matrimonial?" And Charles Dudley Warner wrote Anna "Is it true that you have *not* married W. Reid...?"

Actually, Reid and Anna were drifting further apart at the very time these rumors were appearing in print. Anna began to feel, along with some of her New York friends, that Reid had become a different man since his accession to journalistic power and that he had forsaken his youthful liberalism. In an obvious effort to indicate a lack of concern over his treatment of her, Anna snubbed Reid one day in June, 1873, when he went to Philadelphia and stopped off to visit the Dickinsons. Anna was unresponsive and cold in conversation and seemed quite uninterested in what Reid had to say. Susan was distressed by her sister's behavior and wrote to Reid the evening of his visit to offer a kind of explanation. "I hoped that the meeting would naturally bring Anna and you a little nearer together than you have been of late, and it hurts me more than I cared this afternoon to say, to see her setting aside or throwing away her oldest and truest friendships—and she has none that through all its phases has been more loyal or patient than yours," Susan wrote. "Her manner this evening pained me so much alike for herself and for you, that I must put down tonight what today I would not say....I could not but know that you went away pained and saddened tonight, and I cannot help putting in a plea that you be patient with her...."

Relations between Anna and Reid improved somewhat in the months that followed this unpleasant incident, but they saw each other seldom. In October, Anna went to New York for a brief visit, but could not find time to see Reid. "I am full of regret at having to vanish without another sight of you, but necessity is autocratic, as

autocratic as some people I know (!) and it drives me away at 10,"
Anna said in a note to Reid. "I wanted to say a word to you, too, of
good-bye while I held your hand close. I must write it. Do, I beseech
you ... try to cool the fire that is destroying you. As I before said to
you what will you care for a stately monument if you be lying under
it?" Then, two months later, when Anna again passed through New
York without stopping in at the *Tribune,* Reid wrote to her in evidence
of continued friendship: "It wasn't nice to spend a Sunday here, and
not let me know you were in town till I found it from the papers—
after you had gone. I made a Personal for you wh. Susie asked. I hope
it was of use;—and that the hard times don't trouble you, as I hear
they do other lecturers. Are you not to be here soon?"

But the two did not see each other for months thereafter, and a
solid wall of misunderstanding of motives and acts separated the two
ever more widely. Anna was very ill on the road that winter, but Reid
never wrote to inquire of her health, either because he was too busy,
or did not know where to reach her. The season was a most difficult
one, but the *Tribune,* in contrast to previous seasons and to its treatment of other lecturers, gave Anna's New York talk very small notice.
Anna felt, rightly or wrongly, and Susan shared her belief, that had
Reid given her lecture a proper report, she would have had a successful season despite the panic. From this feeling, it was a short and
easy step for Anna to believe what some friends suggested—that Reid
was purposely withholding mention of her in the *Tribune* out of
fear that other papers would renew the old story of their engagement.
Susan urged Reid to make up to Anna and remove all doubts of his
motives by running a good story about her planned trip to Europe. In
no uncertain terms she told Reid how critically ill Anna had been.
This moved Reid to write to Anna for the first time in many months.
"I am really worried at what Susie tells me of your condition," Reid
wrote. He advised her to postpone her book-writing efforts and he
endorsed the trip to Europe, but feared that she was losing the very
best months for the trip by her delay in departing. "These July days
would be infinitely more tolerable on the Atlantic than in Philadelphia, which I firmly believe to be a hotter city than New Orleans,"
he wrote, "and once on the other side, the worries and cares of this
could no longer fret you.... It is a good many years since I abandoned

all needless ceremony when you seemed to need scolding. Here or abroad, more power to you."

Anna acknowledged Reid's letter, but pointed out that she was only doing work she must do to keep a roof over her head. She asked politely how it was he never came to visit anymore. "Do you take your vacation west, or east, or not at all? And are you a fixture in New York? Philadelphia, so far as I know, sees you no more."

It was during these very days that Reid was having real difficulties of his own with old friends on the *Tribune* staff. Noah Brooks had a run-in with Reid and resigned from the paper to join the staff of the *New York Times*. Brooks wrote to Anna to tell her about the incident. Reid had become impossible to live with; Reid had abused him and imposed on him in all sorts of "brutal and ungentlemanly" ways, wrote Brooks. There was quite a scene when he gave his week's notice. Reid "flew into a rage, sent me an abusive note, and to cap the ridiculous climax, forbade my ever entering the office after my duties in the paper came to an end! Poor child! He had the worst fit."

Anna's special and continuing grievance against Reid concerned the *Tribune's* coverage of her work. What had previously been an intimate personal relationship now had been transformed into a cold, business-like affair. Anna kept her grievances to herself, however, until Susan, of her own accord, wrote to Reid again in August, 1874, to tell him why Anna felt as she did. This moved Reid to write to Anna directly. Was it true, he asked, that she felt slighted? Yes, Anna replied, it was. "I should be heartily glad if the *Tribune* would notice me one dozenth time as often as it does lecturers who are not half as popular —and I should be doubly glad to think you cared enough for me, my work, and success, as voluntarily now and then to mention me— but I am talking again and that I did not intend to do."

With each month, the separation between Anna and Reid thus became broader, each developing different interests and friends, one slipping down, the other rapidly mounting the ladder of public fame —two young people whose paths had first crossed and then traveled parallel for so long a period of time. Now they were to go their separate ways and as the years passed, feelings would harden and memories be distorted or erased.

Anna's public career now seemed to be rapidly disintegrating, and Bernard, her manager, made desperate efforts to revive it. In the spring of 1875 Anna ventured forth on a special tour. She was to go into the South. She had not been there since directly after the war when she toured the defeated Confederate strongholds with Mary Dickinson. Now she traveled with Bernard, and she lectured in Richmond, Raleigh, Charleston, Savannah, Atlanta, Macon, and Nashville, appearing before audiences that never before had seen a woman speak from a platform. While the audiences liked Anna's "Jeanne d'Arc" immensely, they were not large enough to make the tour a success. "My first audience did not pay expenses, and the second barely covered its bills," Anna wrote home from Raleigh. "The great body of the people neither know nor care anything about lectures.... The women hate me and won't come to hear me....My first audience had not a dozen women in it...." The *Richmond Dispatch* was surprisingly cordial in its editorial comment: "Anna Dickinson is beyond all doubt a pure-minded woman, and the record of her good deeds—which are nowhere disputed—attest the truth of this assertion. She is modest, retiring, and graceful in her manner...."

Anna headed West and North after completing the Southern circuit and finally came to Chicago where she was scheduled to give a talk on "The Political Crisis." The lecture came to naught. The men in charge, who had promised to "fill the house" did not even buy tickets themselves. Anna was completely despondent. The lecture platform had collapsed under her and her career as a professional lecturer appeared to be at an end. She poured out her heart in a letter to Susan: "It's no use, Dickey," she wrote, "I have tried faithfully to stick to the platform, but the platform won't stick to me. It is nonsense the *Interocean* [a Chicago newspaper] talks, and a plenty of others talk with it about my abandonment of my work—I have no work here to do and must go where I can find it and money with it."

Though she wrote thus to Susan, Anna did make one more final effort to secure lecture engagements for the coming season. She sent out printed circulars to lecture committees throughout the country announcing her availability:

1326 Arch St., Phila.
June 18, 1875

Owing to long absence from work, and conflicting rumors and newspaper statements, there is, I discover, a widespread uncertainty as to whether I propose quitting the lecture field, and if I do not, how I am to be reached.

I send this general letter to my old friends, and I trust to some new ones, to inform them that I will lecture the coming season.

That my new subjects will be "Madame Roland," and "Father Matthew," and that I will also use my old one, "Joan of Arc."

That all invitations must be sent to me DIRECT, and not through the medium of any bureau; that my address is 1326 Arch St., Phila., or simply, Phila., and that the sooner I hear from those who desire to hear me, the more satisfactory it will be to both of us.

Respectfully,
Anna E. Dickinson

The notice received only a negligible response. There would be a few engagements in the fall, hardly enough to comprise a season. Meanwhile Anna was obliged to stay in Chicago impatiently seeking a buyer for her properties. "What is amiss with me and my plans?" she asked Susan. "They seem to have a curse on them whatever they are." She had hoped to go to California to do some lectures on the West Coast on which she was to obtain advance guarantees, but that scheme fell through. The summer weeks passed in anguish. One lighter moment occurred when Anna dropped into the final session of the Women's National Temperance Convention (now the W.C. T.U.) and dropped a bombshell in the midst of the devout women gathered in Farwell Hall. The prohibitionists had been considering the question of women's suffrage and whether the convention should come out in favor of it. The proposal had been shouted down each time, but toward the end of the convention, the issue was introduced once again and gave rise to a heated debate. Anna, who had dropped in to the meeting out of curiosity, thought she "would take a hand in the game." She rose from her seat and was called to the platform. Reform could only be accomplished by political action, she told the assembled delegates, and not by prayer. At this, there were gasps from the affronted women. "If you are determined to destroy drunkenness by political action," Anna said, "then whatever will assist that political action should belong to your platform. I do not believe in moral suasion in this direction, nor do I believe you can accomplish anything by merely praying. There are hundreds of women suffering from the intemperance of their husbands," she said, when an excited voice cried out from the audience, "We pray for them!"

Anna replied, "Yes, and while you are making one prayer for them, there are thousands of ballots being cast against you.... All the women of this land can pray until the crack of doom, but there will hardly be a drunkard the less. God never interferes in the affairs of this world except by human agency." At this statement there was mingled applause, amazed gasps, and a spreading confusion among the delegates. Anna continued: "Last night when you considered the subject of prohibition, you voted to send prohibition men into office. You did not vote to storm the drunkard's stronghold by the instrumentality of prayer, but by the operation of the ballot. That then was a confession of your faith—that this movement must be worked out by mortal means. Women are mortal and could vote if men would let us. When we have the ballot, temperance reform will surely come." With this Anna concluded and retreated to the rear of the platform.

The chair then recognized a Mrs. Burt who said her ears were shocked by what had just been said relative to prayer. Never before had she heard prayer so degraded as to be brought on a level with politics. The lady concluded, midst loud cries of "Amen" and "Hallelujah" by praying God to soften the heart of Sister Dickinson.

Mrs. Fuller, a lady from Michigan, who had uttered a war whoop at the close of Anna's talk, was terribly put out by Anna's statements. She rose to her feet and shouted: "I cannot sit still in my place and hear prayer talked about as though it was of no use." At this there was another loud uproar of amens and hallelujahs, interrupted by the chairman who said, "I would remind the delegates that this is a temperance convention and I would urge you to be temperate in all things."

Mrs. Fuller continued, asserting that prayer was the most potent power upon the face of the earth. She knew it to be true by experimental knowledge.

"That is not true!" cried a voice.

"You are just shouting!" cried another.

Mrs. Fuller resumed with renewed vigor, and in the middle of a fervent invocation to the Almighty to testify in her behalf, the Chair called "Time," and she was forced to sit down.

Anna felt impelled to come forward again. She denied that she had derided prayer. She simply had protested against leaving women who did not pray—who did not believe in the efficacy of prayer—out in the cold. "I am not here to stand upon a temperance platform," she said, "but to stand up for the right to advocate the cause of those that are down—the women of this land." Tumultuous shouting broke out, and an enthusiastic man hurrahed and waved a white handkerchief. Frances E. Willard, head of the convention, then came forward and offered a resolution of thanks to Anna.

"Of course the papers turned the convention and all of its doings into ridicule," Anna wrote Susan. "The fact is that all the suffrage women there implored me to speak—not having the courage to do so themselves, and the few crack-brained shrieking sisters were sat upon by the rest of the convention. The great body of the people went very heartily with the resolution after my speech, and they one and all fell upon me and embraced me—even the shrieking sisters, when they finally managed to understand my position."

The rest of the time in Chicago Anna worked on a book for which she had obtained a contract from the Osgood publishers. "I have written, while here, a little book—50c book, which is for Osgood," she wrote Susan, "and I am digging away at the other, so as to have it out on the heels of this little one, and I feel sure that both of them will go well. Which is a good sign for them, for I have predicted nothing but disaster for everything I have attempted for the last two years." The small book dealt with the duties of citizenship. "I have decided to call my little book, *A Paying Investment*," Anna wrote Susan. "How dost like it?"

Still there was the land to sell. "I would sell the land for what I gave for it—which will be an actual loss in interest of nearly $5,000, if someone will take it at that, with the mortgage on it, which would give me an amount of nearly $6,000," Anna wrote. "It is a vile sacrifice, but if I can do no better that I will have to do. Everybody it seems who has money to lend is afraid either of a second mortgage, or of a woman." The summer moved along agonizingly. "The land is abundantly worth even twice what I want twice told," Anna wrote some days later, "but they all tell me that men are slow to lend to a woman, to lend on unimproved property and to lend on a second mortgage. However!" A week later: "No news. I sit and bite my thumbs with impatience and do not get the half done I could do if I had a mind at ease. Some people write, or do what they have to do best if they are in great need or great anxiety. I can't. I must have a clear track *inside,* if I am to do any decent running *outside*."

Toward the end of July things looked up. There was some chance of a man taking the land, and Anna was now waiting on him. Finally, in mid-August, the sale was made. "The land is actually sold!" Anna wrote Susan gleefully. "At a sacrifice, of course ... but it will make easy sailing for Marmee and thee, till I make a lot of money again which I *shall* do, I hope, this winter."

Anna returned East in high spirits, but they were quickly lowered by the failure of her hopes. Once again she started out on tour to give some lectures, and once again she had to call them off in despair. There were no audiences. The life of the queen of the lyceum had become a harrowing nightmare, as she traveled from one unreceptive city to another and put up in progressively less expensive hotels. Anna's brief tour finally brought her to Washington, the city of her greatest triumph whose toast she had been only a dozen years before. This time she knew only misfortune. She wrote Susan an account of a horrible night in the capital: "I fell into disasters manifold," Anna wrote, "a vile little hall, a very small audience. Just as I knew it would be, a fairly good hotel as to table, but a feather bed upon which, of course, I did not sleep a single wink. Which took all the backbone out of me, and left me with a raging headache." During the night she lay sleepless, her mind in a torment of despair, thinking perhaps of Melinda Jones and what she had written two years before. "Be warned by me," Melinda Jones had written, "and don't commit the unpardonable sin of poverty...." Suddenly Anna heard a scratching sound, then a splash. She drew her bedclothes around her in fright. Then through the darkness she saw a half-grown rat paddling around helplessly in the slop jar. It had fallen in and was now desperately fighting for life. Anna was transfixed as she watched the rat until, after a half-hour of struggle, it drowned. She made no move to save it or to bring its struggle to a speedier end. She just sat and watched. She could feel no sympathy, only wretched desolation. She wrote Susan: "I wanted *something* to be more miserable than I."

CHAPTER 10

"THE MOST TALKED-ABOUT WOMAN
IN AMERICA"

A DRIVING rain swept the streets of Boston the evening of Monday, May 8, 1876, but those fortunate people who held tickets to the grand debut scheduled at the New Globe Theatre would not be deterred from attending whatever the cost in drenched clothes. Every seat had been bought up by the previous Thursday. Standing room was sold out, the "free list" was suspended, and scalpers, shielding themselves under the marquee, did a thriving business as curtain time approached. The audience that packed the theater from pit to dome was, observed the *Boston Globe,* "the most brilliant gathering ever assembled in this city." The *New York Herald*'s judgment was less reserved: "It was the most brilliant ever assembled in an American place of amusement."

The men and women in the galleries would certainly have agreed. Looking down on the boxes, they could spot Ralph Waldo Emerson, Henry Wadsworth Longfellow, and William Dean Howells. Julia Ward Howe, Thomas Wentworth Higginson, and other prominent social reformers could be recognized. Notably absent was Mark Twain, who reluctantly canceled his tickets at the last minute when his wife fell ill. From the City of Brotherly Love, 150 Philadelphians had made the wearying 350-mile journey to the Globe. From New York, then Boston's leading rival to cultural leadership, a battery of first-line drama critics, led by William Winter of the *Tribune* and F. A. Schwab of the *Times,* had turned up. Newspapers in Chicago, Philadelphia, St. Louis, and Cincinnati hired special reporters to cover the opening, and editors the country over speculated on the evening's outcome. "The Impending Fizzle," snorted a St. Louis paper, but other journals made more sanguinary forecasts. Boston had never seen anything quite so exciting. Only two occasions could compare with it—Jenny Lind's debut a quarter of a century before and Charles Dickens' first visit to Boston. But even the furor over Dickens was not so great as the feeling that ran through literary circles of the city now. At eight o'clock sharp, the orchestra struck up a Donizetti overture and the red silken curtains parted on *Anne Boleyn, or A Crown of Thorns,* by Anna Dickinson, the author of the play and star of the performance, and, according to the *New York Daily Graphic,* "the most talked-about woman in America."

Standing in the wings, crowned with a simple blonde wig waved in front and falling in a cluster of curls behind, Anna presented a far different sight than was to be seen in a dingy Washington hotel room only a few months before. Bedecked in a magnificent green and gold Tudor gown decorated with sparkling diamonds, she was tense and nervous, and felt "as if a hand were on her throat." The script had been completed only three weeks before and there were but four days of practice for the cast. There had been no dress rehearsal to try out the elaborate costumes Anna herself had designed. The final days before the opening she had been torn from all sides—rehearsals, the last-minute revisions of the script, costume fittings. She had slept only two hours in the three days since Friday. In a week she had lost ten pounds. She had not touched food in twenty-four hours. She was weary in body, but her heart quickened at the sound of applause from the packed house. Many times had she known the excitement of stepping on to a platform tense, fearful, yet confident that with all eyes on her, her mind would clear, her throat relax, and her voice emerge full and resonant.

How did Anna come to be on the stage of the New Globe Theatre that May night of 1876? It was a long story.

Anna had, of course, harbored theatrical aspirations ever since she first saw a stage play, but for fifteen years she had been obliged by reason of circumstances and family opposition to avoid all open contact with the theater. "I thought of the stage by day and dreamed of it by night," Anna told a friend some years later. It had been a continual and unrelenting personal battle between the desire to act and her love for Mary Dickinson to whom everything connected with the theater— costumes, make-up, impersonations—was unholy. Even Anna's "Jeanne d'Arc" had terribly distressed Mary Dickinson because press clippings commented on Anna's dramatic powers. Hopeful that some day it might be possible to persuade her mother otherwise, Anna had made secret plans to obtain dramatic instruction in Paris during one of her contemplated trips, but even her warm friend Sam Bowles, of the *Springfield Republican,* who handled the negotiations, was not enthusiastic. "Don't count me as really approving your stage plans," he wrote Anna. "I find my heart rebellious. . . ."

Not until the lyceum had dwindled into nothingness and the economic panic had tumbled the value of her land properties, did Anna begin to see a possible meeting of desire and necessity—if she could no longer make money from the platform, she might be obliged to enter the theater for a living. She quietly arranged to take singing lessons. Years later Anna explained: "I had lived one life. I had lived it intensely and it was over. The people with whom I had worked were old. Well, I was old, too, in that sense. But in reality, I was young. I was in the fullest tide of ambition, of powers, and I had another life to live. So I turned to the stage."

The problem was to find the right place for herself in the theater— an opportunity to make a mark that would rival her reputation on the platform. The American stage in the eighteen seventies was dominated by grandiloquent actors and brilliant actresses; plays were merely vehicles for their talents rather than significant creative expressions. Like the English theater by which it was greatly influenced, the American drama was productive to a fault—a tremendous number of new plays were staged each season, but not one of them achieved any enduring distinction. The dramatists were feeling their way toward new dramatic forms, and most of the plays were crude and stereotyped, though many were immensely popular. Melodramas and farces predominated but there were a number of more pretentious plays that imitated Elizabethan models. The stage was experiencing a Shakespearean revival and and it was common for playwrights to emulate the style and subject matter of the master dramatist.

Anna had tried to approach Edwin Booth when he came back to America to discuss dramatic plans with him. She discussed with a playwright the possibility of his writing an adaptation for her of Hawthorne's *The Scarlet Letter.* She confided her plans to Susan who by now recognized what her mother would not—that if Anna was to continue supporting the family, she would have to find a better source of income than the moribund platform. Susan joined with Anna in keeping her theatrical plans from Mrs. Dickinson until a fruitful arrangement might be made. When Anna was in Chicago the previous summer she made her theatrical desires known to local managers and was favored with an invitation to make her debut in San Francisco. There she might get acting experience before offering herself to the more critical and sophisticated Eastern audiences. "If this is satisfactorily arranged," she wrote Susan, "I think it will be the very best thing that I can do, but I don't want a single hint of it to creep out yet to any one."

The California scheme was called off, however, and in the many long hours that passed while she waited to sell her lots, Anna often thought of the theater; she decided that if no one would give her a chance to act, she would break into the theater as a playwright. "If I can write plays, two or three successful ones for other people," she wrote Susan, "there is a lot of money in *that*." Her next thought was, why not write a play in which she herself might act? She asked Susan: "Now I want thee to give thy 'gigantic intellect' a fair chance at this idea—Which is the idea of a subject for me to make a debut in? All of the plays being new, or entirely new versions of old subjects; Katherine of Aragon, Anne Boleyn, Lady Jane Grey, Jane Eyre, or a romantic, melodramatic love play. Which will take best with the public, in which will I play best, and which will suit me the best?"

Within a fortnight, Anna had decided upon the heroine for her play. It was to be a woman of history, about whose treatment at the hands of men she could be as passionate and indignant as she had been on the platform about slaves and disenfranchised women. Anne Boleyn, second wife of Henry VIII and mother of Queen Elizabeth, had come down through history as an inconsequential flirt who succeeded in winning for her daughter the succession to the throne only through a twist of fate and Henry's unmanageable whims. The nineteenth century historians saw none of the nobility in Anne Boleyn that dramatists a century later would assign to her. But Anna was hardly one to be bound by contemporary orthodoxy in matters concerning the mishandling of women by willful males. She had picked up a copy of James Anthony Froude's *History of England from the Fall of Wolsey to the Defeat of the Spanish Armada,* and was infuriated with what she read in it. She wrote Susan:

I have been reading "Frowde" as they call him here, down to the accession of Elizabeth ... and of all mean, truckling, flunkey, mannish spirits, I think he exceeds. If some one would kick his ——— and do it well, I should feel relieved. His style of treating Katherine of Aragon and Anne Boleyn is alike atrocious, and his method of truckling to Henry is worse than an emetic. Elegant language! But it is as I feel....

As to his gabble about Anne Boleyn, I would like to whack him with a club. He denies the truth, or falsifies the truth whenever he so much as alludes to it. She certainly never could have had anything said against her early life, or it would on her trial have been said. And to suppose that this woman, having for years resisted the importunities of such an ardent lover as Henry, evidently because she was not only chaste, but cold, because she wanted to be a queen, would risk all—would turn into the most vulgar and the most infamous of wantons, would *buy* men, her own brother among the number, to revel with a small army of them in a few weeks of time is so monstrous an accusation that the man who in this day repeats it ought to be hounded from the society of all decent people.

Why should this beautiful woman have to bribe men? Why should she go all her life continent to blaze out in this damning flame for a brother and half a dozen men in scant space of time. Why was every particle of the testimony destroyed that was to prove all this infamy? Flunkey Froude finds it easier to believe her guilt than to believe that the lords and gentlemen who convicted her were dishonest.

There was no uncertainty now about a heroine for her play. Anna would present the image of a noble and chaste Anne Boleyn, "a victim of priestly duplicity, political intrigue, and regal inconstancy," and thus rescue the ill-fated queen from the mistreatment of both husband and historian. The play would be written as an historical drama in the style of the Elizabethan revivals. And Anna, herself, would play Anne Boleyn, if a way could be found to put the drama on the boards. For her first appearance on the stage, nothing less than a star role would do.

After her horrible experience in Washington, Anna discontinued lecturing and joined Betty Chatfield in Elizabeth for the winter. In the spring, she moved to New York where she stayed with Laura Bullard, her old friend from the women's rights movement and a theater enthusiast. Meanwhile, *A Paying Investment,* the book Anna had written for Osgood, came out. It was a plea for compulsory education of all the nation's children, for more and better schools, for technical institutes to train skilled workers, and for governmental measures to prevent poverty and crime. A Chicago reviewer described the slim volume as "an arrow shot from a tense bow." But Anna and the publishers were disappointed by the popular reception to the book. It made no money.

Anna devoted the winter to reading histories of Henry VIII and his queens. By the end of March she was ready to write. Working at a white-hot pace, she turned out a four-act drama in three weeks, completing the script in mid-April. She was confident that she had written a good play; when she read it to some theatrical friends, it immediately became clear that she did not stand alone in her judgment. Financial backing was quickly obtained, General Butler proving very useful in this respect. Under the management of her old agent, O. G. Bernard, Anna went into operation as author, star, and producer of her first play.

The next weeks were feverish. The theatrical season was almost at a close; if the play was to see the light of day before the season was out, it must open without delay. Settings must be designed and constructed; a supporting cast must be hired and copies of the script made for them; costumes must be designed and purchased; publicity must be tended to; script revisions must be made as required. Anna was out of the doldrums and the fire of activity was crackling.

Anna went to Boston ten days before the play was scheduled to open and rented a regal suite for herself on the second floor of the Revere House, with a large bay window overlooking Bowdoin Square. It was the hotel's most sumptuous accommodations and had previously been occupied by presidents of the United States, many foreign princes and potentates, and Jenny Lind. A reporter for the *Boston Evening Transcript* succeeded in getting in to see her and gave his readers a glimpse of the thirty-three-year-old debutante: "Anna Dickinson's face and figure are too well known to need description," he wrote. "The figure is slight and petite in stature. The face is wonderfully mobile and expressive, owing in part to the marked strength and peculiarity of the principal features, chin, nose, and mouth, but more than all to the flashing, frank blue eyes set beneath the thoughtful brow and the clustering dark hair. Seen in full front, the general effect of the face is to make the V-shape, pointed downward from square forehead to chin. Seen in profile, the strong features and short curly hair make the head even more remarkable for intelligence and spirit."

Four days before the opening Anna wrote to Susan: "All goes splendidly." Everything in the house was sold within an hour after the office was opened. On the street people were paying five dollars for a seat and were buying for the entire first week. "Pretty well for an untried goat!" Anna noted boastfully. There had been some difficulty at the first rehearsal, but she had taken care of it in her own way. "One or two of the actors," she wrote, "tried to turn *dirty,* thinking they had a *novice* to deal with, but I *perceeded* to sail in—take possession, and conduct my own rehearsal—as Mr. Waller [the stage manager] said—as though I had been accustomed to it for twenty years. Since which they have behaved. The papers are nice as nice can be, and so are all the people I have seen...."

After writing to Susan, Anna wrote another letter. This one was addressed to Whitelaw Reid. It was a pleasant letter, full of good cheer and friendship. "Do you know what I want?" she asked Reid. "I want you to show your face at the Globe next Monday night. Why? Because I hear of all the dons and the big wigs to the number of legion who are to be there, and I grow rapacious and want one more. Also why? Because I really and honestly think I am going to give a good time in the way of a pleasant surprise to my friends, and I want—since so many of them are to be there—to have one more of my oldest and best. Everything is so far as smooth as glass, and I am too busy to have any time for scares. I hope the sun shines on you." Reid accepted the invitation; he would go to Boston for the opening.

Anna carried on rehearsals until the afternoon of the debut. No word of the plot of *Anne Boleyn* was given to the public, nor were representatives of the press permitted to attend rehearsals. The first-night audience would have to judge the play and the star on the basis of the performance alone. That was what Anna hoped for most—an objective evaluation of her work as a playwright and an actress. But she knew such an impartial judgment would be hard to obtain. She recognized well the array of massed prejudices against which she would be flinging herself when she made her entrance on stage.

There would be all the people who had been infuriated by her merciless campaign speeches of bygone years; they would look to her debut as the signal to rush in and take their revenge. There were the hundreds of Quakers, co-workers in the suffrage movement, and political allies who looked down on the theater and wrote to beg Anna to withdraw from her announced debut. The pressure from these sources created in Anna's mind a profound and anxious uncertainty. It was not her possible failure that so many of her respectable friends dreaded; they feared her possible success.

Then there were the professional theater people who resented a newcomer who took star billing in her first stage appearance. Other actors were wise enough to realize that her work as a playwright was the means by which a large cast of supporting players had obtained employment. But if the actors were willing to forget or forgive her inexperience, some of the drama critics never would. The clique of critics then reigning in New York drama circles was ruled by the *Tribune's* William Winter, a writer with a brilliant and caustic pen, of conservative point of view, wholly "Victorian" in outlook. Winter firmly believed that long training was absolutely essential to success on the stage and would allow for no exceptions to the rule. Anna knew that he would be disposed against her, but she felt she could overcome his prejudice. "On the whole I would rather stand the test of Willie Winter *now,* since I must sometime," she noted in a postscript to her letter to Reid, for whose paper Winter wrote. Around Winter clustered a coterie of New York admirers. Shortly before the opening a report reached Anna that Winter and his critical colleagues were discussing in a tavern how they would "ax" her this night. The critics resented her effrontery in putting herself on the stage with such fanfare, and her impertinence (to them) in choosing Boston instead of New York for the opening. Why Anna flew into the face of this theatrical convention and exposed herself to the cultural rivalry of the two cities one can only wonder. The New York critics were doubly irked by the conditions of the debut.

For Anna the crucial moment had arrived. The years of the dreams and the endless hours of toil had rolled on to an imminent climax. The long-awaited opportunity had come. The tension was almost unbearable. Anna breathed deeply, readying herself for her cue.

On the stage the four-act tragedy of Anne Boleyn unfolded. The time of the play is 1529; the scene is the court of Henry VIII. Cardinal Wolsey plots to annul the king's marriage to Catherine of Aragon in favor of an alliance with a French princess, which will in some way enhance

THIRTY-FIFTH WEEK of the SEASON.

ENGAGEMENT OF

Miss ANNA E. DICKINSON

MONDAY EVENING, MAY 8,

First performance of a historical play, in four acts. written by Miss ANNA E. DICKINSON,
entitled, A

CROWN OF THORNS

Or, ANNE BÓLEYN.

ANNE BOLEYN .... Miss ANNA E. DICKINSON
KING HENRY VIII. .... Mr. T. L. CONNER
CARDINAL WOLSEY .... Mr. J. C. COWPER
LORD HENRY PERCY .... Mr. B. S. MURDOCH
(Afterwards Earl of Northumberland.)
THOMAS CROMWELL .... Mr. J. W. LANERGAN
(Afterwards Earl of Essex.)
DUKE OF NORFOLK .... Mr. J. H. BURNETT
DUKE OF SUFFOLK .... Mr. W. H. GILLETTE
LORD HENRY NORREYS .... Mr. R. J. DILLON
SIR THOMAS BOLEYN .... Mr. JOHN DAVIES
SIR WILLIAM KINGSTON .... Mr. J. B. FULLER
MARK SMEATON .... Mr. R. STRUTHERS
MAGISTRATE .... Mr. C. PIERSON
OFFICER .... Mr. J. TAYLOR
SERVANT .... Mr. G. CONNOR
PAGE .... Miss GRACE DURALL
LADY JANE SEYMOUR .... LILLIAN CONWAY
MADGE .... Miss JENNIE GOURLAY

Nobles, Courtiers, Ladies, Guards, Pages.

ACT I.—At Court.
ACT II.—At Home. Six Months Later.
ACT III.—Seven Years After. May Day, 1536.
ACT IV.—A Fortnight Elapses. THE END.

During the evening the orchestra, directed by Mr. JOHN C. MULLALY, will perform —
OVERTURE—" Anna Bolena " .... Donizetti
REVERIE .... Vieuxtemps
ANDANTE—" Italian Symphony " .... Mendelssohn
GRAND SELECTION—" Huguenots " .... Meyerbeer

Carriages may be Ordered at 10.80 P. M.

STAGE MANAGER - - - - Mr. D. W. WALLER

DOORS OPEN AT 7.15 .... COMMENCES AT 7.45.
Box Office open daily for the sale of tickets, from 8 A. M. to 10 P. M.
MATINEES — Doors open at 1.30 .... Performances at 2 P. M.

Playbill for *A Crown of Thorns*

the cleric's power. To divert Henry from Catherine, Wolsey invites to court the comely Anne Boleyn who is innocent of the political intrigue behind the invitation. Anne Boleyn (Anna Dickinson in a blonde wig) enters on a bare stage reading a horoscope that foretells her fatal end. She discounts the prophecy in a brief soliloquy when the king enters. He notices the paper in her hand. Anne tells him she does not accept the judgment of the stars.

Henry: You are above superstition?

Anne: Rather, your majesty, I am not so vain as to believe that the stars in their courses watch over me, nor sufficiently humble to be willing for them to control me.

Henry: You deny the omnipotence of Fate?

Anne: Fate? I believe our own deeds are our doomsmen.

Henry looks at the horoscope himself and reads that it forebodes great fortune before a dismal end.

Henry: Fortune smiles on thee.

Anne: I trust not her smile. I do know that full often upon whom she smiles at morning she frowns at night.

Henry: But she would enrich thee.

Anne: Only to make me afterward the subject of her spoil.

Henry: She would exalt thee.

Anne [turns away]: To pleasure herself thereafter with my ruin.

Henry: Nay, sweet mistress, turn not away from her—listen to what she promises. I speak as thy friend. I urge her upon thee.

Anne: Nay, sire, thou speakest rather as mine enemy. Wert indeed my friend thou would'st wish me a quiet fortune—sheltered from wind and weather rather than an exalted one, exposed to storms and followed by some dismal fall.

Henry makes love to Anne and offers her regal splendor if she will be his mistress, but Anne spurns the king, and reminds him of his marriage to Catherine, and leaves the stage.

His desires aroused, the king considers ways and means of making Anne Boleyn his, but Anne is in love with Lord Percy and will have none of Henry. "Love is an absolute sovereign," she tells her father, "and being once crowned never abdicates. I wear Percy's ring upon my finger." Wolsey connives to force Percy into a marriage of state and sends him off to war. The unhappy Anne Boleyn, deprived of her one true love ("I had staked my whole existence on him," she cries, "and

A contemporary representation of a scene from the second act of *A Crown of Thorns*

am left with empty hands, bankrupt past remedy. Life is done.") returns to court and accepts Henry's offer of royal marriage following his
divorce from Catherine.

Seven years later, the lecherous Henry is thinking of how to dispose
of Anne Boleyn in favor of Jane Seymour, his new favorite. Anne encounters the king and Jane Seymour in an embrace and hears the king
pledge himself in marriage to his new love. She denounces the monarch to his face. "Is this the fair realm of England governed by Christian King, or is it under the sway of Islam or Mahound that you promise
this minion a husband in the person of one who already hath living
lawful wife?" There is a dramatic flurry as Anne orders Jane from the
court and Henry bids her stay. Percy suddenly returns to plead to Anne
his undying love and to express his horror at finding "a Queen outraged
and dishonored, menaced on all sides." Anne reminds Percy she is a
married woman and a mother, and tells him to leave as soon as he can.
Percy asks how she can send away one who loves her when she is in
such danger. Anne replies in a long speech: "I will not tell you of the
struggles through which I have passed the last four and twenty hours.
I tell you only their conclusion—that we must part. It is your due that
I speak the truth...I love you. You know it. I confess it. I stand de-
fenseless in the midst of foes with naught to save me save the Soul
within. I pray you to help, not hinder me, to aid, not destroy me. To
honor me and to leave me, since solitude must be my salvation. It is not
now the Queen who commands. It is the woman who implores." Percy
kisses her hand and departs. Anne turns to her maidservant and says:
"Is love, then, a sin? That it is so sweet at the beginning and so deadly
bitter at the close?" She is despondent, and soon is entrapped by
Henry's conspirators who make it appear that she has been intimate
with one of the palace guards. The king arrests the whole Boleyn
family and secures a confession of intimacy from the innocent guard on
pain of execution. Anne is dramatically arrested for high treason.

No one believes Anne Boleyn is guilty, but she is tried and convicted
by a rigged court. She awaits her execution in the Tower of London,
knowing that Henry will make Jane Seymour his new queen. She is
imprisoned in a dark cell, her chair of state in the rear, her crown on a
table. At one side is the block on which she is to be axed, placed in the
cell to torment her. She kneels in prayer and the moonlight falls upon
her through the tiny window. It is four in the morning. Execution

awaits at dawn. "Oh, my child, my child! My little one!" Anne
soliloquizes. "Elizabeth, my baby, my baby. What is to become of you?"
She hears a noise without and goes to the window. Percy enters through
a secret door and bids her flee with him.

Anne: "No, no, it cannot be."

Percy: "What, you even now care for what the world will say?" He
takes her into his arms. "You shall be saved. I swear it."

Anne recoils. "No . . . My name is blackened and my fame smirched
past whitening. Still, I am innocent. Other times will know me innocent. My child will live, in other times. This act of mine would do all
that the malice of mine enemies had failed to do. I would stand condemned of all that I have been wrongfully accused because by this I
would seem guilty. Seem? Nay, since I am bound by the truth, not
freed by a lie, *would* be guilty. No more."

Percy shows her a parchment containing Henry's pledge that Elizabeth will be confirmed in succession to the throne if Anne "will give
him good show of just cause against her." If not, her daughter will
forever be debarred the Crown. "For her sake, then," Percy pleads.

Anne: "Nay, then doubly for her sake will I not yield. I would rather
have my child live and die a beggar than wear the Crown of England
stained not by her mother's accused, but *proven* shame."

Percy is beside himself and draws his dagger. He will kill either the
king or himself. Anne appeals to him to desist. "It requires more courage to live than to die," she says. "What do I have to live for?" Percy
asks weakly. "You will live to defend the innocent accused," Anne tells
him, "to fight the battles of the weak, to do your duty well and bravely
. . . to die, when duty is done. God willing I will wait for you—" she
points to the vast unknown, "—there." Percy swears not to kill himself.
He turns to leave, but stops at the door. "I cannot." He rushes back to
Anne and she to him, but they find themselves divided by the block
and they part again. The executioners enter. Outside Anne's brothers,
cousins, and friends go to the block one by one, all having refused to
testify against her. The boom of a cannon signals the execution of the
first one. Anne is told she can save the others by signing a paper that
would annul her marriage to Henry. The cannon booms. Anne signs,
but at once comes the announcement that the brothers, cousins, and
friends have already been beheaded. Anne desperately tries to recover
the parchment that disinherits Elizabeth. Only if she will confess her

Fanny Davenport

Anna Dickinson when she was about fifty years old

infidelity to the king will the paper be surrendered. Anne Boleyn refuses and makes her final appeal. "From court and peer and king and people, yes, from this present time and the great unknown time to come, I appeal to Him." She goes to the block unbowed.

As the play progressed from act to act Anna felt herself carried along by the dramatic momentum. A sustained stillness filled the house as the audience reflected the rising tension in increased absorption. When the fourth act curtain fell, there was a momentary pause, and then the audience broke into enthusiastic applause, three times calling Anna before the curtain. Surrounded by flowers and overwhelmed by the response, Anna looked out happily at the triumphant scene, tears welling in her eyes. The ordeal of the first night had been surmounted. Fortune seemed to lie ahead once again. She returned to her rooms at the Revere House and fell into a deep and restful sleep.

The next morning Anna's eyes lighted with joy when she saw the notices in the Boston papers:

The *Boston Globe*:
From the parting of the red silken curtains at 8 o'clock to the their final closing, two-and-a-half hours later, the scene was, to the eye, one of the most complete ovations possible to imagine....It is a pleasure, no less than an act of justice, to record the pleasant disappointment which greeted those who went to the Globe Theatre last evening prepared to witness an ignominious downfall of the hopes of the debutante.

The *Boston Herald*:
She has safely and creditably passed the ordeal of a first night, and the unanimous verdict of the vast audience will be that her debut was a success.

The *Boston Post*:
But for some trifling exceptions, Miss Dickinson was a magnificent success.

The *Boston Evening Traveler*:
No one would call it a great play, but we think it deserves the encomium of a good work.

The *Boston Journal*:
She has much to unlearn before she can expect to be rated as a great actress and to divest herself of so much we fear will be no

easy task. Yet she has rare intelligence and a very considerable degree of dramatic talent.

Anna returned to the theater that evening with a gladdened heart. She found Bernard waiting in her dressing room. His face was drawn and he seemed ill at ease. Obviously he had some bad news to tell. In his hands he held the recently delivered New York papers. Anna went to the dressing table and sat down facing the mirror. "Well, Bernard, what's wrong?"

He had read the New York reviews. They were not very favorable.

"They can't be too bad," Anna replied, "not after what Boston had to say. Let me see them." She turned to Reid's *Tribune* and found Winter's review of the play. She read.

> A thin tissue of level prose dialogue of the story of Anne Boleyn, involving 17 persons. It is not relieved by strong dramatic incident. Scenes in *Henry VIII* and *Axe and Crown* embody its substance and are better. The language lacks elevation. The last scene is taken from Tom Taylor's play.

"The beast!" Anna cried. "That is a deliberate lie!"

Bernard quietly urged her to read on.

Her face reddened with rage, Anna read Winter's judgment of her acting.

> In art she was callow. Her presence as a Queen was puny. Her voice was often nasal and thin. Her walk was one-sided. Her attitudes were mostly crouched. Her emotion was that of the mind and not of the heart. She does not burn, but she glints. The face was often set in a stare to emphasize a tigerish self-restraint. Great stress was laid on the apostrophe to Jane Seymour and an expostulation with Lord Percy. They sounded like wails from Martha's Vineyard with the brethren in full possession. Had Miss Dickinson adopted the stage in youth she might have become a fair actress. It is not easy to see how she could ever become an agreeable one.

Anna was cut to the quick. To be held up to public ridicule in the paper of a personal and family friend of a dozen years' standing! Had not Reid written that she could always count on his support? What had she done to provoke such a torrent of unmitigated abuse? She turned to Bernard: "What does the *Times* say?"

"It's not hard to see where Schwab takes his cue from," Bernard said. "He writes, 'An eminently dull play....Miss Dickinson won no laurels as a playwright, and her impersonation must be accounted a flat failure.'"

"This is worse than I expected," Anna said. She had recovered her poise. It was a foregone conclusion with the critics that she would fail, and they were determined to make her seem to do so. "You know Winter's pet theory that nobody not bred to the stage ever did, ever could, ever ought to succeed. Power and even genius go for nothing with him. Automatic drill and a knowledge of technique are all that he requires, evidently, that an actress possess. So be it. What do the rest say?"

They were rather better than she anticipated, Bernard replied, as he looked over the clippings. "The *World* is much more generous than we would have reason to expect. It says, 'The general impression is moderately favorable to the debutante,' but it does roast you and the play in some of the other paragraphs. The *Herald,* strange to say, is even more tolerant. 'Miss Dickinson has written a very good play, and it is to be regretted that she also undertook to act in it. In the hands of a competent actress it could not fail to have a brilliant run.' At least the *Herald* credits you with half a triumph. The *Tribune* insists on nothing less than a complete wash-out."

"What will these 'reviews,'" she enunciated the word scornfully, "do to our prospects?" Bernard did not know. They would certainly not do the show any good. Tickets for the first week were already completely sold.

"If you do as well as you did last night, the word will spread and I think there is an excellent chance the play will hold up." Anyway they were near the end of the season, so there couldn't be more than a few weeks of performances before the summer. In the fall, if all went well, they could take to the circuit and then go on to New York.

Anna was not listening. She was still looking at the *Tribune.* "I wonder what Mother and Sue will think when they see this."

Bernard saw no reason for worry. "I'll write to Susan tonight and set things right." He left the dressing room and went to the front of the theater to watch the performance. When it was over he went to his hotel, took a pen in hand and wrote Susan:

"Don't let the New York papers deceive you or Anna's friends. She has made an unquestionable hit—a magnificent triumph—and is cheered between each act vociferously. She improved wonderfully tonight on the first night's performance, and that was even better than her most sanguine friends expected. All's well."

The play went into a second week and business held up. "All goes well here," Anna wrote to Susan. "That is to say, I have made a *success*, and will do ten times better in the not far off future. The New York papers were simply *infernal*, and the reaction is setting in against them everywhere.... As to my play, it is just about up to the mark. I have been beset by requests for it, so I know well enough it has money in it or not."

Within a few days, however, Anna and Bernard made the unpleasant discovery that the business manager of the Globe had bound them into a sharp contract. Not until $850 was taken at the box office each night could Anna or Bernard touch a penny. Even a well-filled house barely produced that sum; except for the opening night when, at premium prices, the tally had gone over $2,000, Anna and Bernard found themselves working without pay. This was to be merely the first of several such sharp practices that wily managers tried to impose on the inexperienced woman producer; in time, Anna learned the tricks of the trade. Now she could do nothing but abide by the contract, play out the fortnight, and move the play elsewhere. *Anne Boleyn* closed in Boston on its second Saturday and Anna prepared to take part of the cast to ten New England towns where the show would play one-night stands. She explained to Susan:

What I need is *time* on the stage, and *money*, and I shall get some of both in this New England prowl. I have a lot of good offers now for next season—and one from Daly for New York through June, but I will not go there now. It is too late. It will be too warm, and I am not going to New York till I can just *when* and *as* I like to go. If I hold out I will get my own place and terms.

As to my being a failure, if it had not been for Winter and Schwab's diabolism the thing would have been heralded as the greatest success ever known at a debut, which—dispassionately—was exactly what it was.

I am a thin beast—as I have lost fully ten pounds since I came here, but fortunately it doesn't show in my face, and I am picking up again. I couldn't eat or sleep for a fortnight—none to speak of—and the result was "wearin'," but I see pretty smooth sailing ahead. The Arch St. Theatre offers me 40 per cent—enormous terms—but I am not going to Philadelphia till I can go to the Academy or the Walnut.

After the New England tour, the company disbanded, and Anna spent the summer out of the public spotlight. In late June she wrote to a friend: "Don't you believe it. I am not half the 'failure' they set me forth, and I have all the engagements I want for next season, and I am not an absolute *scarecrow* tho' I *am* minus twenty-odd pounds of flesh and blood—and I am good for ever so much fighting yet—of my enemies—and of loving—one or two people whom I could name.... I am just straggling off to see my marmee up in the mountains and then I am going to dear hideous old Atlantic City—dear to all Philadelphians—hideous to everybody else."

But Anna was not entirely idle that summer. Having known the thrill of writing a much-discussed play in three weeks, she could not resist trying her hand once again. Before the summer was out, she had completed a second play and started a third. The completed work was a five-act drama based on *Jane Eyre*, called *Love and Duty*; the outlined play was a light comedy entitled *Laura, or True to Herself*, which dealt with the career of Laura Chester, a popular English actress of some years before.

In the fall Anna took *Anne Boleyn* on a tour of the major cities of the Midwest. She traveled with Bernard, and in each city they hired a supporting cast to put on the play. This system of local stock companies, then very much in vogue, was much less expensive than transporting an entire company across the country, but it meant constant rehearsals with new actors, and inevitably produced poor and uneven performances. Anna might find herself directing the rehearsal of a new cast from ten in the morning until six, then rushing back to her hotel for dinner, and returning again to the theater at seven to prepare for the performance. "The companies at Cincinnati and Louisville were admirable, and very kindly disposed towards me," Anna wrote to Susan, "The St. Louis company was so so, but so friendly that I was very sorry to get away from it. This at Cleveland is too vile to be permitted to live—rude, coarse, illiterate, mean, boorish, jealous, brutal.

There are but three decent people in the whole crowd. I began by being polite to them. I go on by not knowing they are about me, any more than if they were so many cockroaches." Her yellow jaundice had returned when she reached the Midwest. "Of course I turned green in St. Louis, as I always do, but am a little better now," she wrote. "When I get Mrs. Davies' pills I shall be better still. I might as well jump into a tomb as into this western climate." The tour had been taxing and laborious. "I have been so overworked," Anna wrote, apologizing for the rarity of her letters to Susan, "and so disinclined to write to anyone as to make me hate the sight of a pen." She had, however, put the finishing touches on her new play, *Laura*. "The new piece is a modern piece, and will be one I think to take at once with the 'great vulgar,' " she told Susan, "and since I need money more than anything else at present I have had an eye to them in writing it."

Audiences for *Anne Boleyn* were relatively small at the beginning of each weekly engagement on the road, but they grew in size through the week, thereby signifying increasing popular satisfaction with the play. In Louisville, Henry Watterson, editor of the *Courier-Journal*, saw *Anne Boleyn* and ebulliently declared it to be "the finest historical drama of modern times." Estimates of the play's quality generally seemed to improve as it became better known. The *Philadelphia Item* endorsed Watterson's comment. "It has attracted large and enthusiastic audiences, and has proved a decided success," the paper said. "It is a very good play."

The tour of the Midwest finally came to an end, and Anna started on the long journey east, playing in Buffalo, Rochester, and on the Albany circuit. In December she produced *Laura* in Philadelphia, but it proved an instant failure, and she went back to *Anne Boleyn*.

Finally the time came to bring the drama to the den of her persecutors: New York. There the play opened in April, 1877, at the Eagle Theatre, but not until Anna had been put through a most trying ordeal. The manager of the theater, Joshua Hart, had failed to prepare the resident cast for her arrival, nor had he made adequate provision for staging the play. Two days before opening, seven pieces of scenery were still to be paid for, and the cast was so raw that Anna had to spend twenty-three hours rehearsing with them right up to curtain time.

The performance consequently was anything but a finished one. Winter and the other critics enjoyed a second feast at Anna's expense. Indeed, the severity of their treatment, coupled with the demonstrable inaccuracy of some of their remarks, suggests that their purpose was not simply to write dramatic criticism, but by humiliating and ridiculing her, to drive Anna off the stage. Anna's refusal to be crushed by the reviews of the Boston debut only seemed further to provoke Winter and Schwab, and they returned to their critical chores with sharpened knives. This time their colleagues from the *Herald* and the *World* reversed their opinions of the year before, and attacked both the actress and the play.

"That long threatened event, the appearance of Miss Anna Dickinson on the metropolitan stage, took place last night," announced the *New York Herald,* panning both the star and the play. "Nothing very novel or original in it except the very questionable taste shown in the selection of the title." The *Times* dismissed both the play and the performance as worthless: "Miss Dickinson, as an actress and dramatist, has not the slightest claim upon public attention." Reid's *Tribune* damned the actress with faint praise and calumnied the playwright: "Miss Dickinson at certain points in her performance, addresses the adjacent *dramatis personae* with a physical thrill and with an oratorical tremor of the voice which are exceedingly effective.... Aside from this, her action is 'level tameness.'...In one scene—the last one—Miss Dickinson revealed dramatic instinct. This passage is an imitation of the last act of *Mary Stuart* and it looks very much like a deliberate crim from *Axe and Crown."*

Some of the lesser New York papers were much more friendly to the play. "It is gradually winning a genuine and deserved success," said the *Home Journal.* "It has apparently passed the period of novelty and curiosity, and has entered upon that of a *succès d'estime."* The *Evening Mail* said a "warm and generous reception" was extended to Anna and that her acting was "admirable in some respects." The *Spirit of the Times, The American Gentleman's Newspaper,* which had often twitted Anna for her lyceum talks on women's rights, was now much more kind: "If Miss Dickinson cannot be congratulated on having proven herself, on Monday night, to be a great actress, at any rate, she can safely be complimented on having placed her name as a dramatist amongst those of the foremost of the day. Certainly no play of equal merit to *Anne Boleyn* has been produced in New York for a long time."

After a week of playing to meager houses following the critics' revel, Anna decided to take matters in her own hands, and do something she had long desired. She called in Bernard.

"I have decided that I am not going to let Winter and Schwab step all over me without fighting back," she said. "Whatever the inadequacies of my acting, and I certainly am aware of them, they do not call for such malicious treatment. I will let the public know what kind of men serve them as critics, and how they distort and falsify the facts."

Bernard was mystified. "How do you propose to do this?"

"I will make a speech next Monday night after the curtain falls," Anna replied, "and I will talk to the audience and the public directly, not through the voice of the critics. I will make a speech and it will sizzle!"

Bernard was taken aback. He knew it was futile for an actress to try to beat down the men of the press.

"It may be futile," Anna snapped, "but I would rather go down fighting for a just cause than to submit out of fear of defeat. I have their animosity in full at the moment. What more can they do? Each day they destroy my hopes and plans. They desire nothing more than to destroy me for having attempted and accomplished what they said was impossible. It is not as if their opinions were the true and only voice of dramatic wisdom. That is rank nonsense. This morning I received a letter from a man who knows more about the theater than Winter, Schwab, and the whole caboodle of critics. When Dion Boucicault stands with me, should I be cowed by miserable flunkeys? Listen to what Boucicault wrote to me."

Anna reached for the letter from the famous Irish playwright and read it with evident satisfaction. "I saw the *Crown of Thorns* last night and thought the play and the actress had been hardly treated," ran Boucicault's letter. "There is a resolute and earnest grip in your treatment of the subject that would, alone, entitle you to consideration and respect. As a piece of work it is—in a literary and artistic regard— equal to *Axe and Crown*—I might say, superior to that play.... Don't mind the turkey buzzards of the Press. You flatter them by appealing from the decision. By doing so you acknowledge their capacity to judge, which I decline to recognize."

It was a wonderful letter, Bernard agreed, and perhaps they could use it in their publicity. But he still thought she should forget about the speech. "You are an actress now, Anna, not a lyceum lecturer."

Anna would not be dissuaded. "I want you to buy space in the papers, right over the drama listings, to announce that next Monday night, after the performance, I will have something to say about the newspapers and the critics."

Throughout the next week the papers carried the featured advertisement, THE CRITICS CRITICIZED ON THE FALL OF THE CURTAIN, and by the time Monday evening rolled around, theatrical circles were buzzing. Newspaper editors were intrigued with the idea of an actress replying to her critics, and news of Anna's intentions was carried by the Associated Press across the nation. Anna's name was still so well known that even country editors thought it fit to comment on the impending speech. What would Anna have to say? The critics were supplied with tickets that Anna had to pay for herself because the manager of the Eagle Theatre had maliciously let out word that she did not want complimentary tickets sent to the press. When the curtain fell on the fourth act, shortly before 11 P.M., Anna stepped out on the stage in her black and scarlet costume with her hands full of newspaper clippings, and began to speak in a sad voice.

"Anna Dickinson scarcely knows herself tonight before you," she said. And then, with increased vigor, "I think if I have been known for anything among you—and I doubt not a great many men and women here tonight have listened to me many times on the lecture platform— if I have been known for anything among you, I think I have been known as a defender of the wronged and the oppressed."

She paused. "Candidly and honestly," she went on, "I really know of no more utterly wronged and oppressed person in some respects in this town than the woman who stands before you."

At this the audience broke into applause. Anna turned to the clippings she held in her left hand, and read sarcastically from the *World* of the day before, which said she had been treated with "tenderness by the critics."

"I will try to talk of Anna Dickinson, to discourse of her as I might of somebody else, to a person who never knew her," she continued. "It is not necessary to go over all the ground why I came to the stage. Suffice it to say that I made my first appearance on the 8th of May last at the Globe Theatre in Boston. I believe it has been asserted by the *World* that I object to the criticism of the critics," and with biting innuendo, she added, "the critics that have treated me so *kindly*. No! I object simply and only to deliberate falsification—nothing else!"

She proceeded to describe how the New York critics in their reviews had misrepresented the circumstances under which the play opened in New York and the previous reception given her and the play by Boston audiences. They said her New York opening took place under the most favorable of conditions; she gave the audience the facts about the rehearsals and the scenery. She told how the *Tribune* wrote a second caustic review of her play two weeks after its Boston debut, though Winter in the interim had not seen the play a second time. "It was not a fair or honest thing to do," she said. "It was not generous, it was not manly, it was not just."

She came to Winter's grave charge that she had taken the last scene of *Anne Boleyn* from Tom Taylor's *Axe and Crown*. With indignation in her voice, her eyes flashing anger, she met the charge head on. "In the course of the play this evening," she said, "Anne Boleyn did say to Henry VIII, 'Your Majesty doth right well know in Saxon plainness, this is a lie!'"

Then she turned to the general reviews of the play, and declared that all the comments save half a dozen said her play was a success. Now, she said, the *New York Herald* comes along and says, "Who are these persons who declare this play a success? They certainly have no character or reputation to lose." Holding forth the *Herald* review of her debut the year before, she declared sarcastically, "The *Herald* of the 9th of May last declared this play to be a good one. I am not responsible for the assertion of the *Herald* that the people who declare this play to be a success have no character to lose."

When she reached New York, she had expected to find her old and appreciative lecture audiences, but the papers had made a wall between her and her old public. "It was said that I fought the papers, that I denounced the critics, that I placed myself in antagonism to the papers, to the public. Good friends, what could this one small, sick, weak, miserable, crushed, heartbroken woman do in opposition to the combined papers and the bitter prejudices they had stirred up against me in this place? I did not fight them," she declared with great emphasis, and then, almost sobbing, "God knows I didn't want to fight them. I was almost crushed, but I struggled on as I will struggle on because, having taken up my work in life to do, I put it not down until I utterly fail!"

Here even the hostile people present could not resist joining in the cheers and applause that broke out and continued for a full minute. The hour was almost midnight when Anna brought her speech to a close.

"I have said my say in somewhat disjointed fashion, but I think you all understand it. Don't read what the New York papers say of my play and then sit in judgment on it, but give Anna Dickinson a chance with her own work. Go and see it, and tell your neighbors to go and see it. Listen to it, and then if you condemn, Anna Dickinson has not one word to say in opposition."

She bowed gracefully and disappeared behind the curtains. She had had her say, and she felt better for it.

But still she had to go through the press to reach the general public with her story, and her speech would be summarized and commented on by the very men who were the subject of its attack. New York editors, moreover, had too much at stake in critical reputations to allow their writers to be mauled in their own space by a lady of the theater. Anna's appeal for fairness was destined to bring about only more severe treatment. She became the subject of cartoons—caricatured as a schoolmistress whipping the representatives of the press. Only in papers out of the metropolitan area did she find champions, but these paladins could not make her play live. Editors as far west as Salt Lake City used the speech as a springboard to attack the New York critical circle. But Anna's would-be supporters were severely constrained in their desire to come to Anna's defense, for the Associated Press, which was then the only national wire service agency, had so distorted her remarks in a "one-sided malicious squib," that at least two A.P. members saw fit to publish editorials rebuking the agency for its handling of the speech. The *Hartford Evening Post* commented that "The New York agent of the Associated Press perpetrates an outrage upon the press and the public" in sending a biased and malicious report of the speech with no statement of Anna's argument. "It is the work and opinion of one of the men writhing under the lash of the irate lady," the *Post* concluded. The *St. Louis Times* remarked that "If Anna Dickinson would slaughter an A.P. agent, as she ought to, the pressure of our admiration would at once increase fifty pounds to the square inch."

ANNA DICKINSON CHASTISES THE BOYS.

Oh, dear, what can the matter be?
Dear, dear, why didn't we let her be!
Who'd have supposed she would mad as a
    hatter be?
    Jest cos we treated her bad?

We promised to say the plain truth for our
    lesson;
We promised to put no abuse in excess in;
And now we have caught just the liveliest
    dressin'—

From the *New York Daily Telegraph*, April 14, 1877

Within a week, the engagement of *Anne Boleyn* at the Eagle Theatre came to an end. Anna's appeal had failed. Business continued poor and manager Hart made matters worse by refusing to buy advertising or to paper the house. When, in a final gesture of un-co-operativeness, he changed supporting actors on her, Anna came to the theater, withdrew her manuscript and wardrobe, and left.

Anne Boleyn had run its course. Dreams of fortune had come to naught. "The most talked-about woman in America," who had been raised on popular adulation and to whom good fortune for so many years had seemed commonplace had failed to open the doors of success in the theater. She had orated and lectured for so many years that the public could not identify her with anything save the platform. She was not yet thirty-five, but she had outlived one career and one fortune and stood in desperate need of making a new life for herself. She must still seek ways to keep herself free from that worst of all sins—poverty. Melinda Jones had warned her about it. So had Reid, before he turned his paper against her. So had her mother. But Anna was not one to give up a fight easily. She was not yet through.

CHAPTER 11

ANNA AND FANNY

ANNA withdrew from public view for the next several months, took a furnished apartment on Fifteenth Street in New York and settled down to recover from the overwork and anxiety of the year's excursion in the theater. A rumor appeared in the press that Anna had pawned her jewels. Upon hearing this Bernard immediately wrote to say that she should deny the rumor if false; if true he would lend her the money to reclaim them.

It was not an easy time for Anna. She was approaching forty and realized that the years of youth were slipping away. With them were disappearing the fame she had known since her wartime triumphs. She was becoming just a memory to the public as the war itself faded into the semioblivion of history. Having known and enjoyed success for so long a time, she could not now easily adjust to the fact of popular rejection. The failure of *Anne Boleyn* had planted in her breast pernicious seeds of bitterness that would mature and envelop her whole being unless an end was made to failure and frustrations. Those who come to flower in the sunlight of popular adulation often wither away to bitterness, despair, and even dementia when deprived of that which alone made their growth possible. Bitterness is malicious and destructive. It mistakes friends for enemies, exaggerates all slights, ascribes conscious and evil intent to all acts, suspects conspiracy behind all coincidence, and views compromise, even of the most trivial import, as sacrifice of principle. Friends of Anna feared that her initial failure on the stage might drive her down this frightful road of destruction.

Meanwhile, Ben Butler kept up a warm courtship with "Lizzie"—the

general's private sobriquet for Anna. He was the only person to call her
Lizzie and it is doubtful that this manner of address endeared him to
her. Butler wrote once: "I shall not cross Lizzie off from my books because I cannot. Years of knowledge of her virtues, her failings, of all
that is admirable, and all that is other has left that on my heart which
never can be effaced, and would not if I so desired." Butler was now in
his sixties, a rapidly aging man, very heavy set, almost completely bald,
with great sacs under his eyes. But he retained a certain dash and ele-
gance and he did have money. While Anna tolerated and at times even
encouraged the courtship, she had no real affection for the General and
certainly never contemplated marriage. Butler was having his ups and
downs in politics, carving out for himself one of the strangest careers in
American political history. As a delegate to the Democratic national
convention before the war he had voted thirty-seven times for Jefferson
Davis. After Fort Sumter he became an ardent supporter of the Union,
donned his brigadier's uniform, identified himself with the abolitionists, and later secured election to Congress for several terms as a radical
Republican. Butler's heart was set on becoming governor of his home
state—Massachusetts—but the ruling elements of the Republican party
there distrusted him and would not back his nomination. Twice Butler
sought the Republican nomination on his own strength and twice he
was defeated. Meanwhile he retained his seat in Congress. In 1874 he
was swept out of office in the popular uprising against the Republican
party. For the first time in many years the General found himself without political or military office. He wrote to Anna: "Indeed, I am sad; it
seems as if an adverse fate were following me. I am getting actually
nervous. I dread a great loss as I have just made one and know that
misfortunes never come single." He was downcast. "I have lately met
with great political and other disappointments. Once they would have
made perhaps but little impression. The rebound of a vigorous brain
would have thrown them off, but now they strike upon a defenceless
inelastic one and leave their deadening impressions there as does the
passing footstep in the mud."

But when Anna asked Butler's aid to stage *A Crown of Thorns,* the
General gallantly obliged. He was detained in Washington and could
not attend the debut himself, but he read the press clippings and spoke
to those who had attended. He wrote Anna: "Your play was a very
great success and your presentation of the principal character much more

of a triumph of genius and merit than I had dared hope for. I had hoped much but feared more. A marvellous undertaking marvellously carried out."

As Anna's theatrical fortunes had declined, Butler's political fortunes had risen. By 1878 he was running for governor and Congress again, this time carrying the banner of his third political affiliation—the new Greenback party. He regained his seat in Congress, but missed out in Boston. The General now supplanted Whitelaw Reid in newspaper gossip about Anna. Butler was evidently very fond of Anna, but if he made any formal proposals they were (wisely for him as it turned out) not reduced to writing. He went to considerable effort to be with Anna whenever possible and Anna led Butler a merry chase, tantalizing the portly sexagenarian until he was driven almost to the point of despair. It seems certain that Anna had nothing but revulsion for the physical aspects of any possible relation with Butler, but she would not break off the courtship. It was more profitable to let it go on. She enjoyed being in demand and, in moments of need, the General always proved very sympathetic.

In the summer of 1878 Butler's business plans fortuitously coincided with his romantic impulses and he tried to persuade Anna to go on a little escapade with him to Atlantic City. He wrote Anna happily: "Our committee adjourned today to meet a week from Tuesday, and as the weather is very warm here today came to the conclusion to go to the sea shore for their next session and as the most available point chose Atlantic City. What do you say to that? Was it not a singular coincidence? ... Write please at once where you are to be for the next week after Monday? I would like much to know whether you are pleased with the arrangement."

The prospect of vacationing together that so pleased Butler only terrified Anna. Long-distance alliance was one thing; a week end at Atlantic City with the General was another. She could not simply refuse without bringing the relationship to an end, so she begged off with a handier if rather time-worn excuse. She wrote Susan, who was then living in West Pittston with Mrs. Dickinson, asking Susan to telegraph her that her mother was very ill and Anna's presence was required at home immediately. From the safety of the small town in Pennsylvania's Wyoming Valley, Anna wrote to Butler to say that the sojourn would unfortunately have to be postponed. The hopes of the General fell with a crash.

"When one has planned schemes, brought out any enterprise from which he promised himself advantage either of pleasure, profit, or still more happiness, and fails therein because of accidents or circumstances wholly beyond his control, the failure is very bitter," he wrote. "I give it up. The fates or some stronger power are against me. To attain what I wish is shown to be impossible by any effort of mine. I give it up."

But he did not give up. He seemed never to reconcile himself to the futility of the chase. As Anna's attitude toward him turned from indifference to scorn to ridicule, the patient, bumbling old man continued to woo her. The next year Butler was running for governor again, this time as a Democrat, and Anna wrote to Susan to tell her how "that preposterous old pirate" kept pursuing her. She wrote: "If Massachusetts does elect him there will be diverse and sundry who would like to give the old commonwealth a bath in the 'back-bay.'" Susan's reply indicates she was well aware of the goings on between the two. "So B. B. keeps at it," Susan wrote. "My dear, I don't know 'what to do' except ignore him as long as completely possible. Unless indeed there be some means of getting him to 'aspire to the White House' next year—which might employ his valuable time and attention till after the Convention." When Butler again lost out on the governorship, Anna told her mother: "So B. B. stands now for 'Busted Breeches' and 'Beaten Bunny.' Poor B. B.! Verdict—'serves him right.' If he had behaved himself and remained a Republican he might have had a strong show in *that* line, but to turn Democrat again—bah!" And, on another day soon thereafter: "I had a letter this morning from the formidable B. B.—but he does not settle the question as to whether he is to be known as Broad Back—or Beatrice Benny, a Broken Bummer, or Busted Breeches—or what. Ask Susan, what's to be done about it? He's a nice one! I thought he had retired to the shades and that I was to hear from him no more; but I suppose he must have *some excitement*—or *die*. What a pity, for the sake of good politics, excitement does not fail him!" Anna enclosed a newspaper clipping that reported that Butler's campaign expenses for two years had reached $275,000. She commented: "Just think of that atrocity spending all this money! What a lot of good and happiness *we* could get out of it."

The connection with Butler did not keep Anna from trying to advance her own fortunes. After a fall and winter of recuperation, she returned to writing. She signed a contract with Harper and Brothers for a book of reminiscences, and produced a breezy volume called *A Ragged*

Register of Persons and Places I Have Known in which she recounted amusing experiences on the lyceum circuit, described interesting people she had met, and generally commented on social customs and conditions of travel in the United States. Reviewers treated the book pleasantly, recommending it for light summer reading. Sales were limited.

Anna devoted most of her time, however, to research and reading for a new historical drama she planned to write. While she had not been able to make *Anne Boleyn* a successful vehicle for herself, she had impressed the theatrical world with her writing ability. With the passage of time, *Anne Boleyn* had established itself in critical circles as a major work. Many critics felt that had Anna not acted the leading role herself, the play would have been judged entirely on its merits and would have fared more successfully. After she had brought her own appearances in the play to an end, Anna received several offers from prominent actresses for the production rights to the drama. Mary Anderson, one of the most popular actresses of the day, made numerous attempts to persuade Anna to let her have the play, as did the actress Rose Eytinge. Anna was willing to sell the rights to Rose Eytinge for a production in England, but neither to Miss Anderson nor to Miss Eytinge was she of a mind to surrender production rights in this country. Perhaps she feared she would suffer by comparison, but if pride was the cause of her decision it was exacting a great price: she sorely needed the money. She was adamant about releasing *A Crown of Thorns*. "If I were starving in a garret, I could not part with *Anne Boleyn,*" she told a friend some years later.

Anna's second historical drama was a tragedy called *Aurelian*. It was set in Rome, in the third century A.D., and told of the stormy love between the gallant, just, and handsome emperor Aurelian and Zenobia, the beautiful, courageous, and independent queen of Palmyra. Rome invades Palmyra and Zenobia, in an effort to save her people, surrenders herself to Aurelian who is struck by her beauty and nobility. Aurelian speaks to his adviser, Tacitus, of his longings: "Hitherto have I had but one aim, one object, one desire. If it be a sin to covet glory, then I have been the most offending soul alive. I have hungered for it, as starving men in dungeons hunger for bread; thirsted for it, as one parched for days with these desert heats and sand, thirsts for the crystal stream of water that he hears afar, with strength too spent to reach it. . . . I would not pause nor turn aside even for golden fruit or any sort of rest, pleasure, or what others call happiness. In an instant all this life is dead, and

the one living thing in the whole universe is a woman's face, and its sole
sound a woman's voice, that I have scarce heard, save in tones of en-
mity." Aurelian confesses his love for Zenobia and asks Tacitus: "Am I
mad? And is this to be a man?"

Zenobia meanwhile tells her maidservant, Valeria, that she is bestirred
by fears, desires, dreads, and longings that she aches to tell another but
cannot. Valeria suggests nervously that the queen try to accept the love
of a man. Zenobia disdains the suggestion. "The eagle does not mate
with a crow, a raven, a bird or any weaker wing, or meaner plumage.
I have seen, and see a plenty such—the air is thick with them. I have not
seen one eagle. . . . Likenesses of men there be by millions—here and
there a man."

Zenobia's pride keeps her from admitting her love for Aurelian. The
emperor sympathizes with the dethroned queen whose lands his armies
have ravaged. He deplores the ingratitude of the Palmyrian people who
have deserted their queen and he voices a sentiment Anna must certainly
have meant to apply to her own experience: "What strange fatality
drives the multitude to create an idol, having created him, fills them with
longing to find flaws in him, and, having found, destroy him—or harden
him to crush them." Aurelian and Zenobia finally acknowledge their
love and the play ends as Zenobia vainly gives her life to save the emperor from assassination.

Anna completed the play toward the end of 1878 and submitted it to
John McCullough, one of the theater's foremost tragedians, an actor of
heroic build and excellent reputation who Anna thought was the only
man capable of doing justice to the role of Aurelian. As for Zenobia—
well, she thought she might do the part herself. McCullough read
Aurelian, said it was "a splendidly written play," and took the script
with him to Boston to prepare it for production. Anna was ecstatic and
wrote home the latest: "McCullough agrees to bring out the play in the
spring in New York and to have me play in it."

Everything seemed wonderful until Anna's old nemesis, William
Winter, appeared on the scene. It is not clear upon whose invitation,
McCullough's or his own, that Winter became involved in the negotiations, but the fact seems to be that the critic somehow obtained McCullough's copy of *Aurelian* and gave him a private, unenthusiastic report
on the play. Leander P. Richardson, editor of the *New York Dramatic
News* and a good friend of Anna, visited McCullough in Boston. Mc-

Cullough told Richardson he thought the play was very good, but needed some basic changes. "Somebody . . . has been filling him up with this kind of rot," Richardson wrote Anna, and advised her to take the script back. Anna went up to Boston and withdrew the play from McCullough. Her high hopes had come to naught once again. The cause of the failure she felt was the maliciousness of Winter who must be acting at Reid's direction. When she gave a private reading of *Aurelian* for some friends one evening, word of it appeared in the columns of the *Tribune* where the play was panned, though the reading had not been open to the public and the paper was basing its report on second-hand information.

Temporarily balked in her desire to put on theatrical costumes again, Anna decided to return to the platform for a lecture about the theater. "The Platform and the Stage," she called the talk, and arranged to deliver it for the first time at Chickering Hall in New York on January 17, 1879. The announcement of the lecture evoked considerable comment in newspaper and theatrical circles. Anna, after all, had suffered deeply at the hands of the theater. Would she, with her unrivaled powers of invective and sarcasm, now rip the theater to shreds?

Chickering Hall was filled to capacity, despite almost impassable streets and a threatening storm outside. Anna's entrance was greeted with mild applause. She wore a black dress, trimmed with a gold fringe, and a long train that she dragged now slowly, now with an impetuous rush, from one side to the other. Her hair as usual was worn short, and brilliant diamonds sparkled in her ears, on her throat, and on her fingers. A tiny gold watch hung at her side, and she had narrow gold bands on her wrists. Though her bank account could scarcely support such display, Anna was not one to go before the public in anything but the best.

"I am here tonight," she said, "not as a repentant prodigal, not as a bitter and disappointed woman, not as a rejected suitor of the brilliant and dashing and worldly girl returning to entreat the pardon and embrace of the eminently severe and proper and right-minded one. No! I am here tonight on my feet with the platform under them, because, as of old, I think I have something to say that ought to be spoken, and that I hope you will care to hear."

She compared the theater with lectures, books, the press, and the pulpit, and taking her listeners somewhat by surprise, declared that the stage was potentially more influential than any of the others. Anna took issue with those who complained there were too many love scenes in modern plays and wanted more "impersonal" drama. "People don't dare to face the truth of the relations of men and women," Anna said. "They try to shut it up and lock it away and put a mask on it.... I hope the stage will... show the lives of men and women, not as people say they are, but as they really are, until thought and conscience are gathered together to try to find a solution of a great many painful problems." She called for the establishment of schools of drama, then almost unheard of. "Since this power of the stage is there, vast and overpowering as it is, let it have its schools, its training, its colleges, as lesser and minor sciences have everywhere on the face of the land, and thereby lift it in the estimation of the people to the position it ought to hold."

The next day the *Tribune,* strange to say, reprinted a stenographic copy of the talk and reports appeared in the press throughout the nation. Anna's ultramodern views provoked divided comment. Neither editors nor ministers were pleased by Anna's elevation of the stage at the expense of their profession. Theater people, of course, were delighted with what they felt was the most able and courageous presentation of their cause they had ever heard. One dramatic journal, previously very hostile to Anna, headlined its comment, A NOBLE TRIBUTE FROM A NOBLE WOMAN, and Anna was invited to repeat the talk at the Fifth Avenue Theater before a full house of theater folk.

When Mary Dickinson read reports of the lecture, trouble brewed. In the course of her remarks, Anna had referred to her Quaker habits, and her mother, shocked by Anna's treatment of the church and theater, felt that Anna had publicly derided her religious upbringing. Susan wrote: "Ma has been 'going for' me and other people ever since last Saturday evening when she read thy lecture in the *Tribune....* Each new mention of the plays, or theatrical people, sets her off in a way that there is no sense in starting needlessly. It only makes her unhappy, and uses up my nerve...." In an effort to calm her mother, Anna wrote: "I did not allude to my Quaker training to bring reproach on it, but simply as a statement of fact, and to show how strong my natural taste must have been to make headway against even *its* influence."

Anna toured several Eastern cities with the lecture. This brought her a modest return and kept her name before the public eye. Nothing of consequence developed, but she still hoped to have *Aurelian* produced. In the summer of 1879 she fell ill. She wrote Susan: "My malaria has gone and roosted in my face, and I'm hanging on a hook for fear my teeth will growl, tho' they have stood the soreness very well so far." The illness was a further drain on her limited finances, but she confidently assured Susan, "Do not fret about expenses. I am as poor as Job's cat, but have enough to see you *well* and *comfortably* through the summer. Does thee need any money before I get up?" When Susan asked her for $250 to pay off a note that fell due that week, however, Anna was obliged to reply: "I couldn't scare up $250 at date to save my bones, but if the transfer of the note to me, with a margin of six months, will straighten the matter out for thee all right, I can easily pay it in that time."

Anna spent a few weeks with Susan and Mary Dickinson in August and then returned to Elizabeth, New Jersey, where she visited with the Chatfields. Pa Chatfield was willing to tolerate Anna's presence for the happiness of his wife. Meanwhile Anna negotiated with Leander Richardson to make a trip to California to do some theatrical work on the West Coast. From her letter to Richardson we can get some idea of her state of mind. She wrote: "My decision in regard to California is the outgrowth of a deliberate determination to do no more in this country in regard to theatricals unless I have an open door before me. I will never again try to force one, nor ever try to open one with a golden key. All that ability, endurance, and courage can do, I have done. It is useless for me, single-handed to try to beat down the barrier that a half-dozen worthless fellows in New York have succeeded from the outset in putting in my way. I can use energy and life to better profit elsewhere."

What Anna wanted was a prominent manager who would back her with his theater and his name, provide financial support and assume some of the risks. Such a manager would promote her ventures properly, she felt, instead of fleecing her, as had twice been her experience. The California plans collapsed when Richardson was unable to get adequate financial assurances for Anna. The guarantee he did obtain of two weeks' work at a minimum of $400 per week was grossly inadequate to cover the risks and expense involved in a transcontinental trip, and Richardson himself advised Anna against the project.

Events now were moving slowly and painfully. The family was not well and Anna was hardly in a position to help. Edwin had died from tuberculosis two years before and Mary Dickinson showed a steady decline in health. She was now eighty. Anna confided her personal difficulties to her sister: "I do not yet know how the autumn will come out, but am plodding away and hoping for the best. Expect some money before very long." Susan proposed that she and her mother take permanent leave of Philadelphia and settle down in Pittston where Susan was doing odd newspaper jobs as a writer of obituaries and part-time correspondent for several New York papers. Susan suggested that they obtain hotel accommodations in Pittston. As Susan's chores took her away from home for brief periods of time, a hotel could provide better care for an invalid than could be expected at a boardinghouse. Anna endorsed the idea: "I should say the hotel was the best for all concerned—if we can compass the means—and I think they will be forthcoming." In the intervals of Susan's absences, Anna wrote endearing notes to her senescent mother to cheer her up. "So Dickey has been away for a little prance? Did my marmee get along like a fierce little lion—all alone—or did she get slimpsy? I hope she is frisking this morning, and I send her my heart." When some time passed and no word came from Susan, Anna wrote to her playfully, "Dear little Midge, Am she sick? She has been silent awhile and I am afraid she has collapsed—or is the bad lion ill and is the Midge nursing it—I am afraid thee is in present trouble about money. Is it so? I have none and do not expect any in amount for some little time to come, but if thee is in actual want of any I will see what I can do—with my old shoes—or some such venture."

Anna managed to obtain some lecture bookings that winter of 1879 and she gave readings of *Aurelian;* occasionally she would render "Jeanne d'Arc." *Aurelian* seemed to make a very effective dramatic reading, winning critical acclaim in the provinces. "The play itself is a masterpiece of literary workmanship," commented the *Des Moines State Register,* "written in so pure and good English that it will take its place on the narrow shelf which, as yet, contains all that we can justly claim as class in America literature." Audiences were small, however. Nevertheless, during Christmas week Anna found it possible to give $200 to her sister and $300 to her mother while she deposited in her bank over $3,000. Writing to Susan from Bay City, Michigan, the next February, Anna described her new plans:

"I am doing nothing in the way of making money, but am laying a good solid foundation I think for next season. Of course, the whole thing is *new.* I have long been away from the public, and I have a cruel weight to carry in the shameful lies the New York papers told about me and my work. Luckily, *Aurelian* is the sort of thing that is mighty hard even for prejudice to attack, and the readings *take.* Only I want thee to notice the difference between the leading Republican and Democratic papers of Detroit. The meanest foes I have are those who used to profess to be my friends. There never was a paper fuller of queer contradictions than that of the *Post and Tribune.* It *has* to follow the lead of its dear New York namesake. Yet don't dare to tell downright lies in the face of what I gave the audience and *its* absolutely *wild* delight. Well, time tries all things. If I can only hold out and wait, but when I think of many things—my two dear little vimmins among them—I am sometimes at the point of despair.... Ann Arbor was dull as ditchwater, and all of my *dear old friends* carefully staid [*sic*] away...."

Mary Dickinson took the ups and downs in Anna's fortunes with a display of stoicism. Acknowledging receipt of a $25 check, she sent Anna words of comfort: "I think much and tenderly about thee, and with no small feelings of sympathy, thy broken health, changed circumstances, and broken family ties, but such is life's experiences and may they work together for our ultimate and everlasting good." During a lull in her tour, Anna wrote to Susan. She seemed encouraged by the way affairs were picking up. "I should judge the western people are well disposed towards both me and *Aurelian,* and, if I do not make a deal of money I have no responsibility so I can't *lose,* and it will be a good entering wedge for next season.... It is the only way—this western play, to circumvent the nasty New York tribe. If I went on in anything in the East they would find and go for me, but a lot of small western towns, they have not counted on, and can't get at and the result will be *Aurelian* will get a national stamp before they can sneeze at it." She passed on to her mother a remembrance from Frances Willard, the prohibition worker who had dropped in to see her and asked for Mary and Susan Dickinson. "She is evidently very busy in her W.N.C.T.U. (Woman's National Christian Temperance Union!)," Anna wrote. "Why couldn't they have called it the alphabetical union and saved time and trouble? Well! I suppose that sort of work does some people's souls good—when they 'have a call to it.' But I doubt whether it makes any less drunkenness." She sent Susan a press clipping about one of her readings: "Read it thyself. I don't think it will delight ma, and yet, on the other hand, she is not like to read any notice that will not speak of my 'dramatic power' for, while in one sense it is a reading, I 'wade in heavy' in Zenobia. The house was poor in numbers, elegant in culture, and the newspapermen ... predict a 'smashing house' if I ever come back with the entertainment. Evidently I will have to do with this what I would have to do with a play and a company—what I had to do with *Anne Boleyn* —work against wind and tide at first, but I have no fear of the ultimate success, and, while I do not expect to make much money this spring, I have none of the anxieties of a company and can't lose. Next season I think will be easy sailing."

A week later Anna spotted a newspaper item about John McCullough and her enthusiasm departed. McCullough was doing well on the stage according to the reports. Anna wrote to Susan in a spirit of bitterness: "Patience, my dear, is hard. To know what work I can do, and to see the years going by as they have for these last ones—to see such creatures as the man for whom the play was written scooping in from $600 to $1,200 a night, and to make enough, perhaps, to pay my hotel and traveling expenses, is steep."

Susan chided her about these moments of depression: "Once for all, *stop* being 'at the point of despair' sometimes, or anytime.... I know, my dearie, how hard it is this waiting and waiting for a recognition and a triumph that must and will come, and I hope the day is now not much farther off. Only, take all possible care of thy health meantime so as to be ready for it."

The triumph Susan predicted *would* come actually *did* come, though not in the form anyone then thought possible. Before the year was out Anna was again storming the gates of the New York theater. The new and unexpected turn in events came by way of the famous actress, Fanny Davenport, one of the reigning queens of the theater, a strikingly beautiful woman who was then at the height of her career and happily married to a dentist by the name of Price. Fanny Davenport was sure-fire with the critics; she had a magnificent stage presence, commanding the attention of all who saw her, and she had a delightful flair for melodrama and light comedy. It seems that Fanny had seen Anna in *Anne Boleyn* and was much impressed with the play. Thus began the relationship between two prima donnas that continued for a year in a most unpredictable manner, or perhaps not so unpredictable. Anyone who knew both Anna and Fanny might easily have foreseen as inevitable the events that followed.

Fanny started things off in November, 1879, by writing to Anna that she needed a new play. "I want a play that is a lasting, not a frothy comedy drama, but such a one as you can write should you choose,"

Fanny wrote. "I want a picturesque, dramatic, strong character. I think something of your fine language combined with startling effects...." Having heard of Anna's lecture on Jeanne d'Arc, Fanny thought that perhaps the Maid of Orleans might be a fit subject for a play for her.

Anna demurred. She preferred to write a comedy of manners for Fanny Davenport. "I will not do Jeanne d'Arc at present, for you, myself, or anyone else to play," Anna wrote Fanny. "I can't. It will require a great deal of work and I have not the time to give it. I am doubtful of a *go* for an historical piece on any subject. Have you set your heart on that line, have you a leaning towards a modern play? Melodrama or American comedy-drama, and have you a choice between these? If you care for that sort of work I think I could do it for you...."

The correspondence continued, and Fanny encouraged Anna to proceed with a play. Anna wrote Susan: "It is pretty nearly settled that I let Fanny Davenport have a play for next season—and in that case I am about sure of a *hit* and a lot of money. There are but two ways to make money—that is by writing and acting plays." Since Fanny preferred a powerful melodrama when the historical play was ruled out, Anna began writing one called *Esther Arnim*—a play revolving about European royalty with a Russian Jewess as the heroine. By the end of January, 1880, Fanny was anxious to know how Anna was coming along with the play. She was convinced now of the wisdom of Anna's earlier suggestion to avoid historical drama. Fanny wrote: "Do you intend it to be purely imaginative or historical? I am more and more convinced that strong melodrama is again coming on to popularity. It, I think, is my forte."

Negotiations with Fanny had so far been entirely informal, but now the two women were ready to discuss the contractual basis on which they might work together as author and actress. Though she was in no position to bargain for terms, Anna successfully concealed this fact from Fanny and set some of the stiffest conditions then known for a playwright's contract. Fanny was to hand over $1,500 on receipt of the manuscript and to pay Anna royalties of $350 for every week the play was performed. Furthermore Fanny would have to agree to use the play to open the fall season. Anna would hold the copyright to the end and when Fanny no longer desired to appear in the play she would return the script to Anna.

Mr. and Mrs. Price mulled these terms over carefully. Fanny must

have wanted a play from Anna very badly because she finally accepted
the terms with the friendly proviso that the author must deliver the
script to the Prices in person by mid-August and must visit with them.
Anna must promise to read the play to the Prices in their home.

Well pleased with the contract, Anna went to work industriously, but
the August deadline approached and she found herself behind schedule.
Esther Arnim simply had not jelled as she hoped. She wrote to Fanny:
"You are not to think I am scolding ... when I say I wish you had consented, last winter, to take a comedy part. The play would long ago have
been done. You know about the Russian piece. Never in my life did I
work so hard at any thing as to make Esther an emotional star part."
Two problems had arisen. Esther had to share the stage equally with
another character, the Princess Marina, and even worse, she must wear
drab clothes which, for Fanny, was out of the question. Fanny suggested
that perhaps Esther could use a moderately decorative wardrobe, but
Anna replied that "even those of which you spoke would be out of all
keeping with her, and in the third act she ought to be in shabby dis-
guise."

How resolve this dilemma? Anna had a bright idea, but it was a
delicate one and she couched her suggestion in the most carefully
chosen words she could find. "If you cared to play the role of the
Princess Marina," Anna wrote to Fanny, she could expand the role
in the third and fourth acts to make it as strong or stronger than
Esther's. The Princess Marina "of course, is richly dressed through
three acts—and throughout is brilliant and sympathetic comedy...."

And who would play the part of Esther? Anna wrote: "Friday night
as I tossed to and fro (not being well from neuralgia of my right
writing shoulder) saying, 'What shall I do? What shall I do?' it suddenly occurred to me what you said last winter, 'What would you
think of doing something in a piece with me?' or words to that effect."
If Fanny would do Princess Marina, Anna would be willing to do
Esther. "Understand distinctly I do not go as a star nor a 'feature,' except as the author of the piece," she added. "If I am to act, my name
in the company, on the bills, etc., is simply that of a member of your
company."

Anna's delicately worded proposal hit Fanny like a bombshell. There
was to be but *one* prima donna on the stage if Fanny appeared in a
play. Fanny replied: "Words written or spoken cannot convey to you

my entire disappointment. I feel as though I had received a blow in the face and from the last person in the world I expected it. I had depended so much upon our joint work—not as actresses, but as author and actress. This dream is over.... In place of the palace I had reared I find only a magnificent ruin ... of my hopes.... 'Tis better to let all business between us end here, good friends still, I hope." In a final note Fanny asked, "I wonder if you would entertain my producing *Anne Boleyn* in Philadelphia," and then a final cut: "Hoping this release from all future writing and anxiety may speedily restore you to health."

Fanny's summary dismissal of her proposal must have humiliated Anna, but she was now very conscious of her weak bargaining position. She controlled her feelings and penned a conciliatory reply. "You are very wide of the right understanding of my offer," she explained. "In making the suggestion that I would play as a member of your company, if you desired it, I had no thought whatever, save that I might be of some service to you." She continued: "I have been at work day and night since Sunday on the American play [Anna had several scripts in the fire at the time—one American, one Russian, one English]—the part that baffled and annoyed me and that I destroyed being rewritten in an entirely different shape—and you can have it within a week...." The new play to which Anna referred was *An American Girl*. A telegram came from Fanny's husband: WIFE SATISFIED AND ANXIOUSLY AWAITING YOU ON FRIDAY NIGHT.

Anna brought the script with her that Friday and read it to the Prices. A highly improbable comedy-drama with juicy roles, brisk dialogue, and highly emotional scenes, the play was set in a Long Island country estate and the characters represented various upper-level social types. The author could not resist using the play to voice some social criticism, and in an apparent jibe at Whitelaw Reid she introduced into the cast a newspaperman described as a "journalist millionaire and man; words not *always synonymous.*" The role of the American girl, Kate Vivian, called for the full gamut of Fanny's talents; moreover, she would be able to wear a different gown in every scene.

Fanny was satisfied that the play would do. She would begin work immediately to prepare it for production before the end of September, only one month away. Tremendously relieved by Fanny's decision and confident that she would be well set for the rest of the year at least, Anna returned to Elizabeth, New Jersey. The Prices went into action. Casting, rehearsals, costuming, and publicity proceeded at rapid pace. The announcement of the impending production was greeted with much interest in press and theatrical circles. Word spread about the magnificent wardrobe Fanny had purchased for her part and advertisements billed the drama as "the most superbly costumed play ever presented in America."

But the four weeks between Anna's reading of the play and Fanny's appearance in it saw more than the customary amount of personality clashes incidental to a stage production. The playwright and the star, as might have been expected, had a falling out. In the course of rehearsals Fanny decided that the script did not fully satisfy her. The plot required tightening and she felt her own part needed certain alterations. When she asked Anna to make these changes, Anna declined to do so, holding that the play was better in its original form. She curtly reminded Fanny that by her own statement their relationship must be one of playwright and actress and not otherwise. As Fanny would not tolerate Anna on the stage with her, Anna could see nothing that would qualify Fanny to be a co-author. Fanny proceeded to make changes on her own authority and Anna walked out in a huff, refusing thereafter to attend rehearsals or communicate with Fanny. The star seemed anxious to make amends, however. The day before opening Fanny wrote to Anna: "I do hope you will be pleased with what I have done—you know you have trusted entirely to me and left every bit of business situations, etc., in my hands. I have changed but slightly little bits here and there not to mar your work, but to render the general effect better. I have cut out an entrance for myself as in the rehearsing I found it bad to enter three times."

When Anna finally dropped in to see the dress rehearsal, she was shocked to discover that Fanny had made more changes in the play than she had indicated, transposing and cutting lines and altering the business of the first act. Anna charged that she had not sold the "right to improve" the play to Fanny and walked out, declaring that the play must be acted as she wrote it, or not at all.

Fanny had a big investment in the play by now; the production was advertised, tickets had been sold, and the show was to open the next night. Casting Anna's threats aside, Fanny decided to follow through with the play in the form she and her husband thought best. With the author refusing to put in an appearance, *An American Girl* opened on September 20, 1880, before a glittering audience of notables. Fanny was magnificent. She swept back and forth across the stage in her resplendent gowns and displayed the full range of her emotional powers. The production was a striking success though no one could be quite sure whether people came to see Fanny's fashion parade or Anna's comedy. The reviewers remarked on the star's great beauty and passed lightly over the drama. "The central idea of the play," wrote the *New York Times,* "is bold and novel; in places, admirable," but as a whole the play was not good. "Its merits preserve it, however, from badness," said the *Times,* "though Miss Dickinson's warmest admirer cannot look upon it otherwise than as a production far below the strength of one who gave the world a fine and original drama, in *The Crown of Thorns.*" Anna must have been furious when she read the *Times* that day. This was the same paper that had called *Anne Boleyn* "an eminently dull play" in its first review and as not having "the slightest claim upon public attention" in its second! The *Daily Graphic* told its readers: *"An American Girl* is worth getting acquainted with. It is often brilliant in its dialogue, has some strong situations and is absolutely perfect in the matter of feminine upholstery. Every woman will want to go as a matter of course, and every man may go in the full assurance that he will enjoy it." The *Evening Post:* "The performance was smooth, the scenery handsome, and the costumes of Miss Fanny Davenport exceeded the glory of Solomon or anybody else.... The audience laughed readily whenever a sentence characteristic of Miss Dickinson was uttered...." And the *Evening Express:* "As to the lady's costumes, only a milliner could describe them, so gorgeous and intricate were they."

Box-office receipts for the first two weeks ran over $13,000, an unusually large figure for that time. One paper remarked that it was "probably a larger box-office return for the same period than that of any other uptown New York theatre." The engagement ran for six weeks altogether—a good run in those days—and grossed a trifle short of $30,000.

Meanwhile Anna sat out her discontent in Elizabeth. Since her run-in with Fanny she had not been near the theater. Bernard tried to persuade her to attend at least one performance. When the curtain

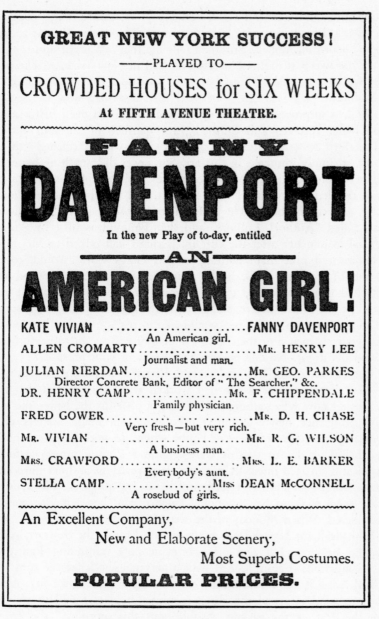

A poster for *An American Girl*

came down on the second night, Bernard wrote Anna a note asking her to relent. "I have just come from the theatre," he wrote. "It was packed to the doors, all money. Frohman tells me that last night and tonight were the two best nights Haverly ever had in New York.... The play has scored a popular success beyond a question. Everybody conceded tonight the play is a 'go.'" Bernard then described how the second night had improved over the opening. It had been even better acted and better received and finished three quarters of an hour earlier. "The third act (the best act of the play)," he wrote, "catched 'em all. F. D. is simply immense in this act. She never did anything better in all her professional life. Mr. Price agrees with me in this. The audience recalled her at the close of this act, and the applause was 'loud, long, and continuous.'" He went on to tell Anna how the audience had called "Author! Author!" and that Fanny was hurt by Anna's refusal to join her after the curtain. Bernard had talked to Mr. Price who assured him that "nothing in this God's world would, could, or should prejudice F. D. against you; that she is greatly devoted and attached to the play, and that she would be supremely happy if you would come to the theatre, and give her the benefit of such suggestions as might occur to you. They would like to see you at the theatre and feel your absence. For their sake I hope you will see fit to be on hand tomorrow night. No one need or will know of your presence."

But Anna would not budge, and Bernard was distressed by her display of temperament. He had worked with her through the lean years and now when affairs were taking a turn for the better she was dissipating her newly acquired prestige. Anna made matters even worse by her rude treatment of Fanny when the weekly royalty checks fell behind a day or two or were sent in a slightly improper form. Anna still smarted inwardly over the script revisions and her unspoken humiliation over Fanny's rejection of her acting proposal. Her frustrations were shaking her emotional balance, and her behavior was ill considered. When Monday of the second week's run came round and a bank draft for $350 did not arrive as called for in the contract, Anna wasted no time, but sent off a brusque note reminding Fanny of her obligations. Fanny replied with a personal check for the sum and asked Anna if she would kindly come to New York to see her. Anna declined and returned the check as unacceptable: "I will thank you for the draft at the earliest possible hour this morning," she wrote.

Several weeks later, on the eve of Fanny's departure with the play for Boston, Anna had a deputy sheriff attach her wardrobe because the weekly draft had not arrived promptly on the due date. This action brought an end to Fanny's disposition to forget all past grievances and be friends; she retaliated by removing Anna's name from all the advertisements and bills of the play. Anna's uncalled-for act seems also to have alienated her own manager, for by the end of the year Bernard, himself, was at legal sword's point with Anna.

Meantime Anna was in Elizabeth preparing herself for a winter's tour of readings and lectures and busily working away on still another play—*Elfrida, or The Test of Honor*, a comedy of manners, set in England. She submitted the new play to the proprietor of the Union Square Theatre who turned it down on the advice of his stage manager as being "highly sensational and highly improbable." Anna took the rejection coldly, quoting in her letter of reply a line she had written for Zenobia: "What is one man's owl is another man's nightingale." She was booked to read *Aurelian* in Philadelphia for $300, one of the best fees she had received since her peak lyceum days; she also worked up a lecture on Danton, the French revolutionary figure, which was to be tried out under a new manager.

Fanny meanwhile toured the East and the South with *An American Girl* and the weekly drafts for $350 arrived with satisfactory promptness until early December when Fanny wrote Anna from Baltimore to say that business was falling off sharply: "You cannot say I have not given the *American Girl* a fair trial for pecuniary success. It is, however, not one. The time has now come when I must throw it overboard or you must reduce the royalty. Will you? I am willing to pay $200 a week or $50 a performance. I do not argue the matter nor need you in answer. It is a business proposition. Upon your answer 'yes' will depend the continuance of the play, upon your answer 'no' will depend my substituting another piece. If I should not hear from you by Saturday I shall assume that your answer is no and act accordingly."

Anna's reply was as brief and to the point as it was ill advised: "IN ANSWER TO YOUR LETTER OF THE 7TH, I REFER YOU TO THE TERMS OF OUR CONTRACT." Anna was cutting off the steadiest and amplest source of income she had known in many years. Events moved to a climax before the month was out. Bernard broke with Anna, but was unable to make what he felt was a satisfactory settlement of moneys due him. He had papers drawn up and served on Anna. To make sure that Anna would not leave him holding an empty bag Bernard wired Fanny not to pay Anna any more royalties. On the basis of this request Fanny only too gladly withheld $1,000. This infuriated Anna who grabbed another ring on the legal merry-go-round and wired Fanny the day before Christmas: "UNLESS ROYALTY IS PAID AT ONCE ACCORDING TO CONTRACT I WILL ATTACH YOUR PROPERTY IN NEW YORK." On December 30, 1880, the suits and countersuits and clashing temperaments came to a formal end when Fanny, after giving her one hundredth performance of the play, decided to shelve *An American Girl* and telegraphed Anna from New Orleans: "THE JUDGMENT OF THE PARTY OF THE SECOND PART DECIDES, AS PER CONTRACT, YOUR PLAY IS A PECUNIARY FAILURE, AND ACCORDINGLY CEASES TO PERFORM THE SAME."

Fanny returned the script and rights to Anna and the play went into oblivion. Though Anna had made over $6,000 from it and had demonstrated an ability to write successfully for the theater, her refusal to compromise, her insistence on having every sentence of the contract observed to the letter, her alienation of would-be and demonstrated friends had turned what should have been a triumph into a dismal episode. She had lost her manager and gained the ill will of the only actress who had ever helped her. The legal squabbles were reported in the papers, of course, and Anna received another dose of bad publicity. Instead of grasping opportunity when it beckoned and making the most of it, Anna misread its message and turned against it in a shameful display of nervous temperament. Her rapidly deteriorating emotional state boded ill for the future.

CHAPTER 12

A QUAKER IN TIGHTS

THE falling out with Whitelaw Reid was now almost complete, and the abuse the *Tribune* heaped on Anna in its drama columns seemed to make a *rapprochement* utterly out of the question. It soon became common newspaper gossip that Reid was using his paper to strike back at Anna for jilting him. "The *New York Tribune* has hounded Miss Dickinson with the utmost persistency for a great many years," wrote the *Chicago Tribune,* echoing Anna's own feelings, "and is determined to prevent her from becoming an actress if it can." Anna was convinced that Reid was using his paper maliciously. "The 'Trib' article I think has our clear and true Whitelaw's earmarks," she wrote to Susan on seeing a strangely complimentary item about herself in the paper. "Having done me all the harm he can and finding that I live—very friskly—in spite of him, he thinks he will take the other tack."

There were two or three notes from Anna to Reid in the course of business. She might ask him to carry an account of a forthcoming lecture or to return some painting or book of hers. The letters were formal. They began with "My dear Mr. Reid," and closed with the cold, "Truly yours, Anna E. Dickinson." The two saw each other no more, and what Anna knew of his personal life came through the press or gossip. Had Susan heard the latest? "Whitey (alias W. R., alias yr young editor) is engaged to Gail Hamilton!" The rumor was false, but not long thereafter announcement was made of Reid's engagement to the daughter of the wealthy Darius Ogden Mills, a philanthropic banker of immense means who had made his money in California after the Gold Rush and later concerned himself with such projects as providing sleeping accommodations for homeless men in cheap hotels. Reid was now a figure of national importance; he had recently declined the ministership to Germany in the hope of greater honors from the Republican administration of President Hayes. Susan commented to Anna with a show of seeming amusement, but more likely of jealousy: "I suspect Whitelaw is *actooally* engaged *this* time. I infer so from what I hear—also that the lady is rich and *humly*."

Nothing seemed to irk Anna more than the thought that Reid, acting through Winter, was waging a remorseless campaign to drive her off the stage through humiliating reviews, inaccurate reports, and behind-the-scene treachery such as had been used to prevent the production of *Aurelian*. That her suspicions might not be based on actual fact was unimportant; she accepted her suspicions as founded in fact, and there was no way openly to disprove them. The worries, troubles, and losses of the preceding five years had created in her a disposition to believe that the cause of her misfortunes was not to be found in herself, but in external forces beyond her control. And these forces— she felt the *Tribune* was the main culprit, giving the cue to other papers that took its utterances for gospel—were determined to destroy her. She had served her country well, but now an ungrateful public stifled her every effort, condemned her to failure, and persecuted her at every turn. She was increasingly given to tantrums, to periods of great depression followed by moments of hope and enthusiasm. She made plans and canceled them, or if they failed she ascribed the fault to others, never herself. Her actions became unpredictable to any but students of abnormal behavior. In the fall of 1880 while *An American Girl* was still on tour, Susan became alarmed over Anna's state of mind and health and wrote a long and bitter letter to Reid berating him for his brutal treatment of her sister. "You evidently forgot— and very speedily—all the volunteered promises that the *Tribune* would gratefully remember her loyal service to Mr. Greeley in 1872, at the expense of so much popularity, and such heavy consequent pecuniary loss to herself," Susan wrote. "You forgot, no less that such friendship as she for years honored you with was a matter which you might well be proud of and grateful for all your life." She reminded Reid that since May, 1876, when *Anne Boleyn* opened, there was "good and abundant cause why he should give the influence of his paper to help Anna. Instead, you have persistently used it to hinder her success," she chided him. "For whatever personal reason I will not stop nor stoop to inquire too closely." His efforts had resulted in unsettling her sister's state of mind and destroying her health so that now her life and career stood in danger of a sudden end. "Perhaps you would like to congratulate yourself on your work," Susan wrote, and then she added: "Perhaps, though, I may do you wrong in supposing that. It is possible that you would rather do what yet lies in your power to delay the coming of the end which you have been precipitating." She did not propose to discuss the McCullough-Winter affair, though it was obvious to her that Winter was merely carrying out Reid's wishes, nor did she intend to argue about the quality of Anna's work, as an actress and playwright. "Again you know, as I do," Susan wrote, "that the work in both cases was better done than much which the *Tribune* has helped the world to praise. The simple question today is Anna Dickinson's life. It stands in peril of the grave by reason of the war on her originated and led on by the *Tribune,* which was bound by every tie of gratitude to help her." If Reid had any doubt of this, Susan suggested that he consult the Dickinson family physician. "It may not be too late to save her yet for some years of usefulness if the *Tribune* choose now to give her the same chances of success, and aids to it," Susan concluded, "which it lavishes in profusion on those to whom it is in no wise indebted."

Reid received the letter, opened it and apparently read it. He took up a pencil and in his neat hand carefully wrote "Unanswered" on the paper and filed it away systematically. Years later, when a two-volume official biography of his life would be published, no mention would be made of Anna's name. Such was the end of the Dickinson-Reid relationship.

In March, 1881, three months after she had parted ways with Fanny Davenport, Anna announced to a startled and somewhat amused public that she was planning to re-enter the theater as an actress and that this time she would enact *male* roles on the stage. She would play Hamlet, Macbeth, and Claude Melnotte, the male lead in Edward Bulwer-Lytton's popular play, *The Lady of Lyons.*

It appears that Fred Zimmerman, a Philadelphia theater manager, was the one to suggest the male roles. He had seen newspaper accounts of Anna's readings of *Aurelian* and was reminded of Charlotte Cushman's success some years before as a female Hamlet. Zimmerman no doubt was motivated by the box-office possibilities of parading before the public a renowned Quaker woman dressed in tights. At first Anna refused to consider the suggestion, but she changed her mind and Zimmerman conferred with her in New York. Zimmerman then went off to arrange bookings and Anna returned to Elizabeth to prepare the roles. Arrangements were made with John Stetson, a Boston theatrical manager, for Anna to make her first appearance with the dramatic company of Signor Salvini, a popular Italian tragedian who was touring the country with several Shakespearean productions. Negotiations for Anna to appear with the company were complicated by two facts: Salvini himself was playing Macbeth and the traveling schedule of the company provided little or no rehearsal time for the cast to practice the special version of *Hamlet* Anna was preparing. A compromise was effected. Anna would not play Hamlet or Macbeth with Salvini's company, but would appear with them as Claude Melnotte in Goodwin's Chestnut Street Opera House in Philadelphia. Both Salvini and Anna were to share equal billing. Anna would receive 25 per cent of the gross receipts until they reached $800; above that she would receive one third of the take. The second week she would appear in Stetson's theater in Boston to play both Hamlet and Claude Melnotte.

Announcements were released and space was bought in the press to tell the Philadelphia public of the FIRST APPEARANCE ON ANY STAGE IN MALE CHARACTER OF MISS ANNA DICKINSON. One can easily imagine the reaction to this news of Mrs. Dickinson and most of Anna's old friends. They were chagrined by Anna's newest venture and felt that she was overstepping all bounds of propriety. The public, however, responded as Zimmerman had hoped; great curiosity was aroused by the prospect of seeing Anna in tights. But on April 7, five days before the scheduled opening, the *Philadelphia Press* carried the headline: WILL NOT PLAY HERE—ANNA DICKINSON REFUSES TO PERFORM IN THIS CITY.

The story behind the headline was involved. It seems that Anna learned that the managers had rearranged the route of Salvini's company due to failing business in the South and that as a result, the company would not arrive in Philadelphia until the day before her debut with it. There would be only the briefest time to rehearse with the cast. Anna also suspected that Goodwin, the manager of the opera house, intended to trick her into playing opposite a Miss Prescott who was much taller than Anna and would make her look silly. Anna preferred a Miss Stuart, a shorter girl, to play opposite her. The matter was discussed back and forth until Anna was convinced the management intended to confront her the day of the performance with the Prescott girl and there would then be no time to rehearse a substitute. Under those conditions she would not appear on the stage. She wired Stetson she was ready to open in Boston for the second week's run, but she would not play in Philadelphia without rehearsals or opposite Miss Prescott. She left the city and went back to Elizabeth.

Anna's abrupt decision made the telegraph wires burn. Goodwin wired Stetson in Boston that Anna must perform or face a lawsuit for breach of contract. Stetson forwarded Goodwin's telegram to Anna, directed her to appear for rehearsal on Monday, and went to Philadelphia himself to see that she did. But Anna did not show up. She locked herself up in Elizabeth, refused to answer telegrams, and positively declined to come to Philadelphia. The management continued to sell tickets to *The Lady of Lyons* starring Anna Dickinson, until the evening of the scheduled performance. At the last minute a substitution was announced and another play was presented in its place. Those who desired were refunded their money and Stetson issued a card to the public stating the terms of his contract with Anna:

To The Public

Mr. John Stetson regrets to be compelled to acquaint the public that Miss Anna Dickinson, without assigning any reason whatever for her conduct, has seen fit to violate her written engagement to appear at the Chestnut Street Opera House in the character of Claude Melnotte. The lady, although repeatedly solicited by Mr. Stetson to carry out the conditions of the contract into which she had entered at her own special desire, has persistently declined to either attend the rehearsals of the play or even to come to Philadelphia.

Miss Dickinson, with lofty contempt either for professional etiquette, commercial integrity or public opinion, utterly refuses to assign any reason whatsoever for her breach of faith, and Mr. Stetson has no alternative but to ask the Philadelphia public to credit him with having used every exertion in his power to further the interests of a lady who is held in such high estimation in our city, but who has, by ill-judged advice, thrown away the best opportunity that will probably ever be offered her of proving her histrionic merit.

Stetson told the press he could account for Anna's actions "in no other way except that she is insane or very much frightened," and he asked Goodwin to hire an attorney to sue her for $8,000 damages.

Anna broke her silence and publicly accepted Stetson's challenge with a long and passionate, almost incoherent letter published in the *New York Herald*. The letter was one that Anna must have greatly regretted in later years. In it she poured forth the anguish and bitterness that were driving her to desperation. It was the letter of a broken woman who felt she had been keenly, mercilessly, maliciously, unjustifiably wronged by a public to whom she had devoted her life and energies.

"I had ample reason in law, justice, and common sense for my action in refusing to appear," Anna wrote. She reviewed the negotiations with Stetson to reveal his shabby plan for exposing her to public ridicule. "So soon as he is ready to bring the threatened suit against me I will be ready with proof of what I here declare." She appealed not to the public, but to the courts to decide the justice of her action. The public had been turned against her and the "experience of the last five years has taught me that it is enough for this public to know I am engaged in any controversy to insure for my antagonist—praise; for me—condemnation."

"I have been absolutely condemned without sight and without knowledge in all I have attempted for years," Anna wrote. For five years she had said to the public, "Forget my past, and look at my present work and judge it for itself, and itself alone." But she had been answered, "No! I will never see the artist nor the art, since I will hold an opaque or a distorted glass, labelled 'Anna Dickinson' between my eyes and all you may attempt to do."

It had been her misfortune to have won a great fame, with neither a great fortune nor an idle nature to accompany it. "Politics and place debarred me, the lyceum platform crumbled to dust, inclination and ability leading me, a homely need and bitter necessity spurring me on, I have tried to do what an unknown woman would have been fully accorded the opportunity to do." But she had been constantly confronted with the words, even in this last attempt: " 'You cannot come into this theatre or secure this engagement or command a suitable presentation of yourself and your work.' Why? Because you are incapable? No. Because we lack confidence in your ability? No. But because you are not rich enough to do this thing alone we will take no risk, since, though we believe you can do it, the American public has decided it don't [sic] want you to do it, and the majority of the American newspapers stand ready, whatever you accomplish, to cry you down."

She had learned her lesson at last, and prayed for an open pathway to another continent in which she would be an absolute stranger, a land where, "since no gratitude is owed me for past faithful services rendered and pleasures bestowed, I may be sure of escaping insults and may hope for a fair opportunity to prove what I can do and for an honest verdict on the thing done. So may it be."

Anna's long wail did not go without comment in the newspapers. Two papers showed surprising sympathy with Anna's plight. The *Philadelphia North American* commented:

Were Miss Dickinson a philosopher, she would recognize in her troubles only the logical outcome of one woman pitted against all the jealousies and prejudices which have accumulated during twenty centuries. She has bravely enough flung herself against the wall, and we can only regret that she has not as bravely endured the shock. The wall cannot be levelled by one woman, or by one hundred, and it goes without saying that there are not a hundred Anna Dickinsons in the whole world.

The *Boston Herald* manifested keen perception in its editorial:

Miss Anna Dickinson's published letter ... is the cry of a brave woman, out of the depths; and, however much one must deplore the lack of judgment and taste evinced in its publication, the despair of such a woman as Anna Dickinson has shown herself to be, throughout her remarkable career, is not, to our mind, a subject for flippant jest or uncharitable comment.... Miss Dickinson's letter betrays an abnormal state of mind in regard to the feelings of the public toward her, and lack of philosophy in accepting the penalties of a public career.

The charity of these two papers stood almost alone. More typical was the comment of a third: "The letter is simply the wail of disappointed egotism. It will make her no friends."

The following week Anna filed a countersuit for damages against Stetson, alleging that his card to the public had maligned her. She wrote Susan a letter stating the facts of her business arrangements and Susan turned the document over to the *Philadelphia Press* which published it in full. Anna seemed to be busier writing letters than doing anything else. In this one she wrote:

> Two things astonish me. One is the stupidity of human nature, and the other is its meanness, but the first is the most annoying. Even the papers that try to say a decent word utterly beg the question. I do not complain of condemnation of my work, but that by reason of premature condemnation I am prevented any chance to show what I can do, the managers fearing the risk and I being too poor to "try it on alone."
> Does John Stetson suppose people have no eyes, and that theatrical people especially never read the papers? It was because...he absolutely would not guarantee me but one rehearsal...to say nothing of the Prescott business, that I kicked over the traces, as it would have killed me professionally, if I had run in them....
> I want him to be taught the value of language, of which he evidently knows nothing, and I think he will discover the difference in due time, between the cross-examination of the witness box and his gabble with reporters.

The case did not go to court. Stetson certainly had no desire to be further belabored in the newspapers and anyway there was nothing to be gained in a court action. Anna had admitted in a press interview that if the case did go to court she had no fear of the result because "the weight of evidence is on my side" and "I have no money whatever, so that I can pay no damages. If I were not so poor as I am, I should not seek the aid of a manager with capital."

Strange as it may seem, Anna found a new "manager with capital" within two months and closed a verbal agreement to tour the country in various dramatic roles the following season. Charles E. Mendum, of the Philadelphia Arch Street Theatre, was a young man with limited means but large aspirations. Mendum felt that he could handle Anna where other managers had failed and make money on the deal. A formal two-year agreement was drawn up in July, 1881, which reserved to Anna the right to approve supporting casts and provided her a range of from 50 to 80 per cent of the profits after salaries of the cast were paid. Mendum was to bear all the expense of advertising and production, Anna would provide for her personal necessities, but Mendum would pay for transportation for her and a maid. The company would include thirty-two people; all the costumes, settings, and properties would be carried from city to city in the tour. It was the best acting contract Anna had ever obtained. Mendum advertised her to appear in a series of male roles—Claude Melnotte, Hamlet, Romeo, Macbeth, and Aurelian, and announced that arrangements were being made for Anna to appear in London. Later it was decided that only three plays would be produced—*Hamlet, Anne Boleyn,* and *The Lady of Lyons.* The tour was announced to begin in January, 1882, and Mendum secured an engagement for Anna in June at the Crystal Palace in London.

Anna spent the winter preparing *Hamlet.* She had her own ideas of how the Shakespearean play should be presented and they were at variance with the views of contemporary tragedians and critics. She would have none of the temporizing, indecisive Hamlet that had become more or less the standard interpretation. "There was no indecision about Hamlet," Anna said. "Where there was any real definite course before him he trod it with a bold foot. Witness the cunning and determination with which he compasses the destruction of Rosencrantz and Guildenstern," she argued. "Not the least trace of hesitation. Hamlet cannot be called vacillating because he hesitates about killing his uncle, the king, since to do so without further evidence of his guilt than a ghost's word would have been absurd."

Anna used the Edwin Booth version of *Hamlet,* but made a number

of revisions in it. She struck out Hamlet's famous advice to the players
on the ground that it retarded the action, and she restored a section
customarily omitted at the time—the full conversation in the grave-
yard between Hamlet and Horatio. Anna also had Hamlet wear a
purple cloak instead of the usual black, arguing that purple had been
the royal color of mourning in Denmark during the years dramatized
by the play. The purple frock draped a few inches below Anna's hips.
Her exposed legs were encased in tights. Her left shoulder supported
a cape that was gathered at the right hip. On her side, she wore a
sword. And though she was now almost forty, she began taking
fencing lessons.

Anna's debut in *Hamlet* took place in Rochester, New York, on
January 19, 1882. Ordinarily one would expect a production in an
outlying city to draw only slight attention, but the Dickinson name
had not lost all its magic. It could, of course, be expected that the
debut would be a major theatrical event for Rochester, but it was
surprising to learn that the *New York Herald* was sending out its
critic to cover the opening. Subsequent events suggest that the *Herald's*
coverage stemmed not from kindness to Anna, but rather from a
desire to strike her down wherever she might raise her head on the
stage. Boston and St. Louis papers, among others, also arranged to
have special correspondents send in reports.

What happened on the stage of that Rochester theater the night of
Anna's debut is difficult to state with certainty. The conflicting reports
of the critics who attended tell an interesting story. The *Rochester
Union and Advertiser* commented:

> It is safe to say that she made a most excellent impression upon
> the large and cultivated audience.... Suffice it to say that Miss Dick-
> inson was repeatedly called before the curtain and received more
> generous applause from first to last than has been vouchsafed to
> anyone playing Hamlet in this city for many a day.

The *Rochester Democrat and Chronicle* also endorsed the opening:
"Anna Dickinson's debut may be considered a success, not unqualified,
but certainly enough of a triumph to justify the congratulations, and
repay her in a measure for the tremendous risks incurred." A special
dispatch to the *Boston Globe* reported: "Rochester pronounces her a

dramatic success—qualified to be sure, but still a success.... She fairly
conquered the audience, and may be justly considered to have set
out anew in her dramatic career, with every prospect of accomplishing
permanent success and acquiring a high position in the profession."
And the correspondent of the *St. Louis Republican* was definitely impressed with Anna's fencing: "Probably no woman in America
handles foils as well as Anna Dickinson today," the reporter wrote.

What did the critic of the *New York Herald* have to say about the
debut?

> Despite the encouragement of an audience anxious and willing
> to be pleased, Miss Dickinson made a dire failure. Her Hamlet had
> none of the attributes it should have possessed, and nothing but the
> fact that the actress was an estimable lady toward whom her
> listeners were kindly disposed saved the affair from ridicule. As
> a lecturer and author, Miss Dickinson's talents are widely acknowl-
> edged, but as an actress she has confirmed the impression before
> created—that she is an absolute failure....
>
> Miss Dickinson did not seem to have the first requisite for the ac-
> complishment of her task. She did not look Hamlet. She did not
> speak as Hamlet should. She did not act as Hamlet must. Her ap-
> pearance was not that of a man or of a boy.... She delivered her
> lines without sense or sentiment.

The maliciousness of this review seemed utterly unjustified to many
Herald readers. The critic's charge that Anna delivered her lines
meaninglessly was impossible for them to believe, as numerous letters
to the editors indicated. They could conceive that Anna might fail
to supply the full emotional depth called for by Hamlet, but that she
should have missed the intellectual meanings of the lines was fantastic. She was too bright a woman for that and had studied her
Shakespeare too long.

The *New York Mirror* was intrigued by the conflict in critical opinion between the *New York Herald* and the Rochester and Boston
dailies. To settle the matter for its own readers, the *Mirror* arranged
to have its own correspondent send in a special report from Rochester
giving "the truth, the whole truth, and nothing but the truth about
Miss Dickinson's debut." This was the report:

She made a favorable impression.... Her acting at times was superb, particularly in the scene with the ghost, where she fairly electrified the audience. The passages between Ophelia and Hamlet were finely rendered and with more tenderness than we are accustomed to.

Miss Dickinson's conception of the character is not remarkable; she displayed genuine dramatic ability, but to pronounce her rendition of Hamlet an unqualified success would be a bold assertion.... When she has become more familiarized with the technique of the cast, she will be seen to greater advantage than at this, the beginning of her stage career, for the episode of her New York appearance some years ago hardly counts.

After Rochester Anna and the company took to the road. They went to Youngstown, Ohio, and then put in a full week at McVicker's Theatre in Chicago where business held up extremely well, starting off at $578.50 and closing with a $914.59 box office, which suggests that audiences were telling their friends to see the show. From Chicago the company hopped through the Midwest: Milwaukee, Minneapolis, Cedar Rapids, Des Moines, Lincoln, St. Joseph, Topeka, Leavenworth. Betty Chatfield accompanied Anna on the tour, and the two women made life as pleasant as they could. A bill for six dollars included in the invoices for the production suggests that Betty and Anna, dressed in the garb of the melancholy Prince of Denmark, enjoyed sandwiches and a keg of beer in their room. Perhaps the cast was invited, too.

By March the company was ready to return East. Over Anna's strenuous objections Mendum brought the troupe to New York. Anna knew well enough what the critics would say, but Mendum was bound by contract to bring the play to the metropolis. It is hard to exaggerate how nervous Anna was at the New York performance; after two months of playing Hamlet, she forgot her lines when it came time to say "To be or not to be," and had to be prompted from the wings. The New York critics shared none of the enthusiasm provincial audiences had shown for Anna's Hamlet. Their collected reviews displayed an utter lack of mercy. The *Herald,* which had gone three hundred miles out of its way to slap her down in Rochester, seemed to relish the opportunity to perform this critical feat once again, though its review indicated that Anna's audience in the Fifth Avenue Theatre was far more favorably disposed than was the *Herald* writer. "She still shows an utter lack of talent for the dramatic stage, and, to speak plainly, she had no proper idea of the character or of the true inflection of voice or of the emphasis of words in reading the lines," the *Herald* said. "She was the recipient of much applause, most of which was not deserved...." William Winter continued his campaign of disapproval in the *Tribune*: "She has shown that she cannot express *Hamlet*, however agreeably she may lecture on the play or read from it; that her choice of the stage has been made too late in life; and that the art of acting is not her destined pursuit." The *Star, Times,* and *Sun* critics seemed to be competing in a test to determine which paper could produce the most abusive review. "Miss Dickinson's impersonation of Hamlet had not a single redeeming feature," said the *Star.* "The supporting company vied with each other in absolute badness, but the worst of them was rather a relief after one had contemplated Miss Dickinson for a brief space." The *Times*: "This performance of Hamlet was one of the worst ransackings of that high and beautiful creation that we have yet endured." None was more brutal than the *Sun*: "One cannot readily imagine a person more completely devoid of any natural gift or ability in the direction of the stage, or obviously less designed by nature for that purpose than is Miss Dickinson."

Yet not all New York critics subscribed to these harsh views. The *Home Journal* recommended the production to its readers declaring "the performance to be above the mass of our Hamlets, and we advise the lovers of Shakespeare to see it without fail. There is so much thorough study in it, so much originality of interpretation and such a fresh impress generally given to the old hackneyed sentences, that no one can fail to find in it abundant suggestion and entertainment."

Outwardly Anna dismissed the critical statements, but inwardly she was terribly angered. She told a friend later "The great trouble with the critics is that so few of them have the least idea of a Shakespearean character. If an actor swaggers or rants through a role in the traditional manner, he is praised unanimously by the critics. But if, by the aid of individuality and talent he works out a new conception of a character, the critics are horrified and shower down ridicule on his unlucky head."

Anna followed *Hamlet* with *Anne Boleyn,* alternating the two plays during the brief New York run. The *Times* now found *Anne Boleyn* "a work of considerable merit"; as for Anna's acting in it, however, the paper did not swerve from its previous condemnation; the *Times* critic felt that Anna was "making herself ridiculous." The *Sun* followed its scornful review of *Hamlet* with more nastiness about *Anne Boleyn:* "It was borne by the critical among the audience with that feeling of exquisite pain which is always the reward of martyrdom.... To the traditions of the past she does full justice, for the only traditions are those of her unique performance at the Eagle Theatre in April, 1877."

The critical onslaught demoralized the entire company and business dropped off badly during the rest of the tour. After a few weeks of playing in Pennsylvania cities, Mendum was dead broke and was forced to dissolve the company. Once again Anna found herself without a sponsor and she temporarily retired from public view, joining Susan at a Pennsylvania mountain resort to recoup her strength. There she lived quietly until a personal notice in the *New York Tribune* stirred her into action again. The *Tribune* had run an item saying that Anna had "resolved never again to appear on the lecture platform, nor on the dramatic stage," and that she was "living quietly at Honesdale, Pa., with her mother, a venerable Quaker lady of 87, and a younger sister." The next day the *Tribune* received a letter from Anna, which at her request, it carried in its columns. Anna wanted to set the record straight: "My mother is not '87 years of age.' I have no 'younger sister.' I am not 'living with them at Honesdale' since my mother has been for weeks past in her home elsewhere—that of my brother, in the city of New York; and my sister is lingering in this pleasant mountain resort, only to keep me company in a vacation necessarily prolonged by reason of ill health. Being a sensible and energetic person with both mental and material need of exercising that sense and energy, and with the good will and friendly regard of a great public, I have, naturally, *not* 'resolved never again to appear on the lecture platform nor on the dramatic stage.' On the contrary, I am at present under engagement to do some talking, and also some reading of plays from what is known as the lecture platform, and later, to do some acting across a very wide space of western territory upon the dramatic stage."

Anna was speaking more out of bravado than facts for by the fall of 1882 she was still without work and was staying with Susan. She even had to borrow $25 from a Philadelphia friend in order to keep a solitary lecture engagement in a small Pennsylvania city. The inactivity was making her more and more sensitive to criticism and on the slightest excuse she would flare out in rage. The bitterness of her failures was cutting ever deeper, distorting her whole personality, making her vengeful and splenetic. In October, rumors appeared in print that Anna had deserted the cause of woman's suffrage. The editor of the *Philadelphia Press* asked her for a statement and this was her reply:

You ask me to state explicitly whether, by means of a letter to the editor of the *Omaha Herald* or through other channels, I have avowed myself an opponent of woman's suffrage. Explicitly, then, the statement is preposterous and not worthy the dignity of a denial. No one at all familiar with my work and my life would, without malice, make it, and no one equally familiar, unless a fool, would believe it. I may have written in some private letter to someone what I have no objection to writing in this public letter to whoever may care to read, that in my judgment there is too much of voting now—voting that is both ignorant and venal; that no man ought to be able to control the destinies of other people by means of a constitution and laws who is not able at least to read them; that, as a question of principle, these ideas apply as well to women who may vote as to men who do vote; and that, as a matter of personal interest, I would rather see the money I have earned in some hardly-contested campaigns, and have never been paid, than any number of ballots, I having learned through much observation that an abundance of paper with a green back is a far better guarantee of comfort, safety, and honor than any amount of material labelled "political rights" without it. All the same, while intelligent men vote I believe in intelligent women voting. While venal men sell their franchise it is but fair that venal women should enjoy a like monstrous privilege; and while brutes are backed with this additional means of brutality and impunity, through rum shops and police courts of travestied justice, I believe in the life companions of these brutes having in hand a staff of protection and defense. All of which is respectfully submitted by

Truly yours,
Anna Dickinson

Six months later Anna re-entered theatrical activity in her final endeavor to make a success on the stage. She signed a contract with Went-

worth and Hunting, theatrical managers, to tour the United States and
Canada for the 1883-1884 season. It was, on paper at least, a good contract. Wentworth and Hunting agreed to provide a supporting company, advertising, scenery, costumes, advance agents, and railroad fares
for Anna and a maid, while Anna agreed to supply her own costumes
and to act in *Anne Boleyn* and other roles. Box-office receipts above the
$950 siphoned off each week to pay the salaries of the company would
be divided equally between Anna and the managers. But again Anna
fell victim to managerial rascality.

When Anna and the company arrived in Detroit they discovered that
Wentworth had skipped town and left them without any money. All
they had were railroad tickets to take the players back to New York.
John McCullough, who was then playing in Detroit, persuaded a group
of Detroit women to sponsor a benefit performance of *Anne Boleyn* to
raise some money for the company. Still there was insufficient backing
to keep the troupe solvent. In a friendly effort to rescue Anna and the
players from their embarrassment, McCullough is said to have advanced
Anna $500 to hold the company together; she engaged another agent
who laid out a two weeks' jaunt through the Midwest. The company
played at Elgin, Illinois, and at Oshkosh and Racine in Wisconsin and
then, when it reached Chicago, called it quits. The players and the agent
went home to New York leaving their star behind.

Anna was on the rocks and utterly humiliated. One dismal failure
had followed another. She had come to the end of the road. Overconfident of her own talents, she had fought futilely against powerful
critical and public opinion. By going on the stage and then by assuming
male roles, she had offended the moral sense of the great body of people
who had supported her through her years of campaigning and lecturing. Misfortune multiplied on misfortune. Now came word of the
burning of a storage warehouse on Fourth Avenue in New York. In
it much of what Anna owned by way of household and theatrical
property was destroyed, without insurance. Under the pressure of these
multiple misfortunes Anna collapsed and was invalided through the
long winter all by herself in a Chicago hotel room. Finally she recovered sufficiently to move.

Now that she was broken and defeated there was but one place for
Anna to go—back to her mother and sister in West Pittston—the same
little town whose local gazette had reprinted with approval the follow-

ing comment on Anna: "It was bad enough to have her come down from her high eminence, from her great work, to represent a very ordinary woman—a pretty flirt like Anne Boleyn—but when she left that place to come still further down and represent a man—a talking machine called the 'Prince of Denmark,' a thing destitute of the simplest and noblest properties of manhood—it was a little more than bad enough."

With what heartache Anna contemplated life in West Pittston we can readily imagine. She loathed the place, and the townsfolk did not take kindly to her cosmopolitan ways. Though they perhaps felt honored by the presence in their midst of such a prominent lady, the people of West Pittston did not approve of Anna's dress, her perfumes, her manners, her advanced ideas. It was a people largely prohibitionist in belief who viewed with displeasure Anna's use of wines and brandies to settle her stomach. The mutual resentment between Anna and the local residents smoldered at first; later it would flare up into violent hatred. Having no alternative, however, Anna resided in West Pittston until her health would permit her to earn a living elsewhere. Occasionally she was well enough to travel as far as Poughkeepsie, in New York, to give a lecture on "Jeanne d'Arc" and pick up an evening's fee. A "stray personal" made the rounds of the newspapers saying that "Anna Dickinson declares that she had to become either a lecturer or a house servant." When Anna spotted the item she sent a denial to the press, and the *Scranton Truth* marked down the rumor as a "malignant example of Whitelaw Reid, whose *Tribune* never misses an opportunity to misrepresent her."

The occasional lecture fees obviously could not pay Anna's medical bills, to say nothing of daily living expenses. Susan tried to earn some extra money by tutoring local students and writing pieces for New York and Philadelphia papers, but her earnings were very small; moreover, Mrs. Dickinson, now hopelessly senile, was a constant drain on her daughters' time and energies. In these circumstances there seemed but one way for the Dickinsons to obtain enough money to keep a roof over their heads—by appealing to General Butler.

Butler had finally squeaked through to election for one term as Democratic Governor of Massachusetts in 1882, but the old General was viewed with solemn contempt by the respectable people of the state. Harvard University broke a long-standing tradition during

Butler's tenure by not awarding an honorary degree to the governor of the state at the annual commencement ceremony. But the General was above insult. He came anyway and, attended by a full military escort, he stood by regally as the embarrassed educators tried to ignore his presence. After two years of the governorship Butler's ambition was still unquenched. He sought the Democratic nomination for the Presidency and when that quest proved unsuccessful he accepted the backing of two splinter parties—the Greenbacks and Anti-Monopolists —and ran as their candidate against the Democrat Cleveland and the Republican Blaine. His defeat was overwhelming and the sixty-seven-year-old man was obliged to return home and pick up the threads of his once very lucrative law practice.

Susan told Anna how to get some money: go to Boston and see the Governor. "Prospect round and discover how and where to walk in on him," Susan wrote, "and get enough for the summer in England." Anna should remind Butler "gently, but firmly of what thee had done for him, and that in *any* case he should be glad to do for thee according to thy need. Remind him of the 5th Avenue winter and money expended there by his request in thy staying at 5th Ave., etc.—and of thy need now of going abroad for health. I shall wait to hear and see if thee will go."

Anna went to Boston several weeks later and saw Butler. She reminded him of his ardor for her ten years before. Some mention was probably made of the possibility of publishing some of the General's less discreet letters in her memoirs. The two had a long talk "as to how far" he "could help Anna financially" if she went abroad. Butler told her that in the event that a pending business deal proved as lucrative as he hoped, he would be able to see her through in style. If not, he would be able only to cover her ordinary expenses. He would give her $5,000 if affairs moved well; otherwise he would periodically hand over limited sums. Anna seemed satisfied with the arrangement and went to New York where she lived quietly at the Victoria Hotel and sent monthly checks to West Pittston. Then it turned out that Butler would not be able to back a European trip after all. Anna wrote Susan: "I have been disappointed in about all my schemes so far. Maybe better luck is ahead."

As winter approached Anna began to ail once again. She wrote Susan: "I am better than I was, but not yet out. I don't send for a doctor because the one who was sent to me nearly killed me with the mess he gave me—morphine or something in it. I have a lot of the same sort of trouble I have had before—catarrh or influenza or whatever it is, of the stomach." Then there came a week when she could not write at all, so sharp was her headache; the dreaded doctor had to be sent for and a friend was asked to write to the family in her stead.

Anna was in a period of steady decline, physically and spiritually. After she had spent $2,500 of Butler's money, she asked him for another thousand. He was recalcitrant, pointing out with some irritation that the $2,500 she had drawn for her expenses was "more than the income that would be had from an investment of $100,000 in the best government securities for a year after paying taxes." Anna charged the General with being "perfectly heartless." Butler's anger flared: "There is no reason why you should spend that amount of money," he wrote, "and there is no reason that I should furnish it. No relation of friendship which exists between us either calls for it or will justify me in giving it." But Butler could not risk closing the door; he continued to supply Anna with funds though the sums grew progressively smaller.

Mary Dickinson was now almost ninety and so enfeebled that it was evident her years of life were at an imminent end. She required constant care—day and night—and even after Susan gave up her outside work to tend to her, there was yet need of more help. Still passionately devoted to her mother, Anna returned to West Pittston and with $1,000 Senator Allison sent her plus some $500 she obtained by liquidating the last piece of her Chicago property she took Mary and Susan out of the boarding home in which they were staying and rented a house for them.

With the persistence bequeathed her by her long-lived forebears, the old lady made a surprising recovery, but the strain of day and night nursing took its toll of Anna's flagging strength. The weather that winter was especially poor and as Mrs. Dickinson rallied, Anna steadily declined. She seemed to have developed an internal ailment that involved the liver or spleen. By spring Anna was unable to stand on her feet. Thinking that any change in climate, however slight, might help, Susan took Anna to Honesdale, in a neighboring valley, but Anna continued to waste away. A persistent temperature sapped her strength and she seemed enfeebled beyond recovery. Weeks passed without sign of improvement. Unable to diagnose the ailment correctly, local doctors finally recommended surgery as a last resort. The operation was performed and seemed a failure. Anna did not rally. Day after day she lay at the point of death, and the entire city stood by for news of her passing. On Sunday June 5, 1887, all churches in Honesdale suspended bell ringing. It was feared that the noise would have a deleterious effect on Anna as she lingered in a state of crisis.

Finally the temperature dropped and it was clear that Anna would live. The following Sabbath the church bells signaled the news of her narrow escape from death. But she was weak beyond description and for weeks could not lift her head from the pillow or see anyone but her attendants. Letters of encouragement and sympathy descended on the Dickinsons from all over the country until Susan announced in the *Philadelphia Times* that she could not answer all the "letters pouring in." Susan desired to say that while Anna was "slowly convalescing," she was still very ill, and it would be a very long time before she would again be able to get on her feet. But Anna would live. What she would live for, what she could hope or expect from the future, Susan did not say. She could not. She did not know. For that matter no one knew.

CHAPTER 13

RETURN TO THE STUMP

MONTHS PASSED. Anna recovered slowly. By winter she was well enough to take pen in hand to write a pitiful plea to General Butler to rescue her from her misery. She begged him: "Take me out of a place [the words "my prison house" were scratched out of the first draft] that has been good to me but that is now doing me little but harm.... I want to get away from this place and I can't get away till you take me away. I am totally bankrupt. I need so much, in so many ways, that I am generally one huge want.... I have been a very sick woman and I do not believe you can quite understand without being with me, that I can look pretty well and endure very little.... I hope you have no snarls of your own to straighten out, and that while you find more or less fault with me, that you carry me always in your heart."

To this poignant appeal Butler replied: "On my return home I found your note which gives me pain in all except the assurance of improving health although slowly, and of continued friendship although so many things have happened which might well have shaken it." He then told Anna of his own financial difficulties. For more than a year he had not been able to sell a single piece of property without ruinous loss. He had only his professional income from his law practice "which everybody wonders why I keep up" to make ends meet. He enclosed a check for $500 and advised Anna to go to California or New Mexico or Florida or wherever she could have an early spring, fresh air, and quiet comfort. For such a trip he would try to see her provided. "I have convinced you, if you have doubt, of my continued friendship," the General concluded hopefully, but then as an afterthought, he added discreetly: "So far and so great as it ought to exist between two sensible beings."

But Butler was beleaguered by his own personal and family obligations and he could not or would not relieve Anna of all the medical
debts that bound her to Honesdale. Anna appealed to him once
more. "You have labored all along under some misapprehension of the
embarrassments that hem me round," she wrote, "or you would destroy
them and that *right speedily.*" Even had she the means to go elsewhere she would be forced to remain in Honesdale because she
could not leave without subjecting herself "to I know not what of
scandal—or worse." She had not dared to venture across the mountain
to see Mary Dickinson on her eighty-ninth birthday because she feared
her debtors would think she was absconding and would call her to
account. She pleaded with Butler to comprehend "the horror that en-
compasses me. You may not really care enough for me—as I feared and
said—to find it of any great moment to yourself whether I live or die,
but you have too much heart to subject even an enemy who might
appeal to you—how much more one you know as your faithful friend
—to such a life of torture as these months of delay have entailed....
My head troubles me too much to write as clearly as I wish what I have
said here, but you will anyhow understand that I am in great and
urgent need of relief and change...." She concluded with a request to
see the General when next he would be in New York. "Meanwhile is
it asking too much that you take off from me without more delay...
the thumb-screws that I endure here. There are points reached when
flesh and spirit can endure no more."

Winter wore on to spring and spring to summer, but still Anna was
mired in Honesdale. Butler sent occasional drafts for $100. Then one
day he sent a letter enclosing a news clipping that had caused him much
grief. It was from the *New York Daily Graphic*. The paper had run
an editorial account of Anna's life and recounted her recent misfortunes.
Then the *Daily Graphic* stated:

What makes Miss Dickinson's career so much more interesting
and unique is that she had had many brilliant offers of marriage,
and that to these, flushed with her dreams of ambition, she gave no
heed. It is an open secret that one of these suitors was Benjamin F.
Butler of Mass., and it is the regret of all Miss Dickinson's friends
that she did not listen to the eloquent General. What a distinguished
couple they would have made! General Butler's manners to women

are perfection from the feminine stand point—always gentlemanly, always courteous, always persuasive. A fastidious young woman who spent a winter in Washington has declared ever since that General Butler was the only gentleman she met. That men of brains should have admired Miss Dickinson was not strange. Her fine expressive features, her brilliant conversation, and her womanliness are qualities that are much more striking in her private life than in her public career. Another claimant was the editor-in-chief of a prominent paper, who sought her hand repeatedly. When he allowed harsh criticisms of her theatrical career it was currently stated that these were but kindness masked. To drive, to compel Miss Dickinson from the stage would be the furthering not only of his hopes, but of Miss Dickinson's ultimate happiness.

"My lame and trembling hand bids me stop," Butler wrote, "but I go on." His daughter had sent him the clipping. She was obviously distressed over the report that her father had proposed marriage to Anna. "I care nothing about it," the General wrote, but it pained his daughter and the circulation of a report that he had contemplated a second marriage did embarrass him somewhat. "Will you therefore in the words that your own good sense will teach," Butler asked Anna, "write me a frank denial that I have tried to get another wife so far as you know. I must wish this to come from your pen. Will you do so?"

Anna refused. She would not issue what she said would be a false denial of a report she charged Butler with having originally inspired. His simple request infuriated her beyond reason and she unleashed upon the old man a torrent of abuse and insult that made further relations between the two, even of the most formal kind, utterly impossible. In an emotional frenzy Anna effectually cut off her last means of succor.

It was in this grievous state, tormented, irrational, bitter, rancorous, desperately in need of comfort and affection, that Anna conceived of a dramatic means of rescuing herself from her unending horrors and recapturing her former fame. It was a spectacular scheme; if voiced by a woman of less historical distinction, it would seem to betray delusions of grandeur. With scrupulous care Anna drew up an elaborate plan for a return to the national spotlight.

The year was 1888, and a presidential election was in the offing.

Elections long since forgotten by the public were still treasured campaign memories for Anna. In 1888 Grover Cleveland, the first Democratic President since pre-Lincoln days was running for re-election against the Republican Benjamin Harrison. The Democrat Cleveland suddenly took on in Anna's mind all the evil aspects of her old *bête noir*—General McClellan. In place of the lance that she had countless times picked up to do wartime oratorical battle, she would now wave a "bloody shirt" and venture forth to slay the presidential dragon and the reincarnated Copperheads.

In June, Anna felt well enough to leave Pennsylvania for a brief trip to New York where she sounded out the political situation and sent up a trial balloon. Her visit was duly noted by the *Daily Graphic*: "Miss Dickinson wore a brown street dress and a dark red hat. She seems to have recovered from her serious illness of the winter. 'There,' said a gentleman who observed her, 'is a monument of the ingratitude of the Republican party.'" The editor of the *New York Press* sought an interview to learn Anna's views on current politics and for him Anna defined the issue in the impending campaign: The Negro question, in its old phase, was settled. The new Negro question was the black man's right to a secret ballot, and this was the issue that had to be resolved once and for all. Anna had the facts and figures well in command. By virtue of their control of the Senate and the Administration, ten million Southern whites were governing forty million Northern whites. "Alabama, Arkansas, Georgia, Mississippi, and North Carolina have hardly six and a half million people, yet their 37 Congressmen were elected by 192,000 votes. Enough to return, north of the line, only a dozen members of Congress." Control of the government must be wrested from this Southern command elected by a favored few. The fight could be won the next November if the Republican party made the free ballot in the South the main issue of the election.

The interview was published and distributed widely. Anna returned to Pittston and awaited the response. It was not long forthcoming. The newspapers had picked up the cue and editorials now commented on her statements. The Democratic *New York World* labeled her "a belated Joan of Arc just emerged from a Rip Van Winkle sleep," and charged Anna with trying "to disentomb the bloody shirt." But Republican papers played up her remarks; one paper predicted "an electric success for her and the cause she espouses"; another advanced the suggestion that the Republican National Committee should put her on its list of speakers for the presidential campaign. This was exactly the reaction Anna sought. Several days later when George William Curtis was credited in the press with supplying in a Fourth of July speech at Gettysburg the best keynote for the Republican campaign by pleading for a "free ballot and a fair count in the South," Susan wrote a letter of protest to the *New York Tribune* to point out that two weeks before Curtis' speech her sister had said, "Justice for the Negro this day means the life of the Nation as truly as it meant it in 1863." Susan wrote: "Not Curtis, the Mugwump and free trader, but Anna Dickinson, gave the keynote for the campaign."

Not long thereafter Anna received a letter from Senator Hobart, of the Republican National Committee, asking her to stop in for a talk in New York. Was she interested in doing any speaking for the committee during the campaign? Anna pretended disinterest. Hobart urged her to take part and said she was the only speaker whose services Benjamin Harrison, the party's candidate, had personally requested the committee to secure. The Senator asked Anna to name a figure for which she might consider speaking. Anna replied that she would be willing to do so for $5,000, that being the sum she needed for her mother. The committee was poor almost to the verge of bankruptcy, Hobart said, and could not afford such a price. However, he would inquire of his colleagues on the committee what might be done. Since Colonel Goodloe, head of the Speaker's Bureau was away at the time, Hobart took Anna directly to Matthew Quay, chairman of the committee. Anna's meeting with Quay was strained. Quay offered Anna $20 a night for speechmaking. Anna smiled coldly, reminded Quay that she had once been paid $1,000 for a single speech in their home state of Pennsylvania, and bowed out of the room.

Soon another inquiry came from the national committee. The vice-chairman, Mr. J. S. Clarkson, now asked Anna to see him at the Everett House in New York. He was indisposed with a sprained foot and regretted that he could not visit her himself. Anna called on Clarkson and found him with Colonel W. W. Dudley, the committee treasurer. She related her unpleasant experience with senators Hobart and Quay; Clarkson asked her to forgive the chairman's preposterous offer. It was true that the committee was very poor, Clarkson said, but he was inclined to make the terms as liberal as possible. Anna reminded him that the Pennsylvania state committee still owed her $12,000 from the 1863 campaign twenty-five years before, which she had never been able to collect, and that she was therefore reluctant to make any further engagements without guarantees in advance. She was not inclined to enter the campaign at all, but she would do so for $5,000. "You want to whip the disaffected radical vote into line, to keep the soldiers," Anna told the committeemen. "I have been called one of the Old Guard, a daughter of the regiment. I will make but one speech, with a solitary plaint— 'honest ballot and a fair count.' I will make that speech for $5,000, not one cent less."

Anna seemed to forget that the Republican party of 1888 was hardly the same party she had campaigned for a generation before. It was now the party of big business and would have much preferred a fighting speech for a high protective tariff than one for civil rights. Clarkson promised to consult the other members of the committee. A week later he wrote to say the committee had approved his suggestion to offer Anna $100 a speech for twenty nights. By inducing the committee to go that far, Clarkson said, "the value and effect of your speeches would take care of the rest of the campaign and make it certain that your services would be secured for the whole time.... It is the very best I could do and if you knew what I have had to contend with, you would not call it bad." If Anna would accept the offer, would she be able to make her first speech at the great meeting to be held at Woodstock, New York, on September 5, when senators Howley, Allison (Anna's old friend), and Evart were to speak?

Anna replied that much as she now wanted to campaign for the committee, the offer was below the minimum she could accept. Clarkson was moved by her appeal for more liberal terms. He wrote: "I do understand that it is not all dollars and cents with you, and I want you to know that I fully understand and appreciate it. It makes my own heart ache to know the world has repaid you with ingratitude and worse when you deserve everything fair and generous that it could give."

On September 4, Anna again called on Clarkson and Dudley and final arrangements were made for her to speak. Clarkson said the committee intended "to roast some rich Bostonians and Pennsylvanians. Then we will have some money." The committee offered Anna $125 a night for thirty nights—a total of $3,750—and all expenses for herself and a maid. If Harrison won—about this provision there was later some dispute—Anna would be given an additional $1,250 to bring the total up to $5,000. Clarkson also thought there would be plenty of money available if Harrison won and that Anna would then be able to get at least some of the $12,000 due her from 1863. Anna reminded him of what an old Republican friend had once told her. "Anna Dickinson," he had said, "never wait for your money on the glory of the Grand Old Party for forty-eight hours. If they don't pay you within twenty-four hours after the election, you sue for it."

"Miss Dickinson," Clarkson said, "I pledge you upon my personal honor that you will be paid." Dudley added his assent. Clarkson was so taken by Anna that he struck up a nonpolitical correspondence with her and borrowed a copy of *Aurelian*, which he read and thought wonderful.

Anna returned to West Pittston to prepare herself for the campaign. It was planned that she should make her first speech on September 20 in Richmond, Indiana, and make ten speeches altogether in Harrison's home state. The plans then called for her to come East for ten speeches in New York and possibly a final ten in Connecticut. Anna was all excitement. It was the war all over again, and she was a heroine once again, albeit a forty-six-year-old heroine. She slaved away on the materials for her speeches and took out from her trunks the lavish gowns she had not donned for so many years. This was to be Anna's first appearance as a public speaker in ten years and her first appearance before any audience in almost four years.

Accompanied by a maid named Emma, Anna boarded a train for Richmond, Indiana. She arrived in the city on the nineteenth, and feeling quite ill, confined herself to her room all day. There she "clawed away at her notes," as she later wrote to Susan, and saw various Indiana committeemen who dropped in to wish her luck. When the hour of the speech arrived Anna left the hotel and went to the Grand Opera House. She discovered that the state committee had done an elaborate job of publicizing her speech. The hall was "packed to suffocation" and fully one thousand people were unable to gain admission. The rush to attend was so great that three women were knocked down and a fourth fainted and was carried out by the police. Everyone wanted to see the famous Anna Dickinson—the Joan of Arc of a war that was already history to a whole generation of young people. "It undoubtedly was the most fearful crush that ever occurred in Richmond," noted the local paper.

How shall we say how Anna looked as she crossed the platform when on-the-scene journalists described her in such conflicting ways? One reporter described her as "neatly and plainly attired in black, with jet ornaments and a neat boutonniere in her bosom." Another saw Anna "in a gobelin blue silk princess gown, square in the neck and with open sleeves. A bunch of jacqueminot roses formed a corsage bouquet, and a red, white, and blue handkerchief was pinned to her belt with a chatelaine pin. She wore a ring or two, a pair of slender gold bracelets, a ruby necklace, and dainty ruby earrings. As she stepped on the platform, she seemed slightly pale, but the thunders of applause that greeted her appearance brought a rosy tinge to her cheeks as she smiled her acknowledgment."

Anna faced the vast audience and paused until there was absolute silence. Then she began in a low tone—so low that she could barely be heard by those nearby. Gradually her voice swelled until it filled the room and could be heard distinctly in every corner. It was a hollow voice that had the belligerence of youth, but a logic of madness, an agitated, splenetic rhetoric that stood unfortified on a base of misapprehensions, irrelevancies, and uncontrollable hate. It was a mockery of the genius of her youth, but the audience, in no mood to discriminate sharply between sense and madness, responded to every outburst with frenzied cries of approval. It was an oratorical phantasmagoria.

"It is as true of a party as it is of an army in the field, that it must fight or surrender," Anna began. "We have had the issue marked out and the battle formed for us by the President of the United States, or the hangman of Buffalo." Cleveland had once served as sheriff of his native city. There was a round of applause. "The sole issue on which the fight is to be made, the President and his party have proclaimed, shall be the tariff. There is no other issue in this contest save that of the tariff, so says this tool of aristocracy, ignorance, and stupid domination." She went on to examine the Democratic party's claim to be the champion of the laboring man. "They are the friends of the laboring man," Anna said scornfully, "as they were of the Negro in the past." She called up memories of the war between the states and the cause for which it was fought. "Don't forget," she said, "you who have lived through those days, and you, young men, if you did not know it, know it this night, that the brave, splendid, heroic, martyred souls that went down to the battlefield and the prison pen from 1861 until 1865 did not go to save the Union. The Union that meant degradation of labor, that meant silenced speech, that meant the pollution of the territories. The Union could have been preserved and saved in peace and quiet at home. They went to the front," she declared, "to die for a Union that allows you this day to spit upon their graves. They fought for your rights, the rights of freedom. They fought for a Union that meant the liberties, the rights and power of free labor against the Union that meant its enslavement, the ignorance and degradation of unrequited toil. The power against which they fought tonight has the impudence to come before you and claim your suffrages and your support as your friends."

At this, cries of "Yes! Yes" and "It's the same party!" burst forth from the audience.

Anna spoke for two hours. When she brought the address to its close a tremendous outburst of cheering shook the hall. "No lady orator ever received such an ovation in this city as she received tonight," noted the *Richmond* (Indiana) *Enquirer*.

As might have been expected, the speech stirred a commotion in political circles. Three years later Cleveland still smarted under the appellation of "hangman" that Anna had brazenly pinned on him. Indiana Democrats were furious. "Anna Dickinson's speech," said the *Indianapolis Sentinel,* "was a coarse, vulgar, brutal, insane harangue, full of vituperation and scurrility, and reeking with passion, malice, and hatred." The paper summarized its judgment with more insight than was generally suspected: "The charitable view, we think, is that Anna Dickinson is insane." To which the *Lafayette Evening Call* replied: "Miss Dickinson may be 'crazy' as the gentlemanly (?) *Indianapolis Sentinel* and others of that ilk insist, but the Lafayette Republicans will be much obliged to the national committee if they will just send along a few more speakers for Republicanism who are affected with the same sort of 'insanity.'"

Anna herself noted in a scrapbook, "Were the 4,000 who applauded insane and equally at fault?" To Susan she wrote that she "went on the platform in a sort of whirl—but got through! The house was a tremendous jam. No room for a fly! The Committee, I take it, to be not rejoiced over my non-tariff talk, but the people and the old soldiers, specially, I think were well content."

Anna spent the morning before her next speech visiting a distant relative whom she had not seen in many years. "I had quite a little call on Aunt A.," she wrote Susan, "and gave her your messages of love and had much store of it in turn confided me to be sent." The aunt was rather badly off and Anna was moved by her plight. "Poor, dear, old soul. She seems so kind, so simple, and good, 'tis abominable her own are not everything they ought to be to her." Anna left behind a token of friendship. "I scared out a $10 bill—tho' I didn't know how to do it—but I thought she must not have less, since she possessed about four cents at the time."

On the way to her next speech Anna had an hour's layover at New-castle while the train changed cars and she "was over run by the whole town shaking hands to my discomfort and Emma's horrible disgust. There were mobs of Friends among them—half the town seemed to be of Mammy's 'Queer Sort' who called everybody 'Sister' and 'Brother' and 'Mother' and 'Father' so and so." Also scheduled to speak for the Republicans that day was Frederick Douglass, the famous Negro orator who had campaigned with Anna during the war. It was a meet-ing of old friends. Anna wrote: "Frederick D. wished his love sent to Miss Sue and to the dear old blessed mother 'whom may God long spare.' He is growing a very old man. He is big and noble looking still, but he shows plainly his years." Douglass was to speak before Anna or, as she put it to Susan, "his 'owl was in the afternoon and mine in the evening—in the rink. My stars, but it was hot! I did not hear him, but he stayed to hear me, and, whatever the unhappy committee thought, he said it was 'the only speech he had heard this campaign and that in all the timidity and fear, it made his heart glow,'" The praise pleased Anna, but she was by no means satisfied with the speech, even though the Muncie audience was no less enthusiastic than the Richmond crowd. "All the same," Anna wrote, "the speech might be better. It serves its purpose to make some money anyhow, and it will probably grow. I had a great cram last night."

Saturday, September 23, was to be Anna's main Indiana address—she would speak in Indianapolis, the home city of the Republican presi-dential candidate. That morning Robert Harrison, the candidate's son, called upon Anna with an invitation from his father and mother to lunch with them. Anna visited with the Harrisons, enjoyed with them a meal of fried chicken, and formed impressions of the man who was to be the next President of the United States. After lunch she went for a long drive with the Harrisons. She wrote to Susan: "The house is a handsome and substantial home, but nothing superfine. The dinner was excellent, but plain. Mrs. H. had a shocking bad cold, but was hospitably speechless. For the rest I will ponder and discuss further anon."

Anna's speech that evening was scheduled for Tomlinson Hall, and word of her fiery addresses at Richmond and Muncie had been spread about by the Republican press. Four thousand people jammed into the hall and many stood up and cheered and women waved handkerchiefs when Anna entered. Anna responded to this demonstration with a bow and as the enthusiasm increased she waved her hand in acknowledgment. There was a storm of applause as she stepped forward to begin her speech after being introduced by the chairman as the "Prophetess of the Republican party."

What happened in Indianapolis that night was reminiscent of another exciting night in Hartford, Connecticut, twenty-five years before. Ever since Anna's first speech in Indiana the Democrats had worked fast and furiously to build up a Democratic parade as a counterattraction to her Indianapolis speech, and it was planned to parade ten thousand Democratic supporters down the street past Tomlinson Hall during Anna's talk. It was a noisy parade, and to guarantee that it would not be ignored inside the hall, the Democrats imported a small cannon that kept booming forth from its position on a float. The explosions carried throughout the city and inside the hall the sound was almost deafening. Anna was tracing the record of the Democratic party during the war when the cannon made its first burst and the hall shook. Undaunted, Anna cried out: "It that a Democratic cannon?"

A voice shouted back, "Yes!"

"Well," said Anna over the acrid smell of gunpowder, "all the noise of hell cannot silence the voice of liberty and truth." The audience cheered and applauded. But this was only the beginning of the battle between Anna and the cannon. Each time the cannon boomed, Anna hurled back a volley of verbal gunshot. The audience was electrified by the brilliant display of fireworks from both sides. The cannon roared. "Let them thunder on this twenty-second of September," Anna roared back. "We will thunder in answer on the seventh of November." The crowd cheered. Again the cannon boomed, and Anna returned with a short burst of sarcasm: "Oh, the Democrats of the North are liberal enough with cannon on the side of the South in 1888; they had their fingers on their lips in 1861!"

The cannon calmed momentarily (refueling was evidently in progress) and Anna went back to berating the Democrats of thirty years before. "This slave-holding power said, 'We silence free speech, we muzzle a free press, and put in its place, if need be, of intelligent discussion—'" (here the refueled cannon blared forth lustily and Anna, quick at the draw, completed her sentence)—"'gunpowder.'" Finally Anna came abreast of the Democratic party of Cleveland and pointed to the Southern Democrats in Congress to show how the old Southern aristocracy had once again gained control of the nation. "These few slave masters of the South dominate not simply the South, not merely a section," she declared, "but the whole country through the pliant and subtle service of this dirty tool—the Democratic party." To this expression of contempt the audience responded with loud applause while outside the cannon added to the confusion with another burst, and Anna cried out over the uproar "And the Democratic cannon says 'Amen!' to that statement." This induced a second wave of applause. Anna sighed: "Oh, they are such fools, one has scarce patience to argue with them." The audience laughed with glee.

Reports of Anna's tilts with the Democrats spread rapidly among pleased Republican managers who were not accustomed to having such oratorical skill at their disposal. They felt Anna was stirring up indifferent Republicans and converting young Democrats. Clarkson wired Anna his congratulations and said he and Dudley had been hearing wonderful accounts of her speeches. The chairman of the Wisconsin Republican Committee wanted to book Anna for six meetings. Michigan wanted five speeches. Meanwhile the Indiana campaign roared on. At Crawfordsville Anna was so overrun by the crowd that she had to get out of the hall through a roundabout way. She wrote Susan: "They almost boiled me at Muncie with the tremendous crowd and I took a fine cold. I tell thee as thee will be sure to see I am 'hoarse.' Monday night at Terre Haute I was in the Wigwam and it was a noble crowd —5,000 within and without—listening like mice, but I said I couldn't talk in wigs anymore—no more than clean out of doors. Last night at Lafayette the audience was something *booful*. The place has a very fine opera house and it never was so jammed." Yet, with all the excitement her speeches had created, Anna clearly was gratified to receive Clarkson's telegram of congratulations because, as she confided to Susan, "in myself I have not yet fully the speech I want to make."

At Logansport, four thousand people came to hear her and hundreds were turned away. The rink at South Bend was "literally packed" a full hour before Anna was scheduled to begin. Indeed, the crowd pushing at the entrance was so great that Anna herself could not enter. Finally she was escorted down an alley to the rear of the rink and on to the platform where she was greeted by a "sea of faces," closely packed from the gallery to the floor, filling every nook and cranny of the huge rink. "So large an audience was never assembled within doors in South Bend," the local paper declared. Many came out of curiosity to see the "great apostle of human rights." At Logansport a hostile Democrat slipped into the audience and interrupted Anna, saying that she should take some of the vinegar out of her talk. It was not vinegar, Anna fired back, but the sugar of truth, and "if it sours on a diseased stomach so much the worse for the listener." By the time Anna came to the end of her ten days in Indiana, a Pennsylvania paper declared: "No campaign orator now in the field, with the exception of Blaine, has succeeded in attracting so much attention in a short time as Anna Dickinson."

Clarkson wrote to Susan that the committee was "proud" of Anna's work and that they had been receiving the "best kind of reports" on the speeches. Everything went well until the Michigan and Wisconsin state committees muddled their plans. When Anna made her first Michigan speech she did not know yet where or when she was to speak during the rest of the campaign. "They seem to have things in a fine snarl," she wrote Susan. "I never saw such unbusinesslike people; one thing is sure and that is I am like to lose time."

The Michigan speeches were simply a continuation of the Indiana triumphs. "The houses have been beyond description!" Anna wrote home. In Adrian, 1,500 people crammed into the local opera house, all standing room was taken, and two thousand stood outside clamoring to get in. At Coldwater the same jam was repeated. But Anna had caught a bad cold and the speeches were becoming quite an ordeal to deliver. Reporters commented, however, that her voice held up well and even strengthened as she approached the end of her two-hour talks.

With her schedule completely up in the air, Anna wired Clarkson to complain about the erratic bookings that kept her on tenterhooks from day to day, not knowing where she was going or before what audience she would appear. Also she did not want to go out to Wisconsin, as was planned, for that would waste several days in traveling time. Clarkson excused her from the Wisconsin engagements, advised her to rest for a week and then to come East to make speeches in New York, New Jersey, and Connecticut where she was "much wanted."

Anna still did not know where in New York she was to speak or on what day she was supposed to arrive. She expressed her exasperation at the committee's blundering in a letter to Susan: "I have not yet any word from those remarkable people," she wrote, "and know 'no more than a fool' where I am to go for Monday night." She added petulantly: "Clarkson evidently thinks it is all one whether the campaign work is done now or next year." She asked Susan to send her "one pair of closed drawers and the one little fine flannel undershirt (no sleeves at all) that were in wash when I left."

Finally word came through. YOUR FIRST NEW YORK APPOINTMENT WILL BE AT BATH MONDAY NIGHT, Clarkson wired Anna. He added a conciliatory note of praise: I SEND YOU THE THANKS OF THE NATIONAL COMMITTEE FOR THE SPLENDID WORK YOU ARE DOING. YOU WILL HAVE A CORDIAL WELCOME IN NEW YORK.

Anna packed the local casino when she spoke in Bath, October 8. The following night she addressed the largest political meeting ever held in Corning, New York. To T. S. Pritchard, the country Republican chairman, Mr. H. S. Hull, publisher of the local Bath paper, sent a letter of warning about Anna's speech. "I think, on the whole," she did us harm. Her speech, from an oratorical point of view, was the best I ever heard. It was simply terrific. But she tore the 'bloody shirt' into inch bits; she called Cleveland a hangman, and heaped such vituperation upon the Democratic party as I have never heard before. She was a holy terror.... You want to sit down on her hard, without letting her know that you have heard from me. Tell her that she must not call Cleveland a hangman and that she must not wave the bloody shirt quite so vigorously. She made some splendid points; and if her speech were properly edited, it would be a powerful effort. There never was a speech delivered in the town that created a quarter of the comment, and this morning business was entirely suspended while everyone discussed it.... During the speech some fellow hissed, and she drove him clear down to the middle of the earth. I never knew anyone to be so thoroughly annihilated by a speaker."

Instead of trying to hold Anna back, Pritchard let her have her head and a few days later he received a second letter from the Bath publisher. Hull had changed his mind about Anna's speech. "The more the Republicans here think about her speech," Hull wrote, "the better they like it. I think it did us more good than harm. Nothing of the kind happened here that occasioned so much controversy." Pritchard forwarded Hull's two letters to Anna and added a note of his own: "Your speech was the best ever delivered in Corning and done the Republican party the most good. I can give the names of six Democrats that have come out for Harrison and Morton, the result of your grand speech."

It is no wonder that with such fine, if possibly unwarranted estimates of the quality of her work Anna felt poorly treated when the New York state committee planned her speaking appointments haphazardly. Instead of engagements in large cities over routes that would involve only short daytime train hops, she found herself scheduled to speak on short notice in small towns with an itinerary that required exhausting all-night journeys. After the Corning speech she called a halt. She learned that the committee had scheduled her for Port Jervis, a town she had "positively shut out" in the original plans for the tour. Moreover, she had been signed up in New York City not for the Metropolitan Opera House as promised, but for the Grand Opera House, a small hall. Anna decided to return home for a few days until Clarkson and the committee could straighten out their plans and make the proper arrangements. She was fatigued from the campaign and the uncertainties of her next moves caused her much anguish. Susan wired Clarkson that Anna must rest for two or three days. The improper schedule had tired her out. Clarkson was penitent. The ways of the New York committee, he wrote, "are past all finding out. In reality they very greatly admire Miss Anna and very much depend on her. It is a part of their lack of organization." He cautioned Susan not to let Anna wear herself out. "She is too precious for that. She has done nobly, and we are all her debtors." He closed with the assurance that he would do something with the New York committee and advised Susan to keep Anna at home until she is "really able for New York." The next day, after talking with the committee, he wired: TAKE GOOD CARE OF OUR

SPLENDID WORKER, AND PET HER UP OVER SUNDAY. WE HAVE ALL REASON TO BE GRATEFUL TO HER.

On Clarkson's advice Anna notified the New York committee that she was ready to speak, but that she would not leave home until she had been supplied with the full list of her remaining engagements. Another precious week of the campaign went by without action by the New York committee. Anna lost her temper and wired Clarkson: IS THIS COMMITTEE TRYING TO RIVAL IN MEANNESS THE WAYNE MCVEAGH PENN-SYLVANIA COMMITTEE [of 1863]? Clarkson was out of the city at the time, but he read Anna's telegram on his return and wired her that he would try to "straighten things out tonight." Anna, however, was too upset by what she soon came to believe was the maliciousness of the New York committeemen: they were keeping her on the string without any engagements in order to muzzle her during the precious days that remained before the end of the campaign. She wrote Clarkson on October 19: "It is cowardice at headquarters that is trying to enforce my silence. I will not be silenced." Unless the committee arranged some speeches for her by the next Monday she would speak "through leading Democratic newspapers. There are two ways of talking to Old Republicans with widely different results." She would be in New York the next day.

At Clarkson's urgent request the New York committee went to work immediately and laid out speeches for Anna in ten leading cities, but it was already too late to arrange bookings in each place and only Pough-keepsie and Auburn were actually scheduled. Anna meanwhile stayed at the Everett House and sent notes to Colonel Dudley, treasurer of the national committee, asking him to straighten out the speaking arrange-ments. Clarkson had to leave the city for a time, and in his absence the other committee members completely confused the schedules. They did not inform Anna of her next engagement until the day of the speech when she was abruptly asked to rush off for a speech that evening in Poughkeepsie. Anna balked at this inconsiderate request and refused to go. Mr. J. N. Knapp, chairman of the New York committee, apolo-gized to her for the mistreatment she was experiencing at the hands of his committee. "If I have been in any way careless about advising you, forgive me, but please don't fail," Knapp wrote. "I profoundly respect and admire you—probably as much as any person living." Anna re-fused to speak on such abrupt notice, however, and demanded to know what other engagements had been made for her. Knapp reluctantly canceled the Poughkeepsie meeting at the last minute. He told Anna that only one more speech was definitely settled, the one at Auburn, and that he was still trying to hire a decent hall for her in New York City.

Anna was thoroughly disgusted at the collapse of her campaign plans. She had been engaged for thirty speeches and with little more than a week left before election she had delivered only about fifteen. She wrote to the committee to say that if there was no further work for her, she would like a final settlement of her contract for the thirty nights. In reply came a last minute proposal for two speeches in New Jersey, but the indefiniteness of it only exasperated Anna still further. She had vainly awaited clarification of her plans for ten days. Now she called on Colonel Dudley to settle the contract. The speaking was over. She would tolerate no more indecision and abuse. Dudley paid her $3,750 and expenses, and Anna returned to her room to await the outcome of the election. When Harrison and Morton won, she called on Dudley again to collect the remaining $1,250 promised her in the event of a Republican victory. Dudley recalled nothing of that part of the agreement and refused to give her another penny. Anna appealed to Clarkson and reminded him of his word of honor to have the contract redeemed. But everyone at committee headquarters was already occupied apportioning the spoils of victory and no one could remember anything about a bonus for Anna.

Anna was enraged by this treatment. After several more days of rebuffs she put the whole affair in the hands of Howe & Hummel, New York attorneys. The lawyers felt that they could get the money "without doubt," but Anna would have to stay in the city while they prepared the case. In the interim Anna investigated the possibilities of lecturing again for some lyceum bureaus, but nothing materialized. She remained in New York through the end of November when Howe & Hummel informed her that the Republican National Committee officially denied any indebtedness to her. The case would have to go to court and Anna would be forced to bring to trial the leading Republicans in the nation if she wanted redress. When word leaked out to the press of this development, the Democratic *World* remarked: "If the Republican National Committee is wise or honest it will at once settle the claim which Anna Dickinson has against it.... She was one of the most effective stumpers sent out to enlighten the heathen during the late campaign. Why should a victorious party seek to cheat and defraud one of its ablest advocates? Keep your contracts, gentlemen of the Republican committee. Robbing a woman! For shame!"

Though such an editorial might comfort Anna, it could not budge the committee. There was now no alternative except to go home to West Pittston. She had come forth from retirement with high hopes and a grandiose scheme. After a spectacular success she stood repudiated and mistreated by the men who had hired her. The word "ingratitude" kept ringing in her ears. What evil power was forcing her to return to a town she loathed and to endure a loneliness and poverty she dreaded with all her soul? With a heavy heart she boarded a Lehigh Valley train on a cold December afternoon and set out for Pittston. Only two months before she had been standing on an Indiana platform before the admiring eyes of thousands. Now she was alone and miserable. Were it not for the press clippings in her scrapbook, the whole brilliant, fantastic episode of the campaign would have seemed a nightmare.

CHAPTER 14

"SEND A TELEGRAM TO . . . "

For the next six months Anna seldom stirred from her home for more than an hour at a time. She brooded over her unhappy fate until she came to believe that the whole world had turned against Anna Dickinson, had singled her out to frustrate her every ambition, to grind her down to insignificance. She had been one of the leading orators of the campaign and had been rewarded with abuse. Whitelaw Reid had made fewer speeches, but he was appointed U.S. Minister to France in payment for his services. The Grand Army of the Republic held an anniversary encampment and invited to the celebration the surviving figures of the war, but no one invited "America's Joan of Arc." Real and imagined wrongs fused into a pattern of grievances that circumscribed all of Anna's thinking. A persistent headache kept her from sleeping at night and drove her wild with pain during the day. The liver ailment of the year before returned with renewed misery. It was clear that unless Anna received proper medical treatment she was headed for a total mental and physical breakdown. Susan pleaded with General Butler to give Anna the money for the medical care she so desperately needed. Butler rejected the plea and said he would not answer any further communications from the Dickinsons. This cold rejection incensed Anna beyond all power of self-control; she sent a venomous, almost incoherent letter to Butler, threatening to publish certified copies of his old letters so that you "may testify for yourself in this matter. . . . An honest man in a good cause can have no better witness than himself." But Butler was resolute and refused to help.

Meanwhile Mrs. Dickinson, after lying on her deathbed for months on end, finally passed away, and Anna was left alone with Susan. While it released her from what had become a tedious and wearying burden, the loss of her dear "Marmee" only added to the shock of the multiple miseries that already were unhinging her mind. She became capricious about seeing friends, sometimes refusing to see them at all, other times being very affable. She took long solitary walks; one day in the fall she wandered away from home and got lost in the vicinity of the railroad junction. She had gone out inadequately clad and was brought home shivering with the cold. She was put to bed suffering from the grippe.

Her mind seemed progressively to be giving way. The physical pains worsened and the memories grew unbearable. She would stick out her finger and ask Susan to "pull it, pull it harder." She had lapses of memory. One day she asked Susan to hold a hat while she trimmed the lace, and then stuck the blade of the scissors into Susan's finger. When Susan said, "'See what thee has done," Anna thrust the scissors into another finger. Several days later, observing the bandages, Anna asked her sister, "What is the matter with thy hand? Has thee burnt it?" She had no recollection of the incident. "I am beginning to get afraid about my head," Anna said. "There are times when I can't remember anything that has happened for hours."

The illusion grew in Anna's mind that people were stealing her ideas to profit themselves. When a play called *Sunlight and Shadow* opened in New York, she read the plot and cried out to Susan that it was stolen from an old play of hers. When Charles Dudley Warner, her old friend, published some articles about Colorado in the *Atlantic Monthly,* Anna accused him of stealing his material from her letters of 1873. She was the innocent victim of omnipresent malice. The clinical symptoms of paranoia evidenced themselves one by one, as Anna's imagination magnified and distorted her adversity. The people of West Pittston—"the stupid little town," Anna called it—were beginning to talk. And it no doubt gave the conservative, prohibitionist townsfolk some satisfaction to talk about the disintegration of the New Woman. On a visit to the local dressmaker Anna suffered one of her excruciating headaches and lost all control of herself. She lay on the floor and kicked at the wall as the frightened woman hovered by. On another occasion she asked the dressmaker to pull her fingers and toes to relieve the pain and to put red pepper on her forehead. She raised her dress to show the scar from her Honesdale operation. Word spread that Anna had taken to drink; the local liquor dealer told about delivering gallons of rye whisky and bottles of brandy to the Dickinson house. The one-armed handyman Anna hired to take her out for occasional drives told how Anna asked him to step on her toes and then she felt his legs and said, "That is a good thigh." One night Susan heard Anna scream out in pain, and she called a Dr. Johnson who brought momentary relief. The next time the doctor came Anna pulled his head down and kissed him. Dr. Johnson noted in his record book that she smelled of whisky.

Anna and Susan were both passing through menopause. It was not long before the two sisters began to turn on each other to find a convenient explanation for their unending tortures. At first there was a slight chilling in the intimacy that had always marked their relations. Then there were mutual recriminations that blazed into vicious argument. Anna recalled that Susan had dropped the hot iron on her foot twenty-five years before and blamed her for all the physical miseries she now suffered. "All the trouble I have had and yet to come is from thee," Anna told Susan. "It is all thy fault." Susan lost her patience and unleashed the stores of envy she had secretly harbored for so many years. "I hate thee! I hate thee!" she cried out to Anna, "but for thee *I* would have had a great name and place in the world!"

Early in February, 1891, Anna received a telegram from her lawyers, Howe & Hummel. It stated that her long-postponed case against the Republican National Committee would finally come to trial the next week and asked that she come to New York to testify in her own behalf. To Anna it somehow appeared, for no real reason whatever, that Howe & Hummel (whose law firm was noted for both courtroom successes and behind-the-scene skulduggery) were in a conspiracy with Clarkson and Colonel Dudley to ruin her reputation. "I won't go," she said to Susan in a loud and excited voice. "It is a trap." She wired the attorneys saying she would not go to New York. A few days later, she went to the telegraph office at five o'clock and stayed there until eleven at night, continually writing and rewriting telegrams and destroying them as fast as they were written. Passers-by noted her excited manner and disarrayed attire and glanced meaningfully at each other.

Each day Anna's disorientation grew worse. Now she spent all her time taking all her belongings from the garret and other rooms of the house and carrying them to her bedroom where she strewed them on the floor. She had all the press clippings of her great speeches dating back to the war, all the letters written to her by men of power and distinction. She read them over and over. Susan sent meals up on a tray, which Anna would take in her room. After eating she placed the tray outside the bedroom door. No one was permitted to enter. Then one evening she failed to return the tray. The next morning the breakfast tray was not returned. At noon Anna refused to open the door for any tray at all. She called down to Martha, the maid: "I want whoever these trays belong to to take them out. If they are not taken out I shall throw them out into the street." Susan tried to enter the bedroom to retrieve the trays, but Anna pushed her back. When Susan placed her foot against the door to prevent Anna from snapping it shut again, Anna grasped her by the throat and held her until a hastily summoned neighbor released her grip.

For the next three days Anna refused to touch any food. She insisted that Susan intended to poison her. Fearful of her own and the maid's safety, Susan took refuge with neighbors and called Dr. Heilman, a young physician, who stood watch for one night and then recommended action. Anna's room was now in total disorder. She had emptied the contents of her trunks on the floor and the bedding was in complete disarray. She closed the windows tight and lowered the shades. For three days she did not leave the unventilated, foul-smelling room to eat or drink or wash. She just sat amid a sea of clippings, busily rearranging the faded records of her former fame.

Thus she was found on the afternoon of February 25, 1891—the climax of a life of triumphs and frustrations—when a group of men led by Dr. Heilman battered down the door and broke into the room. "Infamous!" Anna cried out as she clutched her gown about her. "Who is responsible for this outrage?" The men saw a shadow of a woman, hair uncombed and unbrushed, eyes shining with a queer, unsettling glare. They moved in on her, grasped her by the arms as she struggled to free herself, dragged her out of the room, down the stairs, and into a waiting carriage. They drove off down the bare streets to the railroad depot where their captive said to the conductor: "Send a telegram to Governor Pattison and tell him we must have universal suffrage. Send one also to Jay Gould and tell him I want a million dollars at once." They thrust her into the train and pinned her down to a seat. That night Anna found herself in Danville, Pennsylvania, behind barred doors, in the State Hospital for the Insane.

ANNA DICKINSON INSANE! proclaimed the *New York Times* to a startled world. *A RAVING MANIAC,* the *New York Journal* announced on its front page. " 'Poor Anna Dickinson' are the words on everybody's lips today," said the *New York Herald*. Metropolitan reporters descended on West Pittston to query Susan. "Anna is not in a mental institution," Susan declared in an effort to play down the story. "She is merely out of town taking some needed rest."

But the report could not be denied for long. The *New York World* sent a correspondent to Danville and personally confirmed the commitment. Susan now admitted the facts: she had applied to the local director of the poor to have Anna placed in the state asylum as a pauper and a lunatic. Under Pennsylvania law it was possible to commit any individual on the certification of two physicians of five years' registered practice. Neither physician need have treated the patient nor have ever known her prior to the certification. Anna's commitment had been arranged quickly, too quickly in fact. Of the two doctors who signed her papers, one—Dr. Heilman—did not have the five years of practice. The other doctor had never set eyes on Anna before he broke through the door with the other men. Three days after they had accepted their inmate, the hospital authorities discovered the false certification and hurriedly substituted the name of a third doctor who, though he had never treated the patient, had the requisite years of experience. The announcemen of Anna's commitment as a pauper brought messages of sympathy from long-forgotten friends. The Actor's Fund of New York sent Susan $250 and some friends mailed her $350 to use in Anna's behalf.

Meanwhile, behind the barred doors of Danville strange events were taking place. The shock of the seizure, the train ride, and the commitment seemed to have awakened Anna from her violent frenzy. Once again she was all lucidity—the very personification of reason and virtue come to grips with stupidity and chicanery. The asylum authorities had a real problem on their hands. There would later be bitter dispute over the facts of Anna's condition that day she was taken from her room in West Pittston. There could be no doubt, however, about her general orientation in Danville. She was no longer a raving maniac. Outwardly all semblances of mania disappeared, though inwardly the paranoia from which she suffered was probably no less real. What others saw as delusions of persecution were still to Anna's mind palpable truths. The commitment itself, she reasoned, was irrefutable proof of the persecution she had so long suspected. Now she was surrounded by howling lunatics all day and locked in a solitary cell by night. Denied the right to bathe privately, she refused to allow others to bathe her publicly. She responded to all questioning with the single demand that she be released. On the third day she received her first visitor. It was the doctor whose signature was to be substituted for Dr. Heilman's on the certificate. She refused to be interviewed, demanding first that she be released from her heinous imprisonment. This apparently convinced the doctor that she was insane and he hastened to append his name to the papers. Anna demanded the right to communicate with the outside world. She prepared telegrams to President Harrison, General Butler, the former governor of Pennsylvania, Howe & Hummel, and her brother John asking them to relieve her from distress. When no answers came she rightly deduced that the asylum authorities had held up her mail and that she was incommunicado. On one of the walls of the institution she spotted a poster that published, as required by statute, the lunacy laws of the state. She read the poster intently and immediately realized that her incarceration was illegal. She noted that the law directed the authorities, upon request, to forward unopened one letter per inmate each month. Anna sat down and wrote two letters on scraps of paper she had secretly accumulated. She made copies of both. The first letter she addressed to Howe & Hummel. This she enclosed in a second letter addressed to the chairman and secretary of the state board of charities in Philadelphia. Both missives went forward under a single envelope, which bore the explicit direction that it was to be forwarded unopened as required by law.

The letters went through. This is what Anna wrote:

> State Hospital for the Insane
> Danville, Pa., March 17, 1891
>
> Thomas G. Morton, M.D., or Henry M. Wetherill, M.D.:
> Sir:
> I address this letter to either that if the one may be absent the other may read, and I address it with what looks like superserviceable care to make sure of its reaching you at once. The evening I was brought here, Feb. 25 last, I wrote a telegram to my attorneys, Howe & Hummel, and one to my brother, the Rev. John Dickinson, Los Angeles, Cal. Neither was sent, and as I did not care to write letters for in-

spection or indefinite retention I have been held from all outside contact until now.

Will you please forward immediately to Howe & Hummel the letter enclosed and with it papers for which I call by provision of Section 17 of the State Lunacy Law.

I have yet to learn by any authorized statement who is responsible, in fact, or in name, for putting me here. It certainly never was the purpose of the law to interrupt or prevent the communication between a client and her lawyer or a brother and sister even in such a place as this.

If, as I suppose, my sister's finger is in this dish I demand protection from her in the security of my mail, to send and receive—if I have occasion to wait on my attorneys—though I know of no reason for delay there. Certainly none unless of delay in transit.

You will understand that I have no desire to needlessly be held in a place that I would have found hell had not God been here as everywhere. You will probably regard this as sentiment. It is simply the statement of a fact, though all things considered, it has needed a straight head to realize it.

Will you have the kindness to let me know by return mail concerning my request?

> Yours truly
> Anna E. Dickinson

I have kept a copy of the letter to my lawyers which, if there is occasion to use, you can in due season.

> A. E. D.

Within forty-eight hours Anna received a note from Dr. Morton, chairman of the board, acknowledging receipt of her letter, but no reply was made to her requests. Soon afterward Dr. Wetherill, the board secretary, and a lawyer called at the asylum to talk to her. Anna informed the doctor of his legal responsibilities and refused to discuss anything save her immediate release. The visitors declined to do this and went away, saying they would report to the board itself. Anna returned to her cell.

In New York meanwhile, Messrs. Howe & Hummel were in receipt of an amazing 1600-word document written on scraps of paper.

State Hospital for Insane
Danville, Pa., March 17, 1891

To Howe & Hummel:

Gentlemen:

There appeared to be some curious misunderstanding and play at cross purposes a month ago in regard to my suit against the National Republican Committee in your hands. Whatever was at fault then may be found to be so now by finding the solution of the mystery of my journey and incarceration in this place.

So many matters in my life have been marred for me by the explanations and inferences of others, and pre-eminently of one other, that I beg you to suspend judgment yourselves until you see me.... I am taking for granted that you will assume the care of the new cause, since it is one not of dollars and cents but of a life. I have written Drs. Morton and Wetherill to forward you the necessary papers from Philadelphia, on the supposition that you will accept them, and I send this, sealed, through their hands. As you will see (by part 2, section 28 of L. law) this letter can otherwise be indefinitely retained as my telegram too has been.

Briefly, on the 25th of last month (February), while I was in my own room in West Pittston, with the key turned, attending to my own affairs and interfering with no one, with open trunks and a mass of private papers sorted and unsorted on the floor (why the door was locked shall be related later), the lock was burst and the door broken in by a half-dozen men and one woman, part known, part unknown; a young physician, who seems to know little of medicine and less of law, the woman who was with him said she was his aunt; since I am not acquainted with her I cannot vouch for the statement, but would like to have it proven; an old physician, of whom I knew nothing but his name and who never spoke with me save as he stood for a moment in my open doorway; a neighbor and small shopkeeper, the agent of my sister's landlord.... who announced that he assumed all responsibility for what was done; a man never seen before; another man, who said he was an officer, and these supplemented at the train by yet another neighbor of my sister.

My hands and arms were wrenched till they were bruised and the blood oozing from the pores. Knowing I was half-clad, with but a wrapper over insufficient underclothing, an old Autumn wrap thrown around me, a straw hat put on my unbrushed hair, I was torn out of the room, partly dragged and partly pitched down the stairway (my sister and her insolent and dangerous Welsh servant woman, who also has played and is to play further in this miserably done farce-tragedy, nowhere in sight) and into the carriage. All my worldly possessions, my garments, my few jewels, my mass of private and business letters and manuscripts left absolutely at the mercy of those left in possession. From my own home to this door I will tell you later. Enough that at the lonely West Pittston station the regular ticket agent was absent, a young man who left the train a few miles down the road (easily identified) being in his place. No possibility of telegraphing and absolute refusal to put me within 'phone speech of the Western Union agent at Pittston. Again dragged into the train to find the conductor and brakeman, who had been seen.

Again I will stop. I cannot tell the tale in this fashion, and what heed? I know not by what assumed authority all this has been done, and I have been refused any information. Neither has there been any pretense of a "medical examination" nor of "treatment" since I was first here. . . . Directly after reaching here I wrote four telegrams —to your firm, to my brother, the Rev. John Dickinson, of Los Angeles, Calif., and two others. Evidently none were sent. . . . A few back number newspapers have been placed where I could see that someone had kindly notified the public that I was ill; that I was in an insane asylum; that I was sunk in silent stupor, or lost in some slough of despond; that I had been sent here by the commissioners of the poor of the borough of West Pittston, with more of the same ilk. It is needless to answer any of this stuff.

What I want to know is, who put me here? When you know that I think you will speedily find the means to take me away. I have not talked since I have been here. I need all my strength to observe and to live, but I have listened to what has been said to me, the longest sentence I have heard from the Superintendent being, when I said I wished to communicate with my brother, "Do you not wish to write to your sister?"

"How do you know I have a sister," I asked.

"Oh, yes; we know you have a sister," was the reply.

So then, I think we reached here the kernel of the nut. If, as I judge, my sister is in this matter, she has brought at last to an issue the straight and awful test of sanity between us. So be it, and let it be made fairly and openly, and not with the assassin's knife and in the dark. . . . If there is still something back of this I know of no people in the world who will so surely unearth and so certainly destroy it as you. Will you let me hear from you immediately and by messenger. I need help even to leave this place with the door open. While I own or did on Feb. 25, a good many things that cost money, I have not a dollar in the world. I thought never to say it like this. Sure as I live I will repay you in the end. I call myself a resident of New York, and so always register, though I have a deal in Pittston, and in any case take it for granted in some way you can bring this affair within your professional jurisdiction. Since so much has been said in the newspapers already, will you see that the Associated Press has this letter? It has been written on my knee with a bad pen and the tools I could find, but you will be able to read it. It was begun with no thought of publication, but it ought to be in print. I do not know where in California my brother may be, since he is often far from home. In this way he will hear at once. . . .

I ask help from some one rather than to simply hear from you, as before I venture again into West Pittston to look after my property and papers there I need some sort of legal protection in a place where all law and personal safety have been violated, and where I have found all the insecurity of a lonely country town. This is a long letter, but I have thought it better to say overmuch rather than too little, and even now the gaps are enormous that only speech can fill. I am, sincerely yours,

Anna E. Dickinson

My nerve and will are good enough, but my body is sadly tired, and I beg that what you do you will do speedily.

A.E.D.

While Howe & Hummel went to work for Anna's release from Danville by placing her case in the hands of Pennsylvania attorneys, Susan re-entered the picture. She was sorely distressed by all the publicity given to Anna's imprisonment. When the money from the New York friends arrived, she decided to have Anna transferred to a private sanitarium where her sister might be kept away from the intrusions of the press. She had heard of a retreat for invalids in Goshen, New York, called Interpines, which was run by a homeopathic physician named Seward. The niece of a friend had been sent there a year before and was treated well. Susan asked Louise MacDonald, Anna's personal maid of former days, to call at Danville and prepare Anna for the transfer. Louise was the only visitor Anna received at the institution whom she considered a friend. The two embraced each other and Louise cried.

Plans for the transfer were completed. On April 5, five weeks after Anna's commitment, she was removed from Danville. Dr. Seward, accompanied by one or two nurses and armed with a strait jacket, arrived at the asylum. The transfer papers were signed and Anna was bundled off. Throughout the trip to Goshen Anna demanded her release, as she had vainly demanded it in Danville. This time, however, she found an unexpectedly sympathetic and understanding listener. It was not unusual for Dr. Seward to hear asylum inmates protest their sanity and attribute mania to those who keep them interned. But as the doctor listened to Anna he was tremendously impressed with her unfailing command of language. Anna told him a fearful and dramatic tale of injustice. Her knowledge of the law obviously exceeded that of her keepers. Her general orientation seemed, on the surface at least, satisfactory. Dr. Seward was convinced she was sane.

"Miss Dickinson," he told her as she concluded her appeal, "I came to take away a madwoman and find instead a woman of sanity and genius. You are free to go about as you will. I cannot keep you."

Anna wept at the first kindness she had been shown in years. "I would advise you to leave this state else you might be recommitted to Danville," Seward said. He invited her to accompany him to Goshen and to stay at Interpines not as his patient, but as his guest. "I will be glad to proclaim my opinion of your sanity to the world, if you wish me to do so, and assist you in every way I can to see that justice is done to you," he said.

The unexpected rescue from Danville was almost too incredible to be real. It was more like the novels of Dickens she had read in her youth. The tears streamed down Anna's cheeks as she smiled her gratitude.

The news of Anna's release took everyone by surprise. An incredulous press published Dr. Seward's statement that Anna had never been insane

at all and sent reporters off to Goshen to verify his claims. Susan wired
Seward that she would hold him legally responsible for his statement
and for allowing her sister to be visited by the press. After a few days of
rest at Goshen Anna came down to New York with Seward to plan a
campaign to expunge the charge of insanity from her record and to institute legal action against her incarcerators. She called on Howe & Hummel and held a press conference in their offices. One reporter observed
that she sported a large hat with a black feather and had a deliberate
businesslike manner. She spoke in a steady, coherent, and pointed style,
frequently interrupting herself to ask the reporters if she showed any
signs of being out of her mind. The reporters could see none. When
asked to comment on Susan's hand in her imprisonment, Anna said:

> Susan is out of her mind, that is the long and short of it. She is
> not responsible for her actions and she conceived the idea that it was
> I who was insane and she acted accordingly with the ingenuity
> common to people who are insane. You may wonder then that the
> neighbors sided with Susan and helped her to drag me out and
> place me in a carriage and have me driven away to an imprisonment
> that is worse than death. You know what a difference there is be-
> tween life in a great city and in a little duck-puddle of a country
> village where everything stagnates and men and women are given
> over to small local gossip. Well, I do not hesitate to say that I had
> little sympathy with the people in the little collection of houses in
> Pittston. I had nothing in common with them, and because I was
> different from them and seemed to have other than small, petty local
> aims they probably thought my mind was unbalanced and were
> easily influenced by my sister when she conspired against my liberty.

Anna announced that she would take her case directly to the public on
the evening of April 26 when she would lecture on "Personal Liberty"
at the Broadway Theater. She would have much to say about the forces
that had been behind her incarceration that would be of more than passing interest to the newspapers that had branded her a raving maniac
and to the political leaders who had denied her the rewards she had
properly earned.

The *New York World* was fascinated by the sensational developments
in the Dickinson case and dispatched a correspondent to West Pittston

to interview Susan. He sent back a revealing word picture of a woman
who had also known much mental anguish:

> During the hour or more that *The World's* special correspondent
> spent in conversation with Susan Dickinson at the Eagle Hotel in
> Pittston on Friday night, Miss Susan never so much as even by an
> inflection betrayed the slightest trace of affection for the sister whom
> she declares is afflicted by that most terrible of maladies, insanity.
> Not one word did she utter of sorrow or regret that so heavy a hand
> had been laid upon the one for whom she professed to have done so
> much. The burden of her defense against the awful charges made
> by her sister was resentment rather than justification. It betrayed
> antipathy rather than painful surprise, anger rather than love. . . .
> Physically [she] is a mite—almost a midget. Short, slender, and frail,
> she cannot possibly weigh more than 80 pounds, and perhaps not
> nearly so much. Her little hands are painfully thin and her figure
> is angular—exceedingly so. She sits upon the edge of a chair, her
> toes barely touching the floor, and as she talks to one her head is
> slightly bent, but, be sure of it, her eyes are upon you all the time.
> And such peculiar eyes—they are, round, wide open, and furtively
> questioning always. Those eyes have a color not easily described.
> There is a kind of steel that is too light to be blue and too dark to
> be gray, and Susan Dickinson's eyes are of that medium line in color,
> while her glance, shifting now and then, has all the glitter of the
> hard and cruel polished metal. Her face must have been comely
> once, but now the hard lines around the mouth and the wrinkles
> about the eyes and on the forehead indicate care, sorrow, and dis-
> content, as well as possible acerbity of temperament. She wears her
> hair short, like her sister's, but Susan's hair is painfully straight,
> while Anna's has a curl.
> The expression on Susan's face never changes. Sentences drop from
> her lips as if the words were weighed and specific gravity alone were
> to provide against emphasis.

The *World* reporter quoted Susan as saying that she and Anna had
gotten along well until 1873 when Edwin heard Anna scolding her because she could not keep the household expenses within the $250 pro-
vided each month. "I was taking care of the house, acting as a sort of

housekeeper, amanuensis, and maid of all work, all in one," Susan said. "I remember what my brother said. 'Anna, thee must have more patience. Susan takes care of this big house with but one servant, and thee knows thee has had much company. Verily, I do not see how Susan can get along on the allowance thee has made her.'" Susan's memory was also playing tricks with facts, rewriting the record of family squabbles to make it appear that she had always suffered at Anna's hand.

An audience of curious-minded people and newspaper reporters assembled in the Broadway Theater to see and hear the "insane Anna Dickinson." Anna walked on to the platform wearing a magnificent black lace gown, "elegant in every particular." On her fingers could be seen four large and brilliant diamonds; on her ears were a set of earrings she had purchased the day before for $15. Her *tout ensemble* "was worthy of a ballroom," noted one reporter. Anna had made such a good impression at Goshen that George and Sally Ackley, co-proprietors with Dr. Seward of the sanitarium, had volunteered to finance her fight for vindication. Sally Ackley, a shrewd but otherwise rather ordinary woman who dominated her husband, built up a tremendous admiration for Anna—the only person of renown she had ever known—and put all her resources at Anna's disposal.

"I have faced a great many audiences under all circumstances and conditions with many causes to plead that were pre-eminently unpopular," Anna began. "It has always been for others for whom I spoke. But at last I have been compelled to speak for myself. I'm not young, not handsome, not attractive, but do I look like an insane pauper?"

She unloosed a personal and political invective against the Republican leaders with a fervor that at times almost amounted to frenzy. Some people in the audience were convinced they were listening to the mouthings of a madwoman. "Yet," noted one reporter, "Miss Dickinson never for a moment lost self-control. Her smiles were directed to the orchestra space where the reporters sat, when she said again and again, 'Write it down, brothers of the quill!'" Seeing that one reporter did not write down her remarks, she stopped and shouted, "Write it down, cowardly scribe; I'll stop until you do!" She attacked Quay, Dudley, Clarkson, and Cleveland, and read Clarkson's letters to the audience. She attacked the press for branding her insane without investigating the true facts and announced that she would sue the papers for libel. She attacked President Harrison for failing to help her out after she had worked for him. She called the President "a small thing shivering in a large place." She described the luncheon in Indianapolis with the President-to-be and how she had been shocked to see him quarrel with his wife over the arrangement of some fried chicken legs on the serving platter. She attacked John Wanamaker, Harrison's Postmaster-General, and when she reflected on the legitimacy of his first child, a hiss was heard from the back of the orchestra. Anna stopped, poised her hand and commanded silence with her eyes. "You may hiss, if you please," she said, "but are you hissing John Wanamaker or the truth?" It was a pitiful display of empty rhetoric from a mind that had lost all sense of balance and taste.

The climax of her attacks was saved for Whitelaw Reid. Anna told of her youthful friendship with the *Tribune* publisher, now the country's minister to France and the next year to run for Vice-President on the Republican ticket, of his many visits to the Dickinson home, of the pleasant times they had had together. She told how Reid had urged her to speak for Greeley in 1872 and how she had acted on his advice only to suffer great loss. She described the scene in the editorial room the day after the election when Greeley made Reid promise to treat her fairly in the paper, and how Reid subsequently had used the paper to torment her in all her public ventures. She told the audience why it was she had never married the bright young man. Her explanation stunned her listeners, and newspapers, fearful of libel, refused to report it. Anna said she had rejected Reid because he was an epileptic who had inherited the disease from the "tainted blood of his father and the epileptic blood of his mother." She said Reid had often appealed to her mother for advice; that she herself had seen him in an uncontrollable fit; that she had seen him take medicines during one of his spells. He had told her he took powders "to make a man" of himself. He had said he was ashamed of his parents and had made people believe that his mother was dead. "I have seen his mother," Anna declared, "and you can see her, anyone of you who go out to Cedarville, Ohio, can see his mother in man's boots and gray calico wrapper, and gray hair, wandering about the fields of the farm, a harmless lunatic, from epilepsy."

She related stories Reid had told about her at parties, which had been reported to her by unimpeachable witnesses. Reid allegedly had quipped: "It is said about Anna Dickinson that she rejected, she refused me." Then he would say with a voice full of innuendo, "Anna Dickinson never refused anything I ever asked of her," and he told how one night he called on her in a hotel and stayed late, and at four in the morning when the porter came through to gather up the shoes he had scratched his woolly pate and said, "Golly, I always knew Miss Anna had a great head, but I didn't suppose that she wore size 17 shoes."

"Well," Anna replied, "fatherless and brotherless, with no tongue but my own to defend me, I say there are some lies so atrocious they do not need nailing, and beyond that, with the tainted blood of his father on the one hand, and with the insane epileptic blood of his mother on the other, himself between, taking as he himself asserted medicines to make a man of himself, it was a perfectly safe thing for any woman, however frail her virtue, to leave him inside of her door and his shoes outside for a night, and present a perfectly clean bill of health and morality in the morning!"

The audience was repelled by these insensate statements. "Is there any disgrace or discredit in my saying this?" Anna cried out. Some voices in the crowd came back with "No! No!" and there was a volley of cheers. "The eternal infamy," Anna concluded, "is in the unspeakable wretch who has compelled me to make such a statement here." She announced she was now ready to bring to the bar of justice all the men who had so greatly wronged her. The members of the Republican National Committee would soon have to appear in court to answer her charges. She was filing suits in New York and Pennsylvania courts against everyone who had anything to do with her incarceration, and every newspaper that had libeled her name. With this show of defiance, Anna left the platform.

CHAPTER 15

VINDICATION: EIGHT TO FOUR

SCRANTON, PA., MARCH 30 [1895]—If Anna E. Dickinson is mad, then there is an element in madness that should be courted rather than dreaded. For two days this most celebrated woman—this most wonderful creature—has occupied the witness box of the United States court, sitting in this city, a wonder to judge, jury and lawyers. Thousands of Scranton's best citizens—male and female— have fought, struggled and begged for admission into the courtroom to hear this great woman in her suit against John Courtright, George B. Thompson, Allan Eggleston, Dr. John S. Heilman, Dr. Gideon Underwood and Henry Bryden, all of Pittston, who are charged by the plaintiff with illegally placing and detaining her in an insane asylum. Miss Dickinson was represented by Judge Dailey, of New York, and Hon. W. S. McLean, of Wilkes-Barre. But she was even greater than her great lawyers. Her recital of her arrest and confinement in a mad house was thrillingly dramatic; her portrayal of the awful anguish and sufferings she endured mentally and physically were pathetic. Women wept with her and strong-hearted men stood appalled. For four hours she continued the narrative, during which time a pin might be heard to drop in the courtroom, save every now and then, when Major Warren, of the opposing counsel, objected to conversations which the witness endeavored to introduce.

But when the cross-examination came and Miss Dickinson was turned over to the major, greater than ever was her intellectual superiority displayed. Major Warren was a mere child in her hands. It was she who cross-examined, and for a time turned a very sad and solemn case into a roaring farce. She analyzed every word and every sentence the major used in interrogating her, and picking out the subject words of every sentence asked the opposing counsel which definition of the word he intended. She analyzed to a nicety and decidedly puzzled the gallant major, who, after five hours, gave up the cross-examination without gaining one material point. Her command of words, and the exactness with which she used words, phrases and sentences was a liberal education to those who heard her. A sad feature of the case was to see her brilliant sister, Susan, at the defendant's table, opposing the plaintiff—the star witness against her. It was sister against sister. One battling for what she believes her rights, and the other assisting strangers against her sister.

Thus wrote one correspondent at the spectacular trial of Anna Dickinson vs. her incarcerators. "She was the most brilliant witness ever on the stand in this city," wrote the on-the-scene reporter of the *New York Herald.* The chief defense attorney admitted publicly that Anna was "the most difficult witness he had ever attempted to handle."

For four years Anna had impatiently awaited her day in court. Exasperating legal delays had repeatedly postponed the trial. It was three years since her suit against the Republican National Committee had been argued before a jury in the New York Supreme Court. Anna had faced Colonel Dudley with pint-sized, mustached, tricky Abe Hummel at her side. "Few women at 50 succeed in retaining so youthful an appearance as Miss Dickinson presented," the *New York Times* had noted. "There was nothing in her manner to show that she was not as fully possessed of her faculties as ever," commented the *World.* When Anna had gone on the stand and taken the oath, she had looked at the judge "with those wonderful eyes of hers in a way which almost embarrassed him." The jurors had been unable to free themselves from the fascination of the woman in the box who, in the presence of an audience, had always been captivating. "Those who were there say they never saw and heard so dramatic a witness. Her clear, resonant voice seemed to vibrate in every corner." Hummel, in a clever move, asked Anna to read Clarkson's letters to the jury. "No one who did not hear her can form any adequate idea of the wonderfully dramatic way in which she read them," a reporter had written.

Colonel Dudley had taken the stand for the committee. He confirmed the basic facts of the contract except for the additional $1,250 in the event of a Republican victory. Abe Hummel began his cross-examination.

"Mr. Dudley, did you not leave the State of Indiana on account of an indictment against you?"

Dudley looked savage, but made no reply. His attorney objected to the question and Hummel withdrew it.

"Did you leave the State of Indiana on account of any charges made against you?"

Dudley gave him a black look and made no reply.

"Were you charged with corrupting voters?"

No reply.

"Are you known by any other name than that of William W. Dudley?"

"No."

"Have you not been called "Blocks of Five Dudley?'"

The witness refused to answer and the crafty Hummel released him. He had established through innuendo what he could not prove with facts.

Suddenly the trial had come to a halt. The committee moved to dismiss the complaint on the ground that Anna had sued the committee as a whole whereas the evidence was really against the individual committee members, and any contract the committee had made with Anna was "illegal, null, and void" because an obscure provision of the law forbade the committee from spending any money for campaign speeches. The committee argued in effect that Clarkson, Quay, and Dudley had all broken the law in hiring Anna to speak for Harrison and therefore she could not force payment from them. Hummel jumped to his feet to object to the defense's "pleading the baby act," but the judge ruled for the defense on this technicality and the case was dismissed. The *World* had run an extra edition to announce the unexpected turn and the *Sun* had published an editorial berating the Republican leaders for not paying Anna "the money which they promised and she demands. Points of law and the inexperience of a woman in making a business contract may enable them to get off, but they had better take the money out of their pockets at once and hand it over to the lady." The committee had shown none of the suggested generosity, however, and Anna had sought revenge by applying for a speaking assignment to the Democratic National Committee. But the Democrats could not forgive or forget her bitter attacks of 1888 and her present difficulties and declined the offer.

Then Anna had turned with a vengeance to the suits against the Pittston people and the New York newspapers. A. H. Dailey, a distinguished attorney who had served on the Brooklyn Appellate Court for thirty years, was persuaded of the justice of Anna's claims and accepted the case without fee, paying out of his own pocket the necessary costs of filing legal suits. He invited William L. McLean, a prominent Wilkes-Barre lawyer to join him as Anna's counsel. "She is now without means," Dailey wrote McLean, "but has lost none of her old-time energy or ability, but is in the position of a person who has lost the confidence of the community through plotting of enemies, adverse circumstances and misapprehensions, based upon assumptions of fact which have no foundation whatsoever." The world believed that Anna Dickinson was a raving maniac, and, as such, properly confined in the Danville Asylum for the Insane. "The defendants, as near as I can learn, will defend on the ground that Miss Susan told them that her sister was dangerously insane and that she (Susan) wanted them simply to assist in getting her safely on the train. We can get very little, if any help here in the nature of evidence, as to the state of Miss Dickinson's mind at the time she was swooped up by these chivalric gentlemen defendants, and will therefore have to depend largely upon the testimony of Miss Dickinson and what we will be able to draw out of the defendants at the trial."

"I am very positively of the opinion that Miss Dickinson has good cases against all of the defendants," McLean had written to Judge Dailey after studying the facts. "I think her own testimony will aid us very materially." He accepted the case and filed suits in Anna's name for trespass and false incarceration against the men who broke into her room, the doctors who signed the certificate, and the superintendent of Danville. One hundred and twenty-five thousand dollars were sought in damages. McLean wrote to Anna to say that he had spoken to the defendant's lawyers. "They said if the suits are pushed, many things would have to be told that would be disagreeable to you. I replied you knew all their plans and schemes and that you were brave and would give them an opportunity to air themselves. I think these people are sorely troubled."

"I see by this morning's papers that the suits are entered, and I breathe the freer for it," Anna had written McLean when the papers were served. "I have been almost smothered for two years. In some way I wish the atrocious stigma of 'indigent lunatic' taken off the books at Danville—the record corrected. I was neither 'mentally impaired' when I went there, nor 'improved' when I left.... I do not want revenge. I do want justice all round and with it money enough (which I am afraid you will not get out that little valley alone), not only to make good the shattered plan of a life in my own country, but to have the means and the tools to seek fortune elsewhere." McLean urged Anna to stick to the Pittston suits as her only means of vindication. "If you prevail in your suits," he wrote Anna, "whatever is written upon the books at Danville will be of no effect whatever and all slurs against you with which the newspapers were flooded for some time after you were kidnapped and railroaded to the Asylum at Danville will be wiped out."

When the Pennsylvania cases were over, there would be an opportunity to obtain justice in New York courts. For falsely branding her a maniac, the *New York Journal, World* and *Press* would each be faced with $50,000 libel suits.

Then had come the long legal delays. The Federal Circuit Court for the Western District of Pennsylvania in which the case was to be tried had only two annual sittings in Scranton. Each time Anna's case was ready for trial the defendants succeeded in obtaining a postponement. In March, 1894, at the spring term of the court, Anna had gone to Scranton with Judge Dailey and McLean, but the defendants did not show up. The two doctors who signed the certificate were both too ill to be present and their counsel asked that the case be postponed until they were well enough to attend. Judge Dailey protested bitterly: the case had already been postponed three times. But the court had ruled for the defense and laid the case over until the fall term.

The long delays were deeply unnerving to Anna. She had very few friends left in the world and she began to quarrel even with these. She was abrupt in speech and repelled all efforts to help her. One friend was so surprised by Anna's unaccountable behavior that she was "half-inclined to believe her insane, as so many here declare her to be." Even Sally Ackley, who would give her life for Anna, so great was her love and devotion to her, suffered the whiplash of disaffection. But Sally was somehow so infatuated with Anna that she could not desert her whatever the provocation. Anna squabbled with Dr. Seward who by now had probably revised his judgment of Anna's state of mind. When his guest left Interpines, Seward held on to the papers and effects she had stored there, demanding payment of board and medical care. Anna filed a suit of replevin against the doctor and recovered her property. She moved to New York and took a room for herself at $7 a week a few blocks north of Washington Square and only a short distance from the scene of her greatest successes—Cooper Union. An old friend got her a booking to deliver "Jeanne d'Arc" at Asbury Park and that evening she was in her old glory and richer by $125. Otherwise she was forced to live from hand to mouth. Judge Dailey tried to cheer her up by securing an invitation for her to give a free reading or lecture before a Brooklyn club, but Anna turned the offer down. She snapped: "There is nothing at present that can be of any service to me while awaiting 'the law's delay' but money, and money there is none in these parlor entertainments. If this sounds mercenary I can only say that I have been forced to keep step with the spirit and music of the age. When I see my way to some proper work and reasonable pay, I will go quickly to 'fill the bill,' but I do not care to spend time and strength and money for suitable belongings, for naught but 'empty breath.' "

She could not stay in one place for more than a few months at a time and her few friends found it hard to keep track of her. Then she disappeared. Whether she had lost her mind or was in a state of perpetual intoxication, no one knew. Judge Dailey was forced to seek a delay of the trial. Then, as suddenly as she vanished, she reappeared some months later, sound in body and seemingly so in spirit. And finally the day of reckoning was at hand. For the first time in four years Anna would meet Susan face to face and would confront the men who had seized her. There would be an audience of twelve men to whom she could tell her story. On March 25, 1895, in the packed federal courtroom in Scranton, with batteries of reporters present from New York and Philadelphia, with fashionable ladies carrying sandwiches to tide them through the day, the trial of Anna Dickinson vs. the people of West Pittston got underway.

At the clerk's bidding everyone in the courtroom rose and the Honorable Marcus W. Acheson, the presiding judge, a mild-mannered, elderly man, entered. In the well of the court, seated at the plaintiff's table were Judge Dailey and Mr. McLean and their client. Anna was a bustle of activity as she gave last-minute instructions to the attorneys. She was dressed smartly, her hair freshly waved, her ears adorned with attractive earrings. She had gotten somewhat heavier with the years, but there was still a trimness of figure and a gracefulness of motion. Across the well at the defendants' table Major Everett Warren, a small, self-satisfied looking man with a sharp nose, full mustache, and pince-nez, chief defense counsel and president of the Young Men's Republican League of Pennsylvania, talked quickly with his associate Mr. Ferris. Seated with the defendants and occasionally joining their nervous conversation with a remark or two was Susan Dickinson, sixty-two years old now, tiny of body, neat and plainly dressed. The two sisters, though hardly more than ten feet apart in space, never once looked in each other's direction. The trial began.

McLean called on his client as the first witness for the plaintiff. Anna took the stand knowing that all eyes were on her. She made a dramatic figure as she looked over the jury one by one, surveyed the audience of hushed, eager spectators, and took the oath in a firm and resonant voice. At McLean's request, she reviewed for the jury some of the facts of her public career. Starting from her birth in Philadelphia, she gave a perfectly thrilling account of her life. The jurors and spectators listened wide eyed with awe as the war of thirty years back came to life in the thrilling retelling of events from the lips of a woman who had shaped some of the events herself and who possessed a magnificent gift of speech. They heard of McClellan and Lincoln, of the boys in gray, of fugitive slaves, of the excitement of a nation rent by civil war. Anna told of her work in the New Hampshire and Connecticut campaigns, of her speech in Congress, of her first meeting with Lincoln. The jurymen held on to every word that came from Anna's lips; they felt they were in the presence of greatness. Anna told them how she became Queen of the Lyceum and how she had earned over $20,000 a year from her talks, how she had given up the itinerant life with its night journeys, the lack of sleep and physical discomforts, and how she had to overcome the Quaker prejudices of her mother before she could go on the stage. How she had suffered through all these years the torture of sciatica, muscular fatigue, and bodily ailments that finally required the operating table. She told how she had gone into the campaign of 1888 for the "sole and only purpose of keeping the roof over the head" of her dying mother, and how she had returned home to watch by her mother "till in the following spring she died."

She had spoken without interruption for almost four hours by the time she brought her narrative up to the afternoon of February 25,

1891, and described in vivid detail how she was working on her papers when an "outrageous, infamous assault on her person and property" was made. With meticulous chronology she told how the defendants had seized her and railroaded her to Danville. She gave a brilliant word picture of her entrance into the asylum, the indignities she was forced to face, her first meal with the lunatics, and her first night in a lonely madhouse cell. At times she faltered in her testimony and her voice broke into sobs. Tears could be seen streaming down the faces of the members of the jury. Anna regained her composure and again the clear bell-like tones rang forth in defiant and heart-stirring statements. It was a dramatic monologue in the fullest sense. "I was," she said, "refused certain things necessary to my physical welfare, and cast into the little room and the door locked on the outside."

Major Warren objected to any picture of the treatment offered in Danville, but McLean urged that the witness had the right to tell how she had spent the first night, "whether in peaceful slumber or in agony of mind and body." The court overruled Warren's objection, and McLean asked Anna to "explain, as briefly as possible, how you spent the first night."

Anna's reply was simple, direct, and conclusive: "It was a night in hell." She resumed her narrative and described her release from Danville, the trip to Goshen, and how she went down to New York City to tell the world about the injustice done her. Since her incarceration she had lost lecture opportunities worth thousands of dollars, she told the jury. Finally she brought her tale of injustice to a dramatic close and when she ceased, the enraptured spectators responded to her plea for justice with ringing applause. The demonstration caused Judge Acheson to start up in anger, and order was quickly restored.

Now it was Major Warren's turn to cross-examine the witness. He set out to destroy the impression Anna had made on the jury by pointing out discrepancies in her story, by unnerving and embarrassing her, by confusing her with contradictions, all in the hope that she would fly into a rage that would convince the jury of her essential madness. But the witness would not be awed by a pointed finger, a booming voice, and insinuating questions.

Warren pointed to the woman sitting with the defendants and asked the witness if she recognized her. Anna refused to answer until the woman was told to stand up. Susan rose to her feet and stared

Anna Dickinson

Dr. John Hileman

Susan Dickinson

Dr. Underwood.

Mrs McDonald, Anna's Oldfriend

Judge Daly, Anna's Council

Mrs Ackley, Anna's Friend

Most Conspicuous
Parr of the jury during the Trial

Anna Addressing the Jury

From the *Elmira Telegram*, March 31, 1895

coldly at her sister. Anna returned the look, her own face impassive. "That is Susan Dickinson," she said.

"She is your sister, is she not?" Warren asked.

Anna refused to answer.

"Isn't she your sister?" Warren persisted.

"She is my mother's daughter."

"Then she is your sister, isn't she?"

Anna's eyes flashed hatred. "Well, in flesh and blood, I presume she is. She was born of my mother."

Warren then tried to show that from 1885 until her commitment to Danville, Anna had made regular and excessive use of alcoholic stimulants. This Anna denied. The courtroom broke into laughter when Anna forced Warren to be very explicit in his questioning.

"Miss Dickinson, do you indulge in liquor?" Warren demanded.

With an offended air, Anna fired back, "Sir, what do you mean by 'indulgence'?"

Warren's reply was lost in the laughter.

"Indulgence, sir," Anna went on, "means luxury. No, sir, I never indulged in alcohol as a stimulant."

"What *do* you use liquor for?"

"As a medicine and as a bath," Anna replied.

Warren decided to change the subject. "Didn't the leading papers criticize your play, *Anne Boleyn?*"

"What do you mean by leading papers?"

"The *New York Tribune*. Did it not criticize your play?"

"Criticize, sir, means to analyze," Anna said. "The *New York Tribune* did not criticize me, it abused me, and it sent William Winter, as he himself said, to Boston, 'to tomahawk Dickinson.'"

Warren chose another tack. He queried Anna about her life in West Pittston in an effort to show that her activities were those of an unbalanced or drunken woman. "Major Warren," Anna said, pitching her voice so that it carried to every corner of the courtroom, "kindly look me in the eye like an honest man when you ask me questions." Warren wanted to know if she had not gone riding with a man named Eggleston while intoxicated; if she had not pinched him, and if she had not asked him to pinch her toe. Her answer was no; she had hired Eggleston to drive her about for her health and had paid him for it. Wasn't it true that she had stabbed her sister in the hand with a pair of scissors and had made her bleed? Anna replied that her hand slipped, and whatever blood was seen on Susan's handkerchief the next day came from a nosebleed. Wasn't it true that she had rushed into the street after her cook only partially clad with a knife in her hand? No, it was not true; she had not rushed into the street, she had stood in the doorway; she was only partially clad, but she was properly clad; and she had no knife. Had she not imagined that everyone from the President of the United States down was conspiring against her and attempting to poison her? No, Anna replied.

"Do you remember saying President Harrison, the national committee, and the press of the country were conspiring against you?"

"I never talked to any man about the press conspiring against me. I never used the phrase. I said some of the papers were abusing me."

"Do you recollect using any profanity?"

"No, sir."

"Not even *damn?*"

"I have said, 'May the Almighty damn so and so,' just as if I might say 'May the Almighty bless somebody.' "

"You used the reverential damn?"

"Most emphatically."

"Didn't you call Martha Brown, the servant, a damn liar?"

"I called her a liar to chastise her. I did not use the word damn."

"Had you no means to provide for suitable treatment for the condition you were in?"

"What condition was I in? What is suitable treatment?"

"Had you the means to provide for yourself?" Warren snapped impatiently.

"I had means," Anna replied coolly. She had some money in the bank and some jewels upon which she could readily realize.

Major Warren was insistent. "You were not on pleasant terms with your sister, Susan?"

"What do you mean by 'pleasant terms'?"

"Well, agreeable."

"She was certainly not agreeable to me. I don't know what I may have been to her."

"Didn't you refuse to eat the food sent you?"

"No one sent me food. I was not a beggar. I had food in the house."

Warren decided that his cross-examination was not getting any place and released the witness. Anna stepped down and McLean called to the stand Mrs. Jennie Winterstein, an attendant at Danville, who testified that she saw Anna in the asylum and the plaintiff had seemed sane to her. Sally Ackley told how she had gone to Pittston in 1891 to recover Anna's properties and related her conversation with George Thompson, one of the defendants, in the Pittston bank where she called to get Anna's jewels. "While we were looking over the gems," Sally said, "Thompson remarked to the jeweler, 'You are not in the habit of examining stage jewels?' and the jeweler answered, 'These are genuine.'" She told how Thompson was the only person in Pittston she had heard say that Anna was insane.

Louise MacDonald testified that she had seen Anna before she was taken to Danville and four weeks later when she was in the asylum. "Before she was taken away she looked better than she does now," Louise said, "and she was as cheerful as ever. When I saw her condition at Danville, I had to cry, she looked so bad."

Major Warren tried to shake Louise in cross-examination. He asked her if she had never seen Anna drink whisky. Louise snapped back that it was not her business to watch what Miss Dickinson drank. Warren put the question again, and Louise amused the spectators with the reply that if she saw some liquid in a glass she could not swear whether or not it was whisky.

"Did you ever hear Anna say great people were jealous of her?" Warren asked.

"They *were* jealous of her," Louise said.

"How do you know?"

"Why, from remarks that were passed by other women."

"Who are these people? What women passed remarks?"

"Oh," said Louise, evidencing disgust for any of the New Women except for her former mistress, "the women, of them I know nothing. Some of them ain't of much account."

Now it was time for the defense to present its case. Mr. Ferris made the opening address. His task, he said, was not a pleasant one, as he had known the Dickinson sisters for several years. It was Anna who had dragged his clients into court, however, and forced them to tell the truth, distasteful as it would be. He outlined a damning set of charges the defense would try to prove: that during the summer and fall of 1889 Anna exhibited undue familiarity with men for a woman

of her standing; that she threw kisses to men in public places; that
she addressed one man as an "angel" and grabbed another man above
the knee; that she complained of violent pains in the head and claimed
to have a special nerve in her body that other people did not have.
All the sordid, shameful facts of Anna's last years in West Pittston
were reviewed for the jury to hear. Ferris told the court how Anna
went about in public in a loose wrapper, in garments unfit for the
season; how for several days she locked herself in her room and
refused to take medicine, eat, or drink, declaring the food and medicine were poisoned. All these things came to pass as a time, Ferris
said, when Anna was experiencing a change of life. That physical
and emotional shock acting on a supersensitive intellect had brought
on insanity.

"There is no middle ground," said the defense attorney. "Anna E.
Dickinson, this celebrated, this great woman, who has no equal on
the lecture platform of this country, is either a degraded woman or
was insane at the time of her confinement in Danville. Is she a
degraded woman? No. Surely she would not be cursing, kicking up
her heels indecently and acting in the disgraceful manner if she were
a sane woman. This lady, for she is that, this refined, unfortunate
woman—for we contend that she is unfortunate—would not be chasing
after servant girls, choking her sister, and going on the streets im-
properly dressed if her mental balance was as it should be. Can you,
gentlemen of the jury, imagine Anna E. Dickinson, with her great
mind coming down under natural circumstances to the lowness of a
harridan and a brawler? Surely the only answer is as we represent
what she was at the time of her detention at Danville."

It was an eloquent and forceful address. Anna's face flushed at the
charges and she wrote brief notes to McLean on each of Ferris' points.

As everyone knew, the mainstay of the defense was the plaintiff's
sister and attention now focused on Susan as she took the witness
stand. Under Ferris' promptings, Susan gave her version of Anna's
career. Prior to 1889, she testified, Anna had great genius, but was
of a very nervous temperament, which she could not always control.
After her theatrical failure and on account of the harsh treatment of
the New York press, Anna became more irrational. While she was
in Elizabeth, New Jersey, Anna wrote to her that she wanted to go
into the theatrical business again and wanted money to cross the

Atlantic to consult Henry Irving. Although Anna claimed not to have lost any money in the theater, Susan testified that it was through her financial aid that this was possible. She recounted the difficult years of Anna's illness, and told of Anna's need for money to pay for surgery. "I told her she ought to go to the Republicans for it since she had done so much for them. One night in 1889 I heard her scream as if in great pain, and Dr. Johnson was called. Subsequently she went to Philadelphia for treatment, and on her return brought a man named Benedict home with her. He remained five weeks, and when he went away Anna was so irate she locked herself in a room and refused to say good-by." Anna wasted money on dresses and her breath always smelled of whisky. Susan testified that her sister used chloroform almost constantly for a year to enable her to sleep. She concluded her testimony by describing the days preceding Anna's commitment. She swore that Anna refused to take food, had grabbed her by the throat and threatened her, and that she had become afraid to live under the same roof with her sister. "I have not talked to Anna since she was taken to Danville four years ago," Susan said coldly, "and in view of her behavior toward me and others who genuinely tried to help her, I never shall."

After Susan came a succession of defense witnesses. Martha Brown, the servant girl, told how the plaintiff swore at her. One day Miss Anna had come into the kitchen in search of a loaf of bread for a pudding. "She took the middle out of the loaf," Martha said, "and threw the crust into the stove. I said that was a sin, and she said, 'D—— you, mind your own business.'" The Thursday before she was taken to Danville Anna had rapped on the balustrade and called for her. "She asked for a lamp. Then she ran downstairs and I ran out. When I stopped running and looked back, I saw Miss Anna walking back to the house. She called after me, 'Come back, you little devil!' When I returned to the house, Miss Anna was eating supper. The afternoon before she was taken to the asylum she called me upstairs. I saw her take Miss Susan by the throat when Miss Susan tried to enter her room."

Mrs. Stanton, the local dressmaker, took the stand. Anna had begun to appear strange to her when she complained of severe pains and asked her to pull her fingers and toes. "She threw herself on the floor on her stomach and kicked hard and furious. She laid there over an hour." Sometimes, if the dresses did not fit she would rip off the trimmings and say, "D—— the thing." Once she loosened her clothing and showed her a scar, saying "the d—— doctors cut me all up."

Mrs. Iva Marcy, the dressmaker's daughter, corroborated the story as did Nellie Ellsworth, one of Mrs. Stanton's dressmakers. When Anna showed the scar she said, "The d—— knives did it."

Mrs. Susan Glenn said that she was with the Dickinson family in 1889; that alcoholic stimulants were brought to the house; that she once carried a two-quart jug to Anna's room; one time in the evening while preparing to take a walk Anna talked to her in a manner she did not understand. On cross-examination the witness denied Judge Dailey's insinuation that she herself took "nightcaps" each night before retiring, but did admit she took brandy and sugar several times upon Anna's insisting. She added that Anna was given to extreme statements, that she had said nearly all actresses were vile women and that some actresses had improper relations with their managers.

D. W. John, a liquor dealer of Pittsburgh, swore he delivered gallons and half gallons of whisky to the Dickinson house between 1889 and 1890; also porter by the dozen and half dozen, and brandy by the bottle.

Mrs. Jemmia Griffit, a resident of West Pittston for forty years, admitted she had only a very slight acquaintance with Anna. Susan had asked her to help get Anna ready for the asylum, and she had been with the party of men who broke into the room. She thought Anna was insane because she had acted queer and refused to go quietly.

Mary Beischline, of the Danville asylum, swore she believed Anna was insane. "She called me a fiend when I forced her into the bath," she said. Anna was always writing, and the witness thought that signified insanity.

Henry Bryden, one of the defendants, swore he saw Anna walking the streets very lightly clad for winter weather. Yes, he had broken into her room with the party. His object had been to help take her away, but he wouldn't do it again.

"I don't think you will," interjected McLean.

Dr. Underwood, the Pittston physician who signed the certificate of commitment, took the stand. Anna's state was the worst he had ever seen. No, he didn't examine her, but her glare satisfied him she was out of her mind.

Dr. Johnson testified that he had given Anna a prescription for whisky when she asked for it. Once when he called at the Dickinson house Anna was so glad to see him that she pulled his head down and kissed and hugged him. In reply to a question from Judge Dailey, Dr. Johnson admitted that he was a Prohibitionist, but denied that his testimony was influenced by his beliefs about liquor. Dr. Heilman swore that he once saw Anna all bedecked with jewelry, and that she smelled strongly of whisky. She had confessed to him that she drank to excess. Once she was so intoxicated she could not see him clearly. Dr. Meredith, superintendent of Danville, testified next. In answer to a hypothetical question, he said Anna's behavior showed that she was suffering from paranoia, that she was still suffering from the same disease, and that her condition now was the same as when she was taken to Danville.

The defense rested, and Miss Winterstein was recalled in rebuttal by McLean. She had been an attendant at Danville and she swore that Anna ate of the food offered her and appeared very ladylike, and was very quiet and kind while at the asylum. She saw no violent actions on Anna's part.

Then Judge Dailey put Anna back on the stand for redirect examination. Anna denied she had ever taken intoxicating liquors or alcohol to excess. If she had upon occasion seemed to bear an odor of alcohol it was because she often used whisky for body massages and as a toilet water.

"Is it true, as Dr. Meredith testified, that you are now in the same mental condition as when you were in the Danville asylum?"

"I hope so," was the reply. "My surroundings are somewhat different, however."

"Tell the jury whether there is any truth in the statement by Dr. Johnson regarding undue excitement on your part," Judge Dailey asked.

"It is a filthy lie, manufactured for the manifest purpose for which it was used in this courtroom," Anna said. Yes, she had kissed him on the forehead as he leaned over the bed to take her temperature. "I was grateful to him for relieving my headache, but in the light of the testimony given by him, in the presence of this court I ask pardon of God and man for this act."

Who was this man Benedict Susan testified the plaintiff had brought home with her from Philadelphia? Benedict was an old friend of the family she had known for over ten years, Anna said, and she had invited him to spend some time at her home after her mother died. He was a writer and Susan had one of his pieces printed in a Pennsylvania newspaper. When he overstayed his visit, she had asked him to leave.

Major Warren returned for a brief cross-examination. The attorney was asking Anna about the way she was treated at Danville and had expressed surprise that she received no kindness there when Anna interrupted him.

"You have been in a madhouse," Anna said to Warren as the spectators gasped. "You know the class of attendants there. I understand you were committed to a madhouse because you suffered from nervous prostration, which is the vestibule of insanity."

The trial was temporarily halted until the effect of this sensation wore off. Major Warren, pale with anger, demanded to know where Anna had obtained such information and sent out a hurried call for witnesses to defend his character. Anna finally revealed that her informant was no less than a prominent Scranton attorney who refused to corroborate her statement when he was put under oath. After restoring his own reputation with the jury Major Warren decided to discontinue further cross-examination of the plaintiff. It was obvious that he stood only to lose by keeping her on the stand.

Now it was time for Judge Acheson to present the case to the jury. The trial had gone on for two weeks and the issue was clearly a question of the sanity of the plaintiff at the time of the commitment. Was Anna Dickinson sane on February 25, 1891? If she was sane, was she "illegally, unjustifiably, and maliciously deprived of her liberty and confined among lunatics in an insane asylum under the false pretext that she was insane?" This was the question the jury would have to decide, but the judge made it quite clear where his sympathies rested. "For myself," Judge Acheson said, "I have no hesitation in declaring that I think the defendants were entirely right in forcing open the door of the plaintiff's room. This opinion of mine, which I feel it to be my duty to express, is not binding on you." Why had Anna taken such an inveterate dislike to her sister that she would not suffer her even to enter her room, the judge asked the panel of jurors. Was such conduct natural? Did her language and conduct, as shown by proof of her use of "damn" and "devil" comport with what was naturally to be expected from a woman of purity, native refinement, and culture? If it did not, what was the explanation?

"Is this the law?" Anna kept asking McLean as she heard Judge Acheson's charge.

At 3 P.M. the jury went out to deliberate and the parties to the case awaited the decision with poorly concealed anxiety. Hours passed; the jury sent word that they wished to consult the judge. They were having difficulty agreeing on a verdict. What should they do? The judge sent them back to the jury room and directed them to sacrifice minor points of difference in favor of an agreed verdict. Once again the jury closeted itself; the evening dragged on to the night, and then into the early hours of the morning.

Inside the jury room angry words were being exchanged. After the trial, one of the talesmen, a grocer named McMahon, told what went on inside. The jury had split—eight for Anna and four for the defense. "That man Hoffman from Sunbury," wrote McMahon who was one of Anna's supporters, "we found out after going to the jury room that he was a particular friend of Dr. Underwood." Then there was a Mr. Green whose wife was desperately ill and on the verge of death throughout the two-week trial, but who insisted on staying with the case to the end. "That man Green, whose wife died the Tuesday morning of counsel's address, he was the most inhuman man on earth or else he was bought body and soul or he would never have stayed there one hour after he received the death notice from his home," McMahon wrote to Anna, "unless it was for the purpose of staying to defeat you and I know he was talking to Warren for he told me so, which was in violation of his oath." Then there was "that old ignoramus Neff" and "Old Donahoe" who "did not know anything. Could not get anything through him. I was almost dumbfounded when I found such an ignorant set as these four men. We just kept pounding them for 18 hours. We would have stayed with them until next spring if necessary, before we would give in, but that man Green claiming to the judge that his wife was dead caused our discharge."

At eight o'clock the following morning, the jury reported to the judge that they were unable to agree on a verdict, but the foreman was confident that given more time they could decide the case. Judge Acheson refused the request and declared a hung jury. The case of Anna Dickinson vs. her incarcerators was still unresolved.

Anna was prostrated by the result. She had been so sure of vindication. A dispassionate study of all the facts in the case, however, had led many others to anticipate a different outcome. With a less eloquent witness than Anna Dickinson testifying in her own behalf, the case might have collapsed of its own weight, but Anna's spectacular power over audiences had once again given to a case more persuasiveness than the evidence itself warranted. So convinced of Anna's sanity were the eight jurors who voted for her that they walked down the streets in a procession that morning to the Scranton hotel where Anna had secluded herself. At the hotel the eight men sent up a message of comfort. On the printed jury list, each one signed his name, and next to it wrote the word, "Friend." She had been vindicated by eight, discredited by four. Where did she stand before the world? Anna sobbed bitterly in her heartfelt grief.

CHAPTER 16

ECLIPSE

THE failure of the jury to render a definite verdict was calamitous to everyone concerned. It meant that Anna would once again have to endure the ordeal of the courtroom if the issue of her sanity was to be settled. She felt there was but one purpose left for her in life—vindication before the law and the public. Susan, on the other hand, was conscious that the mantle of guilt would be draped over her shoulders if Anna won the suit. Moreover, Susan felt keenly the responsibility for having involved all the defendants in the case. The split decision also came as a blow to the New York newspapers that faced libel suits; they now stood in danger of losing them. Under the law, a published charge of insanity was libelous *per se;* it was not necessary for Anna to prove she had been sane to collect damages from the papers; it was their burden to prove that she had *not* been sane. And if a federal jury at Scranton could not agree on the issue of sanity, what assurance did the papers have that a New York jury would rule otherwise? In self-protection, the papers closed their pages to Anna Dickinson; nothing would be reported thereafter that might in any way serve to substantiate Anna's sanity; even those metropolitan papers that did not face suit seemed to join in a conspiracy of silence against Anna's name. And when it appeared that Anna was determined to press the libel suits, the papers threatened to throw all their weight behind the Scranton defendants in a second trial. The *New York Press* wrote Judge Dailey that if his client did not withdraw her suit against it, the paper would send attorneys to Scranton to assist the Pittston defendants in the retried case; if she discontinued the action

against the *Press*, the attorneys would not be sent. Anna refused to
withdraw under the threat; and she was supported in her determination by Dailey and McLean. "I think upon another trial with the
knowledge we now have of the situation a like result will be prevented," Judge Dailey wrote, "and that you will come off victorious."

Judge Dailey was right. Two years later, in March, 1897, before the
same Judge Acheson, but with a different set of opposing attorneys,
the second trial of Anna Dickinson vs. her incarcerators took place.
Anna's new attorney compared his client's misfortune to that of
Joseph who was sold into bondage by his brothers. Again Anna told
her story. This time ten of the twelve jurors were carried away by
her eloquence. The remaining two tenaciously opposed her. Behind
the closed door of the jury room a compromise was reached that would
end the litigation once and for all. The foreman announced that the
jury found for the plaintiff: Anna had *not* been insane that day in
February, 1891; Susan and the Pittston folk had acted illegally, unjustifiably, and maliciously in swooping her out of her home and com-
mitting her to Danville. Having succeeded in obtaining a unanimous
verdict for the plaintiff, the majority then compromised with the two
dissenters in determining the damages to be assessed against the
defendants to compensate Anna for the humiliation, physical and
mental suffering, and loss in reputation and earning power caused
by the false accusation and imprisonment. The jury awarded Anna
damages in the amount of six-and-a-quarter cents! (Under old English
common law, defendants in civil actions did not have to pay court
costs when damages for less than twenty shillings were returned by
a jury. The Scranton jury thus placed the full burden for the costs
of the trials—some $3,500—on Anna.)

To the public, Anna pretended to be gratified by the decision. "It's
something to be declared sane, you know," she told a reporter before
turning aside to shake the hand of one of the jurors and thank him
for the verdict. Though psychologically she was fortified by the
dubious technical vindication, in point of fact the outcome of the
second trial only sealed Anna's doom. The case could never be retried,
and the verdict of history on her sanity would forever be clouded with
doubt. Nothing less than complete and overwhelming vindication would
satisfy Anna, and this she could not have. The popular skepticism
engendered by the verdict only served to unbalance her further. She

held that Judge Acheson, whose opinion of Anna's sanity had been poorly concealed at both trials, was the cause of her legal misfortunes, and in later years she impugned the integrity of the judge in letters to every member of the United States Senate to whose power of impeachment she made appeal. Anna's mind, seized by but one idea and one idea only—that of vindication—had become a pitiful shadow of its former brilliance. Emotion displaced all logic; stridency and a wearisome repetition replaced clarity of thought and sober emphasis. A once magnificent command of language was now wasted on a lost and increasingly meaningless cause. With all sense of proportion gone, Anna kept on fighting, refusing to capitulate before impossible odds and undeniable facts.

And some of these seemingly futile fights she managed to win. She won two of the three libel cases in New York. The *World* lost to her in March, 1898, and was ordered to pay her $1,250 in damages plus court costs. Two months later, Anna won her suit against the *Press* and was awarded damages of $2,750, but the *Press* appealed and the case was finally settled out of court. The last libel case, against the *Journal,* was heard in November, 1898, and this time the jury ruled *against* Anna and she lost $162.27 in court costs. In 1901, the last of the Pennsylvania litigations took place when Anna's $25,000 suit against Dr. Oglesby, the Danville doctor who had certified her insanity and who had been too ill to appear in the Scranton courtroom with the other defendants four years earlier, was settled out of court.

With the end of the trials, there was no longer any purpose to Anna's existence. Whatever the verdicts, public opinion had written her off as a litigious paranoiac, and the vindication, which could come only through the press, was forever denied her. The trial of the *World* suit had lasted eight days, and the *Press* suit three full weeks, but not a word of the cases appeared in the New York papers. The woman who had seemed to live on the pages of the nation's newspapers for half her life, whose story could not be retold except in terms of sensational publicity, now could not get her name into print. Except for those few whose memories stretched back almost half a century, Anna Dickinson was a ghost out of the past. Her name yearly grew less identifiable. Only Susan B. Anthony, then the grand old president of the National American Women's Suffrage Association, seemed to cherish Anna's great fame in her memory. Just before the turn of the century, Susan B. Anthony wrote to Anna: "I'm awfully glad to know you still live—and that I have a chance to tell you that my motherly love—my elderly sister's love—has never abated for my first Anna. I have had several lovely Anna girls—'nieces,' they call themselves now-a-day—since my first Anna, but none of them ever has or ever can fill the niche in my heart that you did—my dear."

But to the public at large, the memory of Anna Dickinson—the Joan of Arc of the Civil War, the Queen of the Lyceum, the confidante of senators and governors, the presidential campaigner, the girl who had no equal in Connecticut, who had told Lincoln's Congress how to win the war—grew dimmer with each passing year until eventually her name disappeared altogether from the pages of the nation's history. In 1910, the *New York Evening Mail* published a letter from a reader who asked whether "Miss Anna Dickinson, the lecturer and woman suffrage advocate, is living or dead." The paper replied: "Miss Dickinson died about ten years ago." The living Anna Dickinson filed the clipping away with her other mementoes.

When the body outlives the fame, the result is often tragic. Society makes no provision for heroes and heroines who fall out of joint with their time. After years of pointless struggle, Anna was a thoroughly broken woman, reconciled at long last to injustice and oblivion. Like a lonely animal who turns to any source of warmth and affection, Anna turned to Sally and George Ackley who, alone of all her former friends, still stood by her. She moved into their home in New York, ate the food they were good enough to provide her, and enjoyed the respect and adoration from her last remaining admirers in the whole world. In the circle of this small family, Anna was queen. When the Ackleys moved back to Goshen in the foothills of the Catskill Mountains to run a confectionery store, Anna moved with them. And in the Ackley home over the store and later in a two-story house at 34 Murray Street, Anna lived out her life in the privacy of a small bedroom where she read and reread the letters and clippings that once again called to life the glorious past. Sally served her "Miss D." devotedly. She brought to her room delicate meals of beef tea and fruit; occasionally Anna graced the family table with her presence much as a reigning monarch condescends to visit with her subjects. Sometimes she would step into the store to fascinate the school children and drugstore cowboys with thrilling stories of how she had known Lincoln, how she had told the government of the United States in congress assembled how to win the Civil War. No one, of course, believed her.

To the end Anna kept her pride and her poise, though she often had to retreat to her bedroom to get the comfort that memories alone could provide. To the last she maintained her body in a becoming manner; where she obtained the money for the perfumes and wines in which she bathed, no one ever knew. Despite the miserable liver, the hemorrhoids, the sciatica, the jaundice, the chest colds, the special nerve in her head, which no one else had, Anna Dickinson lived on and on. She wrote plays and articles that were neither produced nor published. She lived to see women get the ballot, but she herself never voted. She lived to see the movies and the radio create a new era of mass communications, which made the lyceum a museum piece. She lived on to see all the great names of her life pass from the scene before her.

First Butler, an unhappy old man, in 1893. Then Allison, soon after the turn of the century, with a funeral befit a United States senator of thirty years' service. Then Susan B. Anthony, with the homage of millions of women who felt indebted to her. Then Whitelaw Reid, the towering, austere figure of American journalism and Republican politics, ambassador, minister, founder of a distinguished family. Then Susan Dickinson, who had stayed on in Scranton working on a local paper. Susan died of pneumonia at eighty, impoverished and lonely. William Winter outlived his day, too, and lost his drama post at the *Tribune* shortly before his death.

Anna outlived them all. When devoted Sally Ackley died, Anna stood at the head of the stairs in the house on Murray Avenue in Goshen and in her cracked, eighty-six-year-old voice delivered a eulogy as her friend of thirty years was carried out of the house. Not long after, Anna's time came. Six days before her ninetieth birthday, on October 22, 1932, two weeks before Franklin D. Roosevelt was elected President, Anna Dickinson, a frail, withered, defeated, forgotten woman drew her last breath, without heirs, without fame, without friends. Forgotten by public and history, she was quietly laid to rest in Goshen's Slate Hill Cemetery, a few feet from Sally Ackley, with only a small footstone to mark the place. There her body lies today, her grave unnoticed, or if noticed, its significance unsuspected by the dutiful mourners who daily pass by on their missions of homage.

Yet with her sense of history and drama, Anna must have known that someday her story would be told and her career resurrected. In all the long years of solitude and longing, of ever-deepening obscurity that cut agonizingly into her heart, Anna held on to all the records of the past that retold her life and that she alone possessed—the clippings, the letters, the memorabilia. They told a story of a woman whom greatness had touched, but humility had passed by; a woman whose power of speech was sheer genius, whose failing was overweening pride; a woman who attained heights unreached by any of her contemporaries and who sank to depths of misery plumbed by few. Hers was the story of a magnificent and tragic failure. She was a woman of contradictions: generous to a fault, but ever self-seeking; desirous of love and affection, but unable to give herself in return; outwardly serene, bold, self-confident; inwardly torn by doubts, fears, a sense of futility. She knew the keenest of frustrations, that of not being able to succeed in the one thing that mattered most to her. She spoke fearlessly for freedom, intelligence, and justice, against corruption, bigotry, and ignorance. She spoke with unrivaled eloquence and a rare power of emotion. Though she could sway the masses and conquer the public heart, she could not master her own frailties, which eventually led to the tragic undoing of all that she had so bravely accomplished. Anna Dickinson's story of courage, energy, devotion, achievement, selfishness, pride, and failure was a part of her nation's history. In her own times she wanted more tribute than she deserved and was offered less than she merited. It would be for her countrymen of a later time to make the final assessment of her life and work and to decide her place in history.

A NOTE ON SOURCES

THE primary source of evidence for this biography was the extensive (though disordered) collection of letters, manuscripts, notes, pictures, clippings, scrapbooks, and memorabilia that comprise the Anna E. Dickinson Papers in the Manuscript Division of the Library of Congress, Washington, D. C. Several letters and clippings were found among the miscellaneous papers in the Manuscript Division of the New York Public Library. Fifty-odd letters written by Anna Dickinson and a somewhat smaller number written by Susan Dickinson were found among the private papers of the senior Whitelaw Reid to whom the letters were addressed. These letters were found and made available for this biography through the kind co-operation of the Reid family. A few unimportant letters written by Anna Dickinson were found in the Manuscript Division of the New York Historical Society. References to Anna Dickinson were found in the Elizabeth Cady Stanton Papers, Volume II, and in the Gideon Welles Papers, both in the Manuscript Division of the Library of Congress. To supplement the collection of clippings in the Anna E. Dickinson Papers, the files of newspapers published during the Civil War in Washington, D. C., Pennsylvania, New York, Connecticut, New Hampshire, Maine, and Boston, Massachusetts, were consulted. Newspapers published in Scranton, Pennsylvania, in 1895 and 1897 were consulted in the Scranton Public Library to obtain additional material bearing on the insanity trials. Supreme Court records on file in the New York Hall of Records were consulted to obtain material bearing on the libel trials. An interview with Miss Bertha Ackley, of Goshen, New York (sister of the late George Ackley), who knew Anna Dickinson and for a time lived under the same roof with her, provided some material bearing on Anna Dickinson's life in Goshen.

Also consulted were three books written by Anna Dickinson: *What Answer?* (1868), *A Paying Investment* (1876), *A Ragged Register* (1879). One of Miss Dickinson's speeches is included in the publication, *Addresses of the Hon. W. D. Kelley, Anna E. Dickinson, and Frederick Douglass, at a Mass Meeting, Held at National Hall, Philadelphia, July 6, 1863, for the Promotion of Colored Enlistments,* which is available at the New York Public Library.

Two unpublished graduate theses dealing with aspects of Anna Dickinson's life were also consulted. They are:

Anderson, Judith. *Anna E. Dickinson, 1842-1932: A Biographical Sketch,* M.A. Thesis, Lehigh University, 1934.

Young, James Harvey. *Anna Elizabeth Dickinson and the Civil War,* Ph.D. Thesis, University of Illinois, 1941.

There seems little point in including here the long list of published materials that were consulted to obtain information bearing on secondary characters and background events. Of most usefulness in their direct treatment of events in Anna Dickinson's life were the following published sources:

Anderson, Judith. "Anna Dickinson, Antislavery Radical." *Pennsylvania Historical Society,* III (1936), pp. 147-63.

Anthony, Susan B., Stanton, Elizabeth Cady, and Gage, Matilda Joslyn (eds.), *History of Woman Suffrage, II, 1861-1876.* New York: 1882.

Brooks, Noah. *Washington in Lincoln's Time.* New York: 1895.

Congressional Globe. 1st Session, 38th Congress, XXXIV, Part I. Washington: 1864.

Dictionary of American Biography, XXI, Supplement One (1944), pp. 244-45.

Harper, Ida A. *Life and Work of Susan B. Anthony.* Indianapolis, I, II: 1899.

Lane, Jarlath Robert. *A Political History of Connecticut during the Civil War.* Ph.D. Thesis, 1941.

New York Times. October 25, 1932, p. 19.

Sandburg, Carl. *Abraham Lincoln. III, The War Years.* New York: Harcourt, Brace and Company, 1939.

Stanton, Elizabeth Cady. *Eighty Years or More.* New York: 1898.

Tarbell, Ida M. "The American Woman," *American Magazine,* LXIX, April, 1910, pp. 801-14.

The Nation. VII, October 29, 1868, pp. 346-47.

Wyman, Lillie Buffum (Chace) and Wyman, Arthur Crawford. *Elizabeth Buffum Chace, 1806-1899, Her Life and Its Environment.* Two volumes. Boston: 1914.

Young, James Harvey, "Anna Dickinson as Anne Boleyn," *Emory University Quarterly,* V, October, 1949, pp. 163-69.

———. "Anna Elizabeth Dickinson and the Civil War: For and Against Lincoln," *Mississippi Valley Historical Review,* XXXI, June, 1944, pp. 59-80.

———. "A Woman Abolitionist Views the South in 1875." *Georgia Historical Quarterly* (December, 1948) XXXII, pp. 241-51.

The dialogue between Anna Dickinson and Senator (later Vice-President) Henry Wilson, as given in Chapter 7, was reconstructed from a letter Anna wrote to her mother. Parts of the dialogue were invented by the author to achieve continuity. The conversation with Horace Greeley in the same chapter was taken from Anna's recollection of the episode at a later date. The conversations between Anna and O. G. Bernard, in Chapter 10, dealing with the critical reception to *Anne Boleyn,* were invented by the author. Some of the dialogue in those conversations was drawn from letters and press interviews; the rest was invented. All other quoted matter in this book was taken from written documents. For the purpose of smoother continuity, one or two minor instances of audience heckling were transposed from one speech to another on the same subject delivered a few days earlier or later. With these inconsequential exceptions, the author has sought throughout to present, in every detail, a factually accurate account of Miss Dickinson's life.

INDEX